Thomas Jefferson Conant

The Meaning and Use of Baptizein

philologically and historically investigated, for the American Bible Union

Thomas Jefferson Conant

The Meaning and Use of Baptizein
philologically and historically investigated, for the American Bible Union

ISBN/EAN: 9783337096366

Printed in Europe, USA, Canada, Australia, Japan

Cover: Foto ©Lupo / pixelio.de

More available books at **www.hansebooks.com**

BAPTIZEIN.

APPENDIX

TO THE

REVISED VERSION

OF THE

GOSPEL BY MATTHEW.

THE
MEANING AND USE

OF

BAPTIZEIN

PHILOLOGICALLY AND HISTORICALLY INVESTIGATED,

FOR THE

AMERICAN BIBLE UNION.

BY T. J. CONANT, D.D.

NEW YORK:
AMERICAN BIBLE UNION, 350 BROOME STREET,
BIBLE REVISION ASSOCIATION, LOUISVILLE, KY.
1861.

Entered, according to Act of Congress, in the year 1860, by
THE AMERICAN BIBLE UNION,
In the Clerk's Office of the District Court for the Southern District of New York.

TO THE READER.

The question may be asked: Why, in a revision of the English New Testament, professedly designed to represent the latest results of critical learning in all respects, is one particular instance of change distinguished, by being made the subject of a separate treatise? *To this I answer:

1. The meaning of the Greek word BAPTIZEIN has been so obscured, by the denominational controversies which have sprung up within the last two centuries, that nothing less than a complete historical exhibition of its use, both in pagan and christian Greek literature, would suffice to place the matter in a clear light.

2. In substituting the literal English meaning of this word for its Anglicized form, in a revision of the New Testament for popular use, the writer feels that a just deference' to public opinion, as well as to christian feeling, requires that the reasons of this change should be fully set forth. It is believed, that the method adopted in the investigation will commend itself to the candid inquirer. By allowing the impartial witnesses of antiquity to speak directly to the reader, he is placed in a position to judge for himself of the writer's deduction from their testimony, which is recorded in the revised text.

3. The exhibition of the grounds for this change is required, moreover, by the action of large and influential organizations in England and America, which chiefly control the work of Bible translation in heathen tongues. By these societies the principle has been formally adopted, that the Greek word BAPTIZEIN shall be universally transferred, and not translated, in versions under their patronage; and so stringently is this rule enforced, that even in mission-fields wholly destitute of the word of God, versions confessedly of the highest merit, in all other respects, have been rejected because in this there was a deviation from the rule. The Bible Society, for which I have the honor to labor, has adopted as its fundamental principle, to be applied to all its versions whether for the home or the foreign field,

the faithful translation of every word capable of being expressed in the language of the version. This is, in the view of its managers and members, the only principle justly claiming to be catholic; and from its nature, it admits of no exception.

It seems proper, therefore, in presenting to the public a revised English version of the New Testament, in which this word is rendered into English, to show that the translation expresses its true and only import, and is not a sectarian rendering.

The entire argument is set before the English reader, in his own language; the authorities for the use of the Greek word being fully given, in translations made as literal as possible. These authorities are all contained in the portion of the page above the dividing line; and in this division of the page no foreign words are used. The translation of this word being indicated by small capitals (followed by the word itself in its Anglicized form), the English reader is as well able to judge of its meaning, from the connection, as the reader of the original Greek.

The examples of the common meaning and use of the word, in Sections I. and II., are from every period of Greek literature in which the word occurs. They include all that have been given by lexicographers,* and by those who have written professedly on this subject; and these, with the examples added from my own reading, exhaust the use of this word in Greek literature.

The quotations have been copied, in every instance, by myself or under my own eye, from the page, chapter, or section referred to. Special pains have been taken to make these references as definite and clear as possible, that any passage may easily be found; the author's name being given, the name of the treatise, and its divisions (if any are made), and the volume and page of the edition in most common use, or of the one accessible to me.

T. J. Conant.

Brooklyn, N. Y., September, 1860.

---

* Basil. p. 256 (Steph. Thes.), "Sympathizing with those immersed in the sea" (τοῖς ἐν τῇ θαλάττῃ βαπτιζομένοις συμπάσχοντες) is not included among the examples, as the writer gives none except such as he has been able to verify, by reference to the passage and its connection.

CONTENTS.

The course of argument, in this treatise, may be seen at a glance in the following sketch of its plan.

	PAGE.
SECTION I. Usage of Greek writers; including the Church Fathers, when they do not speak of the Christian rite.........	1–82
§ 1. In the literal, physical sense...........................	1–42
1. Absolutely, with the ingulfing element implied.........	1–27
2. Construed with some case of the ingulfing clement......	28–42
§ 2. In the tropical or figurative sense.....................	43–72
1. To plunge, to immerse (as in ingulfing floods) in calamities, etc...	43–67
2. To overwhelm (figuratively) with an intoxicating liquor, etc..	68–72
§ 3. Use in composition with a preposition...................	73–82
SECTION II. Usage of the Greek Versions of the Old Testament....	83–86
SECTION III. Summary of lexical and grammatical uses...........	87–96
1. Lexical use...	87–91
2. Grammatical construction...........................	91–96
SECTION IV. Application to the New Testament................	97–101
SECTION V. Usage of the Church Fathers.....................	102–133
1. Where they use the word of the Christian rite, or describe the rite in other words.......................	102–121
2. Where the rite (or what is implied in it) is variously applied for illustration or comparison.................	122–133
SECTION VI. Requirements and practice of the Christian Church...	134–141
1. Of the Eastern, or Greek Church....................	134, 135
2. Of the Western, or Latin Church....................	136, 137
3. Of the Anglican Church............................	138–141
SECTION VII. Usage of the Versions..........................	142–149
1. Of the old Latin versions.	142–144
2. Of the ancient Oriental versions.....................	144
3. Of the Teutonic versions...........................	144–146
4. Of modern versions for the learned..................	146–149
SECTION VIII. Views of scholars of different communions.	150–157
SECTION IX. Obligation to translate the word..................	158–163

MEANING AND USE
OF
BAPTIZEIN.

SECTION I.

Usage of Greek writers, including the Church Fathers, where they do not speak of the Christian rite.

GROUND-MEANING:

TO IMMERSE, IMMERGE, SUBMERGE, TO DIP, TO PLUNGE, TO IMBATHE, TO WHELM.

§ 1. *In the literal, physical sense.*

1. Absolutely, with the ingulfing element implied.

EXAMPLE 1.

Polybius,[*] *History, book I. ch. 51,* 6. In his account of the sea-fight at Drepanum, between the Romans and Carthaginians, describing the advantages of the latter in their choice of a position, and in the superior structure and more skillful management of their vessels, he says:

"For, if any were hard pressed by the enemy, they retreated safely, on account of their fast sailing, into the open space; and

---

* Born 205 before Christ.

=====

GREEK TEXT.

Polybii Hist. lib. I. c. 51, 6 (*ed. Schweigh.*).

Εἴ τε γὰρ πιέζοιντό τινες ὑπὸ τῶν πολεμίων, κατόπιν ἀνεχώρουν ἀσφαλῶς διὰ τὸ ταχυναυτεῖν εἰς τὸν ἀναπεπτα-

A

then with reversed course, now sailing round and now attacking in flank the more advanced of the pursuers, while turning and embarrassed on account of the weight of the ships and the unskillfulness of the crews, they made continued assaults and SUBMERGED (BAPTIZED) many of the vessels."

EXAMPLE 2.

The same Work, book VIII., ch. 8, 4. Describing the operations of the engines, which Archimedes constructed for the defense of Syracuse when besieged by the Romans, and with which he lifted the prows of the besieging vessels out of the water, so that they stood erect on the stern, and then let them fall, he says:

"Which being done, some of the vessels fell on their side, and some were overturned; but most of them, when the prow was let fall from on high, BEING SUBMERGED (BAPTIZED), became filled with sea-water and with confusion."

EXAMPLE 3.

Plutarch,* Life of Marcellus, ch. XV. Describing the same

* Born in the year 50 after Christ.

GREEK TEXT.

μένον τόπον· κἄπειτ' ἐκ μεταβολῆς τοῖς προπίπτουσι τῶν διωκόντων, τοτὲ μὲν περιπλέοντες, τοτὲ δὲ πλάγιοι προσπίπτοντες στρεφομένοις καὶ δυσχρηστοῦσι διὰ τὸ βάρος τῶν πλοίων καὶ διὰ τὴν ἀπειρίαν τῶν πληρωμάτων, ἐμβολάς τε συνεχεῖς ἐδίδοσαν, καὶ πολλὰ τῶν σκαφῶν ἐβάπτιζον.

Polybii Hist. lib. VIII. c. 8, 4 (*ed. Schweigh.*).

Οὗ γενομένου, τινὰ μὲν τῶν πλοίων πλάγια κατέπιπτε, τινὰ δὲ καὶ κατεστρέφετο· τὰ δὲ πλεῖστα τῆς πρώρας ἀφ' ὕψους ῥιφθείσης βαπτιζόμενα, πλήρη θαλάττης ἐγίγνετο καὶ ταραχῆς.

operations, he says (speaking of the arms of the engines projecting from the walls over the vessels):

"Some [of the vessels] thrusting down, under a weight firmly fixed above, they sunk into the deep; and others, with iron hands, or beaks like those of cranes, hauling up by the prow till they were erect on the stern, they SUBMERGED (BAPTIZED)."

EXAMPLE 4.

Aristotle,[*] *concerning Wonderful Reports, 136.* Speaking of what the Phœnician colonists of Gadira (on the southern coast of Spain) were reported to have seen, when sailing beyond the Pillars of Hercules (westward of the strait of Gibraltar), he says:

"They say that the Phœnicians who inhabit the so-called Gadira, sailing four days outside of the Pillars of Hercules with an east-wind, come to certain desert places full of rushes and

---

[*] Born 384 before Christ.

GREEK TEXT.

Plutarchi Vit. Marcelli, XV (*ed. Schäfer*).

Τὰς μὲν ὑπὸ βρίθους στηρίζοντος ἄνωθεν¹ ὠθοῦσαι κατέδυον εἰς βυθὸν, τὰς δὲ χερσὶ σιδηραῖς, ἢ στόμασιν εἰκασμένοις² γεράνων, ἀνασπῶσαι πρώραθεν ὀρθὰς ἐπὶ πρύμναν ἐβάπτιζον.

Aristot. de mirabilibus Auscultat. 136 (*ed. Bekker, Vol. VI. p. 136*).

Λέγουσι τοὺς Φοίνικας τοὺς κατοικοῦντας τὰ Γάδειρα καλούμενα, ἔξω πλέοντας Ἡρακλείων στηλῶν ἀπηλιώτῃ ἀνέμῳ ἡμέρας τέτταρας, παραγίνεσθαι εἴς τινας τόπους

---

¹ Junge στηρίζοντος ἄνωθεν (*Schäfer*).
² Στόματα εἰκασμένα γεράνων sunt *unci adsimilati rostris gruum.* Herodotus III. 28, αἰετὸν εἰκασμένον. Bene Interpres, *figura aquilæ;* h. e. figura adsimilata aquilæ (*Id.*). Baehr, Herod. III. 28, *figuram aquilæ s. figuram adsimilatam aquilæ,* ut reddi vult Schaefer, etc.

sea-weed; which, when it is ebb-tide, are not IMMERSED (BAPTIZED), but when it is flood-tide are overflowed."

EXAMPLE 5.

Eubulus,* (*fragment of an ancient comedy, entitled Nausicaa*) says, with comic extravagance, of one whose vessel is wrecked in a storm and a prey to the ingulfing floods:

"Who now the fourth day is IMMERGED (BAPTIZED),
  leading the famished life of a miserable mullet."†

---

* A Greek writer of comedies, about 380 before Christ.
† Mullet: a fish, fabled to be always found empty, when caught.

EXAMPLE 6.

Polybius,* *History, book XXXIV. c. 3, 7.* In his description of the manner of taking the sword-fish (with an iron-headed spear, or harpoon), he says:

"And even if the spear falls into the sea, it is not lost; for

---

* Born 205 before Christ.

GREEK TEXT.

ἐρήμους, θρύου καὶ φύκους πλήρεις, οὓς ὅταν μὲν ἄμπω τις ᾖ μὴ βαπτίζεσθαι, ὅταν δὲ πλημμύρα, κατακλύζεσθαι.

Eubuli Nausicaa (*Meineke, Fragm. Comic. Græc., Vol. III. p. 238*).

Ὅς νῦν τετάρτην ἡμέραν βαπτίζεται,
νῆστιν πονήρου κεστρέως τρίβων βίον.¹

Polybii Reliq. lib. XXXIV. c. 3, 7 (*ed. Schweigh. Vol. IV. p. 626*).

Κἂν ἐκπέσῃ δὲ εἰς τὴν θάλατταν τὸ δόρυ, οὐκ ἀπό-

---

¹ *Schweigh. Athen., Tom. III. p. 126.*
  Qui nunc quartum in diem undis mergitur
    jejunam miseri mugilis terens vitam.

Gesnerum probavi, monentem (p. 562 init.) πονήρον scribendum esse παροξυτόνως, id est, ἄθλιον, ταλαιπώρου, *miseri, ærumnosi* (*Id. Tom. IX. p. 289*).

it is compacted of both oak and pine, so that when the oaken part is IMMERSED (BAPTIZED) by the weight, the rest is buoyed up, and is easily recovered."

EXAMPLE 7.

The same Work, book III. ch. 72, 4. Speaking of the passage of the Roman army, under the Consul Tiberius, through the river Tebia, which had been swollen by heavy rains, he says:
"They passed through with difficulty, the foot-soldiers IMMERSED (BAPTIZED) as far as to the breasts."

EXAMPLE 8.

The same Work, book XVI. ch. 6, 2. In his account of the sea-fight between Philip and Attalus, near Chios, he speaks of a vessel belonging the latter as:
"Pierced and BEING IMMERGED (BAPTIZED) by a hostile ship."

EXAMPLE 9.

Strabo,* Geography, book XII. ch. 2, 4. Speaking of the underground channel, through which the waters of the Pyramus (a river of Cilicia in Asia Minor) forced their way, he says:

---

* Born about 60 before Christ.

GREEK TEXT.

λωλεν· ἔστι γὰρ πηκτὸν ἔκ τε δρυὸς καὶ ἐλάτης, ὥστε, βαπτιζομένου τοῦ δρυΐνου βάρει, μετέωρον εἶναι τὸ λοιπὸν καὶ εὐανάληπτον.

Ejusdem Hist. lib. III. c. 72, 4: μόλις, ἕως τῶν μαστῶν οἱ πεζοὶ βαπτιζόμενοι, διέβαινον.

Ejusdem Hist. lib. XVI. c. 6, 2: τετρωμένην καὶ βαπτιζομένην¹ ὑπὸ νεὼς πολεμίας.

---

¹ *Being immerged* (in the act of sinking), as expressed by the *pres.*, in distinction from the preceding *perf.*

"And to one who hurls down a dart, from above into the channel, the force of the water makes so much resistance, that it is hardly IMMERSED (BAPTIZED)."

EXAMPLE 10.

The same Work, book VI. ch. 2, 9. "And around Acragas [Agrigentum in Sicily] are marsh-lakes, having the taste indeed of sea-water, but a different nature; for even those who can not swim are not IMMERSED (BAPTIZED), floating like pieces of wood."

EXAMPLE 11.

The same Work, book XIV. ch. 3, 9. Speaking of the march of Alexander's army, along the narrow beach (flooded in stormy weather) between the mountain called Climax and the Pamphilian Sea, he says:

"Alexander happening to be there at the stormy season, and accustomed to trust for the most part to fortune, set forward before the swell subsided; and they marched the whole day in water, IMMERSED (BAPTIZED) as far as to the waist."

GREEK TEXT.
Strabonis Geogr. lib. XII. c. 2, 4 (*ed. Tzschucke*).

Τῷ δὲ καθιέντι ἀκόντιον ἄνωθεν εἰς τὸν βόθρον ἡ βία τοῦ ὕδατος ἀντιπράττει τοσοῦτον ὥστε μόλις βαπτίζεσθαι.

Ejusdem lib. VI. c. 2, 9 (*ed. Siebenkees*).

Περὶ ᾿Ακράγαντα δὲ λίμναι τὴν μὲν γεῦσιν ἔχουσαι θαλάττης, τὴν δὲ φύσιν διάφορον· οὐδὲ γὰρ τοῖς ἀκολύμβοις βαπτίζεσθαι συμβαίνει ξύλων τρόπον ἐπιπολάζουσιν.

Ejusdem lib. XIV. c. 3, 9 (*ed. Tzschucke*).

῾Ο δὲ ᾿Αλέξανδρος εἰς χειμέριον ἐμπεσὼν καιρὸν καὶ τὸ πλέον ἐπιτρέπων τῇ τύχῃ πρὶν ἀνεῖναι τὸ κῦμα ὥρμησε, καὶ ὅλην τὴν ἡμέραν ἐν ὕδατι γενέσθαι τὴν πορείαν συνέβη μέχρι ὀμφαλοῦ βαπτιζομένων.[1]

---

[1] The sense of this clause is given, without imitating the construction, which would be harsh in English.

Example 12.

The same Work, book XIV. ch. 2, 42. Speaking of the *asphalt* in the lake Sirbonis, which floats on the surface on account of the greater specific gravity of the water, he says:

"Then floating at the top on account of the nature of the water, by virtue of which, we said, there is no need of being a swimmer, and he who enters in is not IMMERSED (BAPTIZED), but is lifted out."

Example 13.

Diodorus* (the Sicilian), Historical Library, book XVI. ch. 80. In his account of Timoleon's defeat of the Carthaginian army on the bank of the river Crimissus in Sicily, many of the fugitives perishing in the stream swollen by a violent storm, he says:

"The river, rushing down with the current increased in violence, SUBMERGED (BAPTIZED) many, and destroyed them attempting to swim through with their armor."

Example 14.

The same Work, book I. ch. 36. Describing the effects of the rapid rise of the water, during the annual inundation of the Nile, he says:

* Wrote his history, about 60–30 before Christ.

Greek Text.
Ejusdem lib. XVI. c. 2, 42.

Εἶτ' ἐπιπολάζουσα διὰ τὴν φύσιν τοῦ ὕδατος, καθ' ἥν ἔφαμεν μηδὲ κολύμβου δεῖσθαι,¹ μηδὲ βαπτίζεσθαι τὸν ἐμβάντα ἀλλ' ἐξαίρεσθαι.

Diodori Siculi Biblioth. Hist. lib. XVI. c. 80 (*ed. Bekker*).

Ὁ ποταμὸς βιαιοτέρῳ τῷ ῥεύματι καταφερόμενος πολλοὺς ἐβάπτιζε, καὶ μετὰ τῶν ὅπλων διανηχομένους διέφθειρε.

¹ Zufolge welcher es, wie wir sagten, keines Schwimmers bedarf (*Groskurd*).

"Most of the wild land animals are surrounded by the stream and perish, being SUBMERGED (BAPTIZED); but some, escaping to the high grounds, are saved."

EXAMPLE 15.

The same Work, book XI. ch. 18.

"The commander of the fleet,* leading on the line, and first joining battle, was slain after a brilliant conflict; and his ship being SUBMERGED (BAPTIZED), confusion seized the fleet of the barbarians."

* Of the Persians, at the battle of Salamis.

EXAMPLE 16.

Josephus,* Jewish Antiquities, book XV. ch. 3, 3. Describing the murder of the boy Aristobulus, who (by Herod's command) was drowned by his companions in a swimming-bath, he says:

"Continually pressing down and IMMERSING (BAPTIZING) him while swimming, as if in sport, they did not desist till they had entirely suffocated him."

* A Jewish writer, born in the year 37 after Christ.

Ejusdem lib. I. c. 36.

Τῶν δὲ χερσαίων θηρίων τὰ πολλὰ μὲν ὑπὸ τοῦ ποταμοῦ περιληφθέντα διαφθείρεται βαπτιζόμενα, τινὰ δ' εἰς τοὺς μετεώρους ἐκφεύγοντα τόπους διασώζεται.

Ejusdem lib. XI. c. 18.

Ὁ δὲ ναύαρχος προηγούμενος τῆς τάξεως καὶ πρῶτος συνάψας μάχην διεφθάρη, λαμπρῶς ἀγωνισάμενος· τῆς δὲ νεὼς βαπτισθείσης, ταραχὴ κατέσχε τὸ ναυτικὸν τῶν βαρβάρων.

Βαπτισθείσης Coisl.[1] quod satis elegans; vide Polybium, 1, 51 (*Wesseling*).

Josephi Antiq. Jud. lib. XV. c. 3, 3 (*ed. Oberthür*).

Βαροῦντες ἀεὶ καὶ βαπτίζοντες ὡς ἐν παιδιᾷ νηχόμενον, οὐκ ἀνῆκαν, ἕως καὶ παντάπασιν ἀποπνίξαι.

[1] Consulendus hic Codex est ab iis, qui novam Diodori Siculi editionem parare voluerint (*Montfaucon, Biblioth. Coisl. p. 214, ima*).

Example 17.

The same writer, Jewish War, book I. ch. 22, 2. Relating the same occurrence, he says:
"And there, according to command, being IMMERSED (BAPTIZED) by the Gauls in a swimming-bath, he dies."

Example 18.

The same writer, Jewish War, book III. ch. 8, 5.
"As I also account a pilot most cowardly, who, through dread of a storm, before the blast came voluntarily SUBMERGED (BAPTIZED) the vessel."

Example 19.

The same writer, Jewish War, book III. ch. 9, 3. Describing the condition of the vessels in the port of Joppa, during a storm, he says:
"And many [of the vessels], struggling against the opposing swell towards the open sea (for they feared the shore, being rocky, and the enemies upon it), the billow, rising high above, SUBMERGED (BAPTIZED)."

Greek Text.

Ejusdem de Bello Jud. lib. I. c. 22, 2.

Ἐκεῖ δὲ, κατ' ἐντολὴν ὑπὸ τῶν Γαλατῶν βαπτιζόμενος ἐν κολυμβήθρᾳ, τελευτᾷ.

Ejusdem lib. III. c. 8, 5.

Ὡς ἔγωγε καὶ κυβερνήτην ἡγοῦμαι δειλότατον, ὅστις, χειμῶνα δεδοικὼς, πρὸ τῆς θυέλλης ἐβάπτισεν ἑκὼν τὸ σκάφος.

Ejusdem lib. III c. 9, 3.

Πολλὰς δὲ πρὸς ἀντίον κῦμα βιαζομένας εἰς τὸ πέλαγος, τόν τε γὰρ αἰγιαλὸν ὄντα πετρώδη καὶ τοὺς ἐπ' αὐτοῦ πολεμίους ἐδεδοίκεσαν, μετέωρος ὑπεραρθεὶς ὁ κλύδων ἐβάπτισεν.

Example 20.

The same writer, Antiquities of the Jews, book IX. ch. 10, 2. In his narrative of Jonah's flight, and of the events that followed, he says:
"The ship being just about TO BE SUBMERGED (BAPTIZED)."

Example 21.

The same writer, Life of himself, § 3:
"For our vessel having been SUBMERGED (BAPTIZED) in the midst of the Adriatic, being about six hundred in number, we swam through the whole night."

Example 22.

The same writer, Jewish War, book III. ch. 10, 9. He says of the Jews, in describing their contest with the Roman soldiers on the Sea of Galilee:
"And when they ventured to come near, they suffered harm before they could inflict any, and WERE SUBMERGED (BAPTIZED) along with their vessels; .... and those of the SUBMERGED (BAPTIZED) who raised their heads, either a missile reached, or a vessel overtook."

Greek Text.

Ejusdem Antiq. Jud. lib. IX. c. 10, 2 : ὅσον οὔπω μέλλοντος βαπτίζεσθαι τοῦ σκάφους.

Ejusdem Vitæ § 3.

Βαπτισθέντος γὰρ ἡμῶν τοῦ πλοίου κατὰ μέσον τὸν Ἀδρίαν, περὶ ἑξακοσίους τὸν ἀριθμὸν ὄντες, δι' ὅλης τῆς νυκτὸς ἐνηξάμεθα.

Ejusdem de Bello Jud. lib. III. c. 10, 9.

Καὶ πλησιάζειν τολμῶντες, πρὶν δρᾶσαί τι παθεῖν ἔφθανον, καὶ σὺν αὐτοῖς ἐβαπτίζοντο σκάφεσι· ... τῶν δὲ βαπτισθέντων τοὺς ἀνανεύοντας ἢ βέλος ἔφθανεν, ἢ σχεδία κατελάμβανε.

Example 23.

The same writer, Jewish War, book II. ch. 20, 1.
"And after the calamity of Cestius, many of the distinguished Jews swam away, as when a ship IS BEING IMMERGED (BAPTIZED), from the city."

Example 24.

Plutarch,* *Life of Theseus, XXIV,* quotes the following oracle of the Sibyl, respecting the city of Athens:
"A bladder, thou mayest be IMMERSED (BAPTIZED); but it is not possible for thee to sink."

---

* Born in the year 50 after Christ.

Example 25.

The same writer, Life of Alexander, LXVII. Describing a season of revelry, in the army of Alexander the Great, when returning from his eastern conquests, he says:
"Thou wouldest not have seen a buckler, or a helmet, or a pike; but the soldiers, along the whole way, DIPPING (BAPTIZING)

Greek Text.

Ejusdem lib. II. c. 20, 1.

Μετὰ δὲ τὴν Κεστίου συμφορὰν, πολλοὶ τῶν ἐπιφανῶν Ἰουδαίων ὥσπερ βαπτιζομένης νεὼς ἀπενήχοντο τῆς πόλεως.¹

Plutarchi Vit. Thesei, XXIV. (*ed. Schäfer*).

Ἀσκὸς βαπτίζῃ· δῦναι δέ τοι οὐ θέμις ἐστίν.

Ejusdem Vit. Alexandri, LXVII.

Εἶδες δ᾽ ἂν οὐ πέλτην, οὐ κράνος, οὐ σάρισσαν· ἀλλὰ φιάλαις καὶ ῥυτοῖς καὶ θηρικλείοις παρὰ τὴν ὁδὸν ἅπασαν

---

¹ The version in the text is the best expression we can give of this imperfect metaphor.

with cups, and horns, and goblets, from great wine-jars and mixing-bowls,* were drinking to one another."

* Large bowls for mixing wine and water, into which the drinking-cups were dipped.

EXAMPLE 26.

The same writer, Comparison of Aristophanes and Menander. In this abridgment (by another hand) of one of his lost compositions, speaking of Aristophanes'* faults of style, he quotes from him the following example of *punning,* or *play on words:*

"'For he is praised,' says he, 'because he DIPPED (BAPTIZED) the stewards; being not [*T*amias] stewards, but [*L*amias] sharks.'"†

* Born about 450 before Christ.

† A play on the two similar words (differing only in the first letter) 'tamias' *stewards,* and 'lamias' *sharks,* the former resembling the latter in rapacity as well as in name.
The significance of the Greek verb, in this connection, is aptly expressed by the English translator of these writings of Plutarch : "For he is much commended (saith he) for ducking the chamberlains." The word is, perhaps, used metaphorically here, as in Ex. 157.

GREEK TEXT.

οἱ στρατιῶται βαπτίζοντες ἐκ πίθων μεγάλων καὶ κρατήρων ἀλλήλοις προέπινον.

The reading βαπτίζοντες has been doubted,¹ on account of the unusual construction with ἐκ πίθων; but (as suggested by Coray,² *in loc.*) a part of the action is put for the whole (*synecdoche*), as one must first *dip* the vessel in order to fill it.

Ejusdem Aristoph. et Menandri Comp. (*ed. Wyttenb.*).

Ἐπαινεῖται γὰρ, φησὶν, ὅτι τοὺς ταμίας ἐβάπτισεν, οὐχὶ Ταμίας ἀλλὰ Λαμίας ὄντας.

¹ Suspecta mihi hæc vox, cum ἐκ πίθων ita constructa (*M. Dusoul,* in Reiske's edition).

² Λέγεται μὲν οὖν κατὰ συνεκδοχήν ... πρότερον γὰρ τοῦ πληροῦν ἐστι τὸ βαπτίζειν ἀγγεῖόν τι τὸν ἀρύσασθαι βουλόμενον.

Example 27.

Epictetus* Moral Discourses† (*fragment XI*).
"As you would not wish, sailing in a large and polished and richly gilded ship, to be SUBMERGED (BAPTIZED); so neither choose, dwelling in a house too large and costly, to endure storms of care."

---

* Born about the year 50 after Christ.
† As committed to writing by his pupil, Arrian.

Example 28.

Lucian,* Timon or the Man-hater, 44. Among the resolves for the direction of his future life (to testify his hatred of mankind) is the following:
"And if the winter's torrent were bearing one away, and he with outstretched hands were imploring help, to thrust even him headlong, IMMERSING (BAPTIZING), so that he should not be able to come up again."

---

* Born about 135 after Christ.

Example 29.

The same writer, True History, book II. 4. In this satire on the

---

Greek Text.

Epicteti Dissertat. Frag. 11 (*ed. Schweigh. Vol. III. p. 69*).

Ὥσπερ οὐκ ἂν ἐβούλου ἐν νηὶ μεγάλῃ καὶ γλαφυρᾷ καὶ πολυχρύσῳ πλέων βαπτίζεσθαι· οὕτω μηδὲ ἐν οἰκίᾳ αἴρου ὑπερμεγέθει καὶ πολυτελεῖ καθήμενος χειμάζεσθαι.

Luciani Timon, 46 (*ed. Lehmann*).

Καὶ ἤν τινα τοῦ χειμῶνος ὁ ποταμὸς παραφέρῃ, ὁ δὲ τὰς χεῖρας ὀρέγων ἀντιλαβέσθαι δέηται, ὠθεῖν καὶ τοῦτον ἐπὶ κεφαλὴν βαπτίζοντα, ὡς μηδὲ ἀνακύψαι δυνηθείη.

love of the marvelous, he pleasantly describes men walking on the sea (having cork feet), and says:

"We wondered, therefore, when we saw them not IMMERSED (BAPTIZED), but standing above the waves, and traveling on without fear."

EXAMPLE 30.

Hippocrates, on Epidemics,* *book V.* Describing the respiration of a patient, affected with inflammation and swelling of the throat (*Cynanchè*), and oppression about the heart, he says:

"And she breathed, as persons breathe after having been IMMERSED (BAPTIZED), and emitted a low sound from the chest, like the so-called ventriloquists."

---

* An ancient medical work (attributed erroneously to Hippocrates) written, probably, before the Christian era.

Describing the same case (book VII.), he says: "And she breathed, as if breathing after having been IMMERSED (BAPTIZED)."

EXAMPLE 31.

Dion Cassius,* *Roman History, book XXXVII. ch. 58.* In the

---

* Born in the year 155 after Christ.

GREEK TEXT.

Luciani Veræ Historiæ lib. II. 4 (*ed. Lehmann*).

'Εθαυμάζομεν οὖν ἰδόντες οὐ βαπτιζομένους, ἀλλ' ὑπερέχοντας τῶν κυμάτων, καὶ ἀδεῶς ὁδοιπορούντας.

De Morb. vulg. lib. V. (*Hippocratis Op., vol. III. p. 571, ed. Kühn*). Καὶ ἀνέπνεεν ὡς ἐκ τοῦ βεβαπτίσθαι ἀναπνέουσι· καὶ ἐκ τοῦ στήθεος ὑπεψόφεεν ὥσπερ αἱ ἐγγαστρίμυθοι λεγόμεναι.

Ejusdem lib. VII. (*ed. Kühn, vol. III. p. 658*). Καὶ ἀνέπνει οἷον ἐκ τοῦ βεβαπτίσθαι ἀναπνεούσῃ.

description here given of the effects of a violent storm of wind, he says:—
"So that very many trees were upturned by the roots, and many houses were thrown down; the ships which were in the Tiber, and lying at anchor by the city and at its mouth, were SUBMERGED (BAPTIZED), and the wooden bridge was destroyed."

EXAMPLE 32.

The same Work, book XLI. ch. 42. Describing the defeat of Curio by Juba, King of Numidia (at the siege of Utica in Africa), and the fate of the fugitives, many losing their lives in their eager haste to get aboard of their vessels, and others by overloading and sinking them, he says:
"And many of them, who had fled, perished; some thrown down by the jostling, in getting on board the vessels, and others SUBMERGED (BAPTIZED), in the vessels themselves, by their own weight."

EXAMPLE 33.

The same Work, book LXXIV. ch. 13. Of the foraging ships of Byzantium (during the siege of the city by the forces of the

GREEK TEXT.

Dionis Cassii Historiæ Romanæ lib. XXXVII. c. 58 (*ed. Sturz*).

Ὥστε πάμπολλα μὲν δένδρα πρόρριζα ἀνατραπῆναι, πολλὰς δὲ οἰκίας καταρραγῆναι· τά τε πλοῖα τὰ ἐν τῷ Τιβέριδι καὶ πρὸς τὸ ἄστυ καὶ πρὸς τὰς ἐκβολὰς αὐτοῦ ναυλοχοῦντα βαπτισθῆναι, καὶ τὴν γέφυραν τὴν ξυλίνην διαφθαρῆναι.

Ejusdem lib. XLI. c. 42.

Συχνοὶ δὲ δὴ καὶ διαφυγόντες αὐτῶν ἀπώλοντο, οἱ μὲν ἐν τῇ ἐς τὰ πλοῖα ἐσβάσει ὑπὸ τοῦ ὠθισμοῦ σφαλέντες, οἱ δὲ καὶ ἐν αὐτοῖς τοῖς σκάφεσιν ὑπὸ τοῦ βάρους αὐτῶν βαπτισθέντες.

Roman Emperor Severus), returning overloaded with provisions in a storm, and attacked by the Roman fleet, he says:

"And they, however much they might have desired it, were not able to do any thing; but attempting in one way or another to escape, some were SUBMERGED (BAPTIZED) by the wind, using it too freely,* and others were overtaken by the enemy, and destroyed."

---

* Carrying too much sail, in their eagerness to escape.

EXAMPLE 34.

The same Work, book L. ch. 18. Mark Antony, in his address to his soldiers before the sea-fight at Actium, boasting of the superior strength and equipment of his vessels, and that the enemy would not venture to encounter them, adds:

"And even if any one came near, how could he escape being IMMERGED (BAPTIZED) by the very multitude of the oars?"*

---

* These vessels being impelled with oars, the larger and better equipped could run down and immerge the more feeble, by their greater speed and weight.

EXAMPLE 35.

The same Work, book L. ch. 32. In his account of the sea-fight at Actium, he describes Antony's large and powerful ships as awaiting the attacks of the smaller and swifter vessels of

---

GREEK TEXT.

Ejusdem lib. LXXIV. c. 13.

Καὶ ἐκεῖνοι δρᾶσαι μὲν οὐδέν, οὐδ' εἰ τὰ μάλιστα ἤθελον, ἠδύναντο· διαφυγεῖν δέ πῃ πειρώμενοι, οἱ μὲν ὑπὸ τοῦ πνεύματος, ἀπλήστως αὐτῷ χρώμενοι, ἐβαπτίζοντο· οἱ δ' ὑπὸ τῶν ἐναντίων καταλαμβανόμενοι διώλλυντο.

Ejusdem lib. L. c. 18.

Εἰ δὲ δὴ καὶ πλησιάσειέ τις, πῶς μὲν ἂν οὐχ ὑπ' αὐτοῦ τοῦ πλήθους τῶν κωπῶν βαπτισθείη;

IN THE LITERAL, PHYSICAL SENSE.

Augustus, hurling heavy missiles and grappling irons as they approached, and adds:
"And if they hit them, they came off superior; but if they missed, their own vessels being pierced, they WERE SUBMERGED (BAPTIZED)."

EXAMPLE 36.

The same Work, book L. ch. 32. In his further description of this battle, he says of the two parties in the conflict:
"And hence, they gained advantages each over the other; the one dropping within the lines of the ships' oars, and crushing the oar-blades, and the other from above SUBMERGING (BAPTIZING) them with stones and engines."

EXAMPLE 37.

The same Work, book L. ch. 35. In his account of the efforts to escape from the flames of the burning vessels (near the close of this battle), he says:
"And others leaping into the sea were drowned, or struck by the enemy WERE SUBMERGED (BAPTIZED)."

GREEK TEXT.

Ejusdem lib. L. c. 32.

Καὶ εἰ μὲν ἐπιτύχοιεν αὐτῶν, κρείττους ἐγίνοντο· εἰ δ᾽ ἁμάρτοιεν, τρωθέντων ἂν σφίσι τῶν σκαφῶν ἐβαπτίζοντο.

Ejusdem lib. L. c. 32.

Κἀκ τούτου ἐπλεονέκτουν τε ἀλλήλων, οἱ μὲν, ἔς τε τοὺς ταρσοὺς¹ τῶν νεῶν ὑποπίπτοντες, καὶ τὰς κώπας συναράσσοντες, οἱ δὲ, ἄνωθεν αὐτοὺς καὶ πέτραις καὶ μηχανήμασι βαπτίζοντες.

Ejusdem lib. L. c. 35.

Οἱ δὲ εἰς τὴν θάλασσαν ἐκπηδῶντες ἀπεπνίγοντο, ἢ καὶ παιόμενοι ὑπὸ τῶν ἐναντίων ἐβαπτίζοντο.

---

¹ "Ταρσὸς is 'the whole *broadside* of oars,' if such an expression be allowed" (Arnold, Thucyd. 7, 40).

Example 38.

Porphyry,* *Concerning the Styx.* Describing the *Lake of Probation*, in India, and the use made of it by the Brahmins for testing the guilt or innocence of persons accused of crime, he says:

"The depth is as far as to the knees; .... and when the accused comes to it, if he is guiltless he goes through without fear, having the water as far as to the knees; but if guilty, after proceeding a little way, he is IMMERSED (BAPTIZED) unto the head."

---

* A Greek philosopher, born 233 after Christ.

Example 39.

Heliodorus, Æthiopics (Story of Theagenes and Chariclea**), book V. ch. 28.* Of a band of pirates, who had seized a vessel, and were unable to manage it in the storm that ensued, he says:

"And already BECOMING IMMERGED (BAPTIZED), and wanting little of sinking, some of the pirates at first attempted to leave, and get aboard of their own bark."

---

* Written about 390 after Christ, by Heliodorus, afterward Bishop of Tricca in Thessaly.

===

Greek Text.

Porphyrii locus ex libro de Styge (*Porphyrii de Abstinentia, etc., Cantabr. 1655, p. 282*).

Τὸ βάθος δ' ἔστιν ἄχρι τῶν γονάτων· ... ὅταν δὲ κατηγορούμενος ἐπιβῇ, ἀναμάρτητος μὲν ὢν, ἀδεῶς διέρχεται, ἄχρι τῶν γονάτων ἔχων τὸ ὕδωρ· ἁμαρτὼν δὲ, ὀλίγον προβὰς βαπτίζεται μέχρι κεφαλῆς.

Heliodori Æthiopicorum lib. V. c. 28 (*ed. Bekker*).

Ἤδη δὲ βαπτιζομένων καὶ καταδῦναι μικρὸν ἀπολειπόντων, ἐπεχείρρυν τὴν πρώτην ἔνιοι τῶν λῃστῶν εἰς τὴν ἰδίαν αὐτῶν μετεισβαίνειν ἄκατον.

IN THE LITERAL, PHYSICAL SENSE.

EXAMPLE 40.

Heimerius,* *Oration X. § 2.* Speaking (in a strain of rhetorical extravagance) of the pictorial representations of the battle of Marathon, in the Pœcile at Athens, where Cynægirus was shown grasping a Persian vessel with his hands, he says:

"And I will show you also my soldiers; one fighting life-like even in the painting, ... and another IMMERGING (BAPTIZING) with his hands the Persian fleet."

---

* A Greek rhetorician, born about 315 after Christ.

EXAMPLE 41.

Themistius,* *Oration IV. (XXIII).*

"And neither can the swordsmith determine whether he shall sell the sword to a murderer, nor the shipwright whether he shall build ships for a robber, ... nor the pilot whether he saves, in the voyage, one whom it were better to SUBMERGE (BAPTIZE)."

---

* A Greek rhetorician and philosopher, early in the second half of the fourth century after Christ.

GREEK TEXT.

Heimerii Sophistæ Orat. X. 2 (*ed. Wernsdorf*).

Δείξω δὲ ὑμῖν καὶ στρατιώτας ἐμοὺς, τὸν μὲν τῇ φύσει καὶ ἐν τῇ γραφῇ μαχόμενον· ... τὸν δὲ ἄλλον διὰ χειρῶν τὸν Περσῶν στόλον βαπτίζοντα.

Themistii Sophistæ Orat. IV. (*ed. Dindorf. XXIII*).

Καὶ οὔτε ὁ μαχαιροποιὸς δοκιμάζειν ἔχει εἰ ἀνδροφόνῳ τὴν μάχαιραν ἀποδώσεται, οὔτε ὁ ναυπηγὸς εἰ ἅρπαγι ναυπηγήσεται, ... οὔτε ὁ κυβερνήτης. εἰ σώζει ἐν τῷ πλῷ ὃν καὶ βαπτίσαι ἄμεινον ἦν.

Example 42.

On the Life and Poetry of Homer,* *II. 26.* Among other characteristics of Homer's manner, the writer mentions *Emphasis;* and after one example, adds:
"Similar also is that:

'And the whole sword was warmed with blood.'

For truly in this he exhibits very great emphasis; as if the sword were so IMBATHED (BAPTIZED), as to be heated."

The expression, on which the writer makes this comment, is used by Homer in the Iliad, book 21, line 476, after saying that Achilles drove his sword through the head of Echeclus. He uses it also in book 16, line 333, where he says that Ajax smote with his sword the neck of Cleobulus. In either case the writer's comment is just; the poet's expression implying, that the sword was so plunged in the warm blood as to be heated by it.

* Of uncertain date; attributed (erroneously) to Plutarch.

Example 43.

Suidas, Lexicon. "Desiring to swim through, they were IMMERSED (BAPTIZED) by their full armor."*

* A quotation, by this old Greek lexicographer, from a Greek writer now unknown.

Example 44.

Gregory,* *Panegyric on Origen, XIV.* Describing him as an

* Surnamed *Thaumaturgus;* made bishop of Neocæsarea about the year 240 after Christ.

Greek Text.

De Vita et Poesi Homeri II. 26 (*Plutarchi Moralia, ed. Wyttenb.*).

῞Ομοιον δὲ κἀκεῖνο,
  πᾶν δ' ὑπεθερμάνθη ξίφος αἵματι·
καὶ γὰρ ἐν τούτῳ παρέχει μείζονα ἔμφασιν, ὡς βαπτισθέντος οὕτω τοῦ ξίφους ὥς τε θερμανθῆναι.

Suidæ Lexicon, s. v. Διανεῦσαι (*ed. Bernh. col. 1300*). Διανεῦσαι ἐθελήσαντες ἐβαπτίζοντο ὑπὸ τῆς πανοπλίας.

experienced and skillful guide through the mazes of philosophical speculation, he says:

"He himself would remain on high in safety, and stretching out a hand to others save them, as if drawing up persons SUBMERGED (BAPTIZED)."

EXAMPLE 45.

Chrysostom,* Discourse on the paralytic let down through the roof. Comparing the Saviour's cures with those effected by human art, through the aid of the knife and the cautery, he says:

"But here, no such thing is to be seen; no fire applied, nor steel PLUNGED IN (BAPTIZED), nor flowing blood."

---

* An eminent Greek writer of the Christian Church, born 347 after Christ.

EXAMPLE 46.

The same writer, on Eph. ch. V. Discourse XIX. Showing that the visible heavens do not rest (according to the popular error) on the waters of the ocean, he says:

"For things borne on the water must not be arched, but must

GREEK TEXT.

Gregorii Thaumaturgi Orat. Panegyr. in Orig. XIV. (*Gallandii Biblioth. Vet. Patr. Vol. II. p. 430*).

Μετέωρος αὐτός τε ἐν ἀσφαλεῖ μένοι, καὶ ἄλλοις ὀρέγων χεῖρα διασώζοιτο, ὥσπερ βαπτιζομένους ἀνιμώμενος.

Chrysost. Homil. de paralyt. per tect. demiss. 4 (*ed. Montfaucon, Vol. III. p. 39*).

Ἐνταῦθα δὲ οὐδὲν τοιοῦτόν ἐστιν ἰδεῖν, οὐ πῦρ προσαγόμενον, οὐ σίδηρον βαπτιζόμενον, οὐχ αἷμα ῥέον.

Ejusdem in Epist. at Ephes. c. V. Hom. XIX. 3 (*ed. Montfaucon, Vol. XI. p. 138*).

Τὰ γὰρ ἐπὶ τῶν ὑδάτων φερόμενα οὐ κυρτοῦσθαι δεῖ,

be hollowed [downward]. Wherefore? Because, on the water, the entire body of that which is hollow* is IMMERGED (BAPTIZED); ... but of that which is arched, the body is all above, and only the extremities touch."

---

* Concave above, and hence convex underneath.

EXAMPLE 47.

The same writer, on David and Saul, Discourse III. 7.

"Even this was worthy indeed of praise and of greatest admiration, that he did not PLUNGE IN (BAPTIZE) the sword, nor sever that hostile head!"

EXAMPLE 48.

Epistle to Damagetus* (by an unknown Greek writer).

"Shall I not laugh at him, who, having SUBMERGED (BAPTIZED)

---

* Of uncertain date, falsely attributed to Hippocrates the physician and medical writer, and printed with his works.

===

GREEK TEXT.

ἀλλὰ κοιλαίνεσθαι. τί δήποτε; ὅτι τοῦ μὲν κοίλου τὸ σῶμα ὅλον βαπτίζεται ἐπὶ τῶν ὑδάτων· .... τοῦ δὲ κεκουρτωμένου τὸ μὲν σῶμα ὅλον ἐστὶν ἄνωθεν, τὰ δὲ ἄκρα ἐπίκειται μόνον.

Ejusdem de Davide et Saule Hom. III. 7 (*ed. Montfaucon, Vol. IV. p. 779*).

Ἐπαίνου μὲν ἄξιον καὶ μεγίστου θαύματος καὶ τὸ μὴ βαπτίσαι τὸ ξίφος, μηδὲ ἀποτεμεῖν τὴν πολεμίαν ἐκείνην κεφαλήν.

Hippocratis Opera (*ed. Kühn, Vol. III. p. 809*).

Μὴ' γελάσω τὸν τὴν νῆα πολλοῖσι φορτίοισι βαπτί-

---

¹ Hermann ad Vig. Annot. 252.

his ship with much merchandize, then blames the sea for having ingulfed it full laden?"

EXAMPLE 49.

Life of Pythagoras,* 2. In his account of the philosophy of Pythagoras, Aristotle, and Plato, the writer states that things *sublunar* are subject to four controlling forces, deity, fate, human choice, fortune; and in illustration, says:

"As, to enter into the ship, or not to enter, is in our own power; but the sudden coming on of storm and tempest, in fair weather, depends on fortune; and that the IMMERGED (BAPTIZED) ship beyond all hope is saved, is of the providence of God."

* By an unknown Greek writer, and of uncertain date.

EXAMPLE 50.

Æsopic Fables; fable of the mule, who, finding that he lightened his load of salt by lying down in the water, repeated the experiment when loaded with sponges and wool.

"One of the salt-bearing mules, rushing into a river, accidentally slipped down; and rising up lightened (the salt becoming

---

GREEK TEXT.

σαντα, εἶτα μεμφόμενον τῇ θαλάττῃ ὅτι κατεβύθισεν αὐτὴν πλήρη;

De Vita Pythagoræ, II. (*Jamblichi Chalcid. de Vita Pythagorica liber, ed. Kiessling*).

Οἷον· τὸ μὲν εἰσελθεῖν εἰς τὴν ναῦν ἢ μὴ εἰσελθεῖν, ἐφ' ἡμῖν ἐστί. τὸ μέντοι ἐν εὐδίᾳ χειμῶνα καὶ ζάλην ἐξαίφνης ἐπιγενέσθαι, ἐκ τύχης. τὸ μέντοι βαπτιζομένην τὴν ναῦν παρ' ἐλπίδα σωθῆναι, προνοίας θεοῦ.

Αισωπου Μυθοι, 254 (*ed. Coray, p. 167*).

Τῶν ἁληγῶν ἡμιόνων εἷς, ἐμβαλὼν εἰς ποταμὸν, ὤλισθεν αὐτομάτως· καὶ τῶν ἁλῶν διατακέντων ἀναστὰς

dissolved) he perceived the cause, and remembered it; so that always, when passing through the river, he purposely lowered down and IMMERSED (BAPTIZED) the panniers."*

* Of uncertain date (related in Plut. Moral. *Skill of Water and Land Animals, xvi*).

EXAMPLE 51.

*Fable of the Ape and the Dolphin.** The dolphin bearing the ship-wrecked ape to the shore, and detecting the attempted imposition of the latter, it is said:
"And the dolphin, angry at such a falsehood, IMMERSING (BAPTIZING) killed him."

* Writer and date unknown.

EXAMPLE 52.

*Fable of the Shepherd and the Sea.** The shepherd having embarked, with the merchandize obtained from the sale of his flocks, it is said:
"But a violent storm coming on, and the ship being in danger

* Writer and date unknown.

GREEK TEXT.

ἐλαφρὸς, ἤσθετο τὴν αἰτίαν, καὶ κατεμνημόνευσεν, ὥστε διαβαίνων ἀεὶ τὸν ποταμὸν, ἐπίτηδες ὑφιέναι καὶ βαπτίζειν τὰ ἀγγεῖα.

Fabularum Æsopic. collect. 363[1] (*recog. Halm*).

Καὶ ὁ δελφὶς ἐπὶ τοσούτῳ ψεύδει ἀγανακτήσας, βαπτίζων αὐτὸν ἀπέκτεινεν.

Αἰσώπου Μῦθοι (*ed. Coray, 49; recog. Halm, 370*).

Χειμῶνος δὲ σφοδροῦ γενομένου, καὶ τῆς νεὼς κινδυ-

[1] Fab. 156 of the Oxford edition (1698), the preface to which speaks of Bentley as, *Virum in volvendis lexicis satis diligentem!*

of BECOMING IMMERGED (BAPTIZED), he threw out all the lading into the sea, and with difficulty escaped in the empty ship."

EXAMPLE 53.

Plutarch,* On the comparative skill of water and land animals, XXXV. Speaking of the bird called the *Halcyon*, and of her skill in constructing her nest, shaped like a fisher's boat so as to float safely on the water, he says:
"That which is moulded by her, or rather constructed with the shipwright's art, of many forms the only one not liable to be overturned, NOR TO BE IMMERSED (BAPTIZED)."

* Born in the year 50 after Christ.

EXAMPLE 54.

Achilles Tatius;* Story of Clitophon and Leucippe, book III. ch. 1. The vessel being thrown on her beam ends in a storm, the narrator says:
"We all, therefore, shifted our position to the more elevated parts of the ship, in order that we might lighten that part of the ship that was IMMERGED (BAPTIZED)."

* Author of the Greek romance here quoted, middle of the fifth century after Christ.

GREEK TEXT.

νευούσης βαπτίζεσθαι, πάντα τὸν φόρτον ἐκβαλὼν εἰς τὴν θάλατταν, μόλις κενῇ τῇ νηῒ διεσώθη.

Plutarchi de sollertia animalium, XXXV. (*ed. Wyttenb, Vol. IV. Pt. II. p. 987*).

Τὸ πλαττόμενον ὑπ' αὐτῆς, μᾶλλον δὲ ναυπηγούμενον, σχημάτων πολλῶν μόνον ἀπερίτρεπτον καὶ ἀβάπτιστον.

Achillis Tatii de Leucippes et Clitophontis Amoribus, lib. III. c. 1 (*ed. Jacobs, p. 58*).

Μετεσκευαζόμεθα οὖν ἅπαντες εἰς τὰ μετέωρα τῆς νηός, ὅπως τὸ μὲν βαπτιζόμενον τῆς νηὸς ἀνακουφίσαιμεν.

Example 55.

The same writer (ibidem).
"But suddenly, the wind shifts to another quarter of the ship, and the vessel is almost IMMERGED (BAPTIZED)."

Example 56.

The same Work, book IV. ch. 10. The heroine, Leucippe, having fallen down, apparently in a fit, the cause is thus explained:
"For the blood when quite young, and boiling up through intense vigor, often overflows the veins, and flooding the head within, WHELMS (BAPTIZES) the passage of the reason."

Example 57.

The same Work, book IV. ch. 18. Describing the manner in which the Egyptian boatman drinks water from the Nile, he says:
"For their drinking-cup is the hand. For if any of them is thirsty while sailing, stooping forward from the vessel he directs his face towards the stream, and lets down his hand

---

Greek Text.

Ejusdem (*ibidem*).

Αἰφνίδιον δὲ μεταβάλλεται τὸ πνεῦμα ἐπὶ θάτερα τῆς νηός, καὶ μικροῦ βαπτίζεται τὸ σκάφος.

Ejusdem lib. IV. c. 10 (*p. 90*).

Τὸ γὰρ αἷμα πάντῃ νεάζον, καὶ ὑπὸ πολλῆς ἀκμῆς ἀναζέον, ὑπερβλύζει πολλάκις τὰς φλέβας, καὶ τὴν κεφαλὴν ἔνδον περικλύζον βαπτίζει τοῦ λογισμοῦ τὴν ἀναπνοήν.

Ejusdem lib. IV. c. 18 (*p. 101*).

Ἔκπωμα γὰρ αὐτοῖς ἐστιν ἡ χείρ. Εἰ γάρ τις αὐτῶν διψήσειε πλέων, προκύψας ἐκ τῆς νεὼς τὸ μὲν πρόσωπον εἰς τὸν ποταμὸν προβέβληκε, τὴν δὲ χεῖρα εἰς τὸ ὕδωρ

into the water; and DIPPING (BAPTIZING) it hollowed, and filling it with water, he darts the draught towards his mouth, and hits the mark."

EXAMPLE 58.

Demetrius, the Cydonian,* On contemning death, ch. XIV. 4.

"For the dominion [of the soul] over the body, and the fact that, entering into it, she is not wholly IMMERGED (BAPTIZED) but rises above, and that the body separate from her can do nothing, but she, in efforts the greatest and gravest and kindred with herself, is wholly withdrawn from the body and from the vanity thence proceeding, are a clear proof, that there is an essence of the soul by itself, not dependent on the body, and able of itself both to subsist and to abide."

* Middle of the first century of the Christian era.

GREEK TEXT.

καθῆκε, καὶ κοίλην βαπτίσας καὶ πλησάμενος ὕδατος, ἀκοντίζει κατὰ τοῦ στόματος τὸ πόμα, καὶ τυγχάνει τοῦ σκοποῦ.

Demetrii Cydonii de contemnenda morte, c. XIV. 4 (*ed. Kuinoel*).

῎Η τε γὰρ κατὰ τοῦ σώματος ἀρχὴ, καὶ τὲ δῦσαν εἰς αὐτὸ μὴ παντελῶς βεβαπτίσθαι ἀλλ' ἀνέχειν,[1] καὶ τὸ μὲν σῶμα χωρισθὲν ἐκείνης μηδὲν δύνασθαι πράττειν, αὐτὴν δὲ κατὰ τὰς μεγίστας καὶ σεμνοτάτας ἐνεργείας καὶ ἑαυτῇ συμφύτους τοῦ σώματος καὶ τῆς ἐκεῖθεν φλυαρίας παντελῶς ἀπηλλάχθαι, τεκμήριον ἐναργὲς, εἶναι τινὰ καθ' ἑαυτὴν τῆς ψυχῆς οὐσίαν, ἀνενδεᾶ μὲν σώματος, δυναμένην δὲ ἐφ' ἑαυτῆς καὶ εἶναι καὶ μένειν.

[1] Comp. Plutarch. de Gen. Socrat. XXII. med. Μίγνυνται δ' [σαρκὶ] οὐ πᾶσα [ψυχή] τὸν αὐτὸν τρόπον· ἀλλ' αἱ μὲν ὅλαι κατέδυσαν εἰς σῶμα, κ. τ. λ.

2.

CONSTRUED WITH SOME CASE OF THE INGULFING ELEMENT,

WITH OR WITHOUT A PREPOSITION.

EXAMPLE 59.

Polybius,* *History, book* V. *ch.* 47, 2. Speaking of a body of cavalry sent by Molon to attack Xenœtas, in a position where he was protected partly by the river Tigris, and partly by marshes and pools, he says:

"Who, coming into near proximity with the forces of Xenœtas, through ignorance of the localities required no enemy, but themselves by themselves IMMERSED (BAPTIZED) and sinking in the pools, were all useless, and many of them also perished."

---

* Born 205 before Christ.

GREEK TEXT.

Polybii Hist. lib. V. c. 47, 2 (*ed. Schweigh.*).

Οἳ καὶ συνεγγίσαντες τοῖς περὶ τὸν Ξενοίταν, διὰ τὴν ἄγνοιαν τῶν τόπων οὐ προσεδέοντο τῶν πολεμίων· αὐτοὶ δ' ὑπ' αὐτῶν βαπτιζόμενοι καὶ καταδύνοντες ἐν τοῖς τέλμασιν, ἄχρηστοι μὲν ἦσαν ἅπαντες, πολλοὶ δὲ καὶ διεφθάρησαν αὐτῶν.

IN THE LITERAL, PHYSICAL SENSE.

EXAMPLE 60.

Epigram on the comic poet Eupolis;* occasioned by his offensive allusions in a play called *Baptæ (Dippers?),* to the title of which the epigram refers.

"You dipped me in plays; but I, in waves of the sea IMMERSING (BAPTIZING), will destroy thee with streams more bitter."†

---

* Attributed to Alcibiades, about 400 before Christ.

† It is related that on a sea-voyage, the soldiers of Alcibiades, by his command, gave the poet several immersions in the waves, a rope being attached to his body to insure his safety.

EXAMPLE 61.

Strabo,* Geography, book XII. ch. 5, § 4. Speaking of the lake Tatta in Phrygia (which he calls a natural salt-pit), he says:

"The water solidifies so readily around every thing that is IMMERSED (BAPTIZED) into it, that they draw up salt-crowns when they let down a circle of rushes."

---

* Born about the year 60 before Christ.

GREEK TEXT.

Epigramma in Eupolin (*Meineke, Hist. crit. Comic. Græc. p. 119*).

Βάπτες¹ μ' ἐν θυμέλῃσιν, ἐγὼ δέ σε κύμασι πόντου
βαπτίζων ὀλέσω νάμασι πικροτέροις.

Strabonis Geogr. lib. XII. c. 6, 4 (*ed. Tzschucke*).

Οὕτω δὲ περιπήττεται ῥᾳδίως τὸ ὕδωρ παντὶ τῷ βαπτισθέντι εἰς αὐτὸ ὥστε στεφάνους ἁλῶν ἀνέλκουσιν, ἐπειδὰν καθῶσι κύκλον σχοίνινον.

---

¹ Sic enim legendum pro βάπτε με (*Meincke*).—Βάπτεις (*Bergk, Poet. Lyr. p. 473*).

Example 62.

Pindar,* Pythic Odes, II. 79, 80 (144–147). Comparing himself to a cork of the fisher's net, floating at the top, while the other parts of the fishing-tackle are doing service in the depth below, he says:

"For, as when the rest of the tackle is toiling deep in the sea, I, as a cork above the net, am un-DIPPED (un-BAPTIZED) in the brine."

---

* Born 522 before Christ.

Example 63.

Archias, Epigram X.* Among other implements of his art, which the old fisherman is said to have hung up as a votive offering, are mentioned:

"And fishing rod thrice-stretched,† and cork un-DIPPED (un-BAPTIZED) in water."

---

* Of uncertain date, what Archias is meant not being indicated.

† An extension-rod, capable of being stretched to thrice its length when folded.

Greek Text.

Pindari Pyth. II. 144–147 (79, 80, *ed. Boeckh*).

Ἅτε γὰρ εἰνάλιον πόνον ἐχοίσας βαθὺ
σκευᾶς ἑτέρας, ἀβάπτιστός εἰμι, φελλὸς ὣς ὑπὲρ ἕρκος,
ἅλμας.¹

Anthol. Græc. Tom. II. p. 94 (*ed. Jacobs, Vol. II. p. 82*).

Καὶ δόνακα τριτάννυστον, ἀβάπτιστόν τε καθ' ὕδωρ
φελλόν.

---

¹ Ego Bothio assentior conjungenti ἀβάπτιστός εἰμι ἅλμας, quod non durum, quum verba φελλὸς ὣς ὑπὲρ ἕρκος quasi in parenthesi dicta sint; ideoque post ἕρκος interpunxi virgula (*Boeckh*).

Jam vero ἀβάπτιστος ἅλμας hoc loco eo aptius sententiæ est, quod ἅλμη dicitur *amarities.* ... *Ego,* inquit, *ut cortex supra rete, non immergor salis undis* (*Boeckh*).—Βαθὺ est βαθέως (*Id.*).

Example 64.

Plutarch*, On Superstition, III. The superstitious man, consulting the jugglers on his frightful dreams, is told:
"Call the old Expiatrix,† and PLUNGE (BAPTIZE) thyself into the sea, and spend a day sitting on the ground."

---

* Born in the year 50 after Christ.

† An old woman, supposed to have power to avert evil omens by magic lustrations.

- ## Example 65.

The same writer, Gryllus, VII. He says of Agamemnon:
"Then bravely PLUNGING (BAPTIZING) himself into the lake Copais, that there he might extinguish his love, and be freed from desire."

Example 66.

The same writer, Physical Questions, X.
"Why do they pour sea-water into wine, and say that fisher-

Greek Text.

Plutarchi de Superstitione, III. (*ed. Wyttenb. Vol. I. p.* 656).

Τὴν περιμάκτριαν κάλει γραῦν,¹ καὶ βάπτισον σεαυτὸν εἰς θάλασσαν, καὶ καθίσας ἐν τῇ γῇ διημέρευσον.

Ejusdem Grylli, VII. (*ed. Wyttenb. Vol. V. p.* 23).

Εἶτα καλὸν καλῶς ἑαυτὸν βαπτίζων εἰς τὴν Κωπαΐδα λίμνην, ὡς αὐτόθι κατασβέσων τὸν ἔρωτα καὶ τῆς ἐπιθυμίας ἀπαλλαξόμενος.

Ejusdem Quæst. Nat. X. (*ed. Wyttenb. Vol. IV. p.* 696).

Διὰ τί τῷ οἴνῳ θάλασσαν παραχέουσι, καὶ χρησμόν

---

¹ Quasi dicas anum *circumpistricem*. Istiusmodi lustrationis pars erat, ut corpus lustrandum circumlineretur, et quasi circumpinseretur, imprimis luto, πηλῷ, tum abstergeretur; quorum illud est περιμάττειν, hoc ἀπομάττειν; sed utrumque promiscue de tota lustratione dicitur (*Wyttenb.*).

men received an oracle, commanding to IMMERSE (BAPTIZE) Bacchus in [or at] the sea?

EXAMPLE 67.

Parallels between Greek and Roman History, III.* Relating a story of a Roman General, who fell mortally wounded in an ambush of the Samnites at the Caudine Forks, the writer says:
"But in the depth of night, surviving a little longer, he took away the shields of the slain enemies, and DIPPING (BAPTIZING) his hand into the blood, he set up a trophy inscribing it, 'the Romans against the Samnites, to trophy-bearing Jove.'"

* Attributed (falsely, as is supposed) to Plutarch, and printed with his writings.

GREEK TEXT.

τινα λέγουσιν ἁλιεῖς κομισθῆναι προστάττοντα βαπτίζειν τὸν Διόνυσον πρὸς τὴν θάλατταν;[1]

The oracle is given thus (Schol. Hom. Il. 6, 136, ed. Bekker): ἢ ὅτι χρησμὸς ἐδόθη, "ἁλιεύειν ἐν τόπῳ Διόνυσον ἁλιέα βαπτίζοιτε," ὡς Φιλόχορος.[2]

Ejusdem Parall. Græc. et Rom. III.

Βαθείας δὲ νυκτὸς ὀλίγον ἐπιζήσας, περιείλετο τῶν ἀνῃρημένων πολεμίων τὰς ἀσπίδας, καὶ εἰς τὸ αἷμα τὴν χεῖρα βαπτίσας, ἔστησε τρόπαιον ἐπιγράψας· 'Ρωμαῖοι κατὰ Σαμνιτῶν Διὶ τροπαιούχῳ.

[1] Similiter conjunctum cum πρὸς verbum βάπτειν ab Sophocle notabimus sub illo (*Dindorf, Steph. Thes.*). Perhaps, at (or by) the sea.

[2] Immergere Bacchum, ἁλιβδύειν seu ἁλιδύειν [as conjectured by Lobeck], nihil aliud est quam vinum temperare; et videtur Scholiastes verbum antiquatum, nobisque a solis grammaticis servatum, cum nonnullis aliis ex oraculo retinuisse, cujus sensum tantum per caliginem videre licet:

Ἐν δέπαϊ Διόνυσον ἀλωέα βαπτίζοιτε.

De δέπαϊ non recuso quin alii a me dissentiant; sed ἀλωέα recte mihi reposuisse videor, aptum imprimis Baccho nomen, a vinetis tractum (Lobeck, Observ. crit. et gram in Sophocl. Aj. p. 347).

IN THE LITERAL, PHYSICAL SENSE. 33

EXAMPLE 68.

Josephus,* Jewish War, book II. ch. 18, 4. He thus describes the death of Simon by his own hand, after he had put his family to death in sight of the people:
"And stretching out the right hand, so as to be unseen by none, he PLUNGED (BAPTIZED) the whole sword into his own neck."

---

* Born in the year 37 after Christ.

EXAMPLE 69.

The same writer, Antiquities of the Jews, book IV. ch. 4, 6. Describing the mode of purifying the people, during the thirty days of mourning for Miriam, sister of Moses, he says:
"Those, therefore, who were defiled by the dead body, casting a little of the ashes into a fountain and DIPPING (BAPTIZING) a hyssop-branch, they sprinkled, on the third and seventh of the [thirty] days."

GREEK TEXT.

Josephi Bell. Jud. lib. II. c. 18, 4 (*ed. Oberthür*).

Τήν τε δεξιὰν ἀνατείνας, ὡς μηδένα λαθεῖν, ὅλον εἰς τὴν ἑαυτοῦ σφαγὴν ἐβάπτισε τὸ ξίφος.

Ejusdem Antiq. Jud. lib. 4. c. 4, 6 (*ed. Imman. Bekker*).

Τοὺς οὖν ἀπὸ νεκροῦ μεμιασμένους, τῆς τέφρας ὀλίγον εἰς πηγὴν ἐνιέντες καὶ ὕσσωπον βαπτίσαντες, ἔρραινον τρίτῃ τε καὶ ἑβδόμῃ τῶν ἡμερῶν.

This reading of the passage, in Bekker's edition, is the one suggested by Bonfrer (on Num. ch. XIX), some words having evidently been repeated, in the common Greek text, by an error in copying. The common reading,[1] however, shows the same use of *βαπτίσαντες*, and is thus rendered in the Latin version: Paulum igitur hujus cineris in fontem immittentes cum hyssopi ramulo, ejusdemque cineris aliquantulum in aquam immergentes, a mortuo pollutos die tertia et septima *puri aliqui* conspergebant.

---

[1] Τοὺς οὖν ἀπὸ νεκροῦ μεμιασμένους, τῆς τέφρας ὀλίγον εἰς πηγὴν ἐνιέντες καὶ ὕσσωπον, βαπτίσαντές τε καὶ τῆς τέφρας ταύτης εἰς πηγήν, ἔρραινον τρίτῃ καὶ ἑβδόμῃ τῶν ἡμερῶν.

Example 70.

On Diseases of Women,* book I.

"Then dipping [the pessary] into oil of roses or Egyptian oil, apply it during the day; and when it begins to sting, remove it, and again IMMERSE (BAPTIZE) it into breast-milk and Egyptian ointment."

* An ancient medical writing, ascribed (erroneously) to Hippocrates, and printed with his works.

Example 71.

Homeric Allegories, ch. 9.* The writer explains the ground of the allegory (as he regards it) of Neptune freeing Mars from Vulcan, thus:

"Since the mass of iron, drawn red hot from the furnace, IS PLUNGED (BAPTIZED) in water; and the fiery glow, by its own nature quenched with water, ceases."

* The work of an old Greek grammarian, of uncertain date; attributed (falsely) to Heraclides Ponticus, fourth century before Christ.

Greek Text.

Hippocratis Opera (*ed. Kühn, Vol. II. p. 710*).

*Ἔπειτα βάψας ἐς ἄλειφα ῥόδινον ἢ αἰγύπτιον προσ-
θέσθω τὴν ἡμέραν, καὶ ἐπὴν δάκνηται ἀφαιρέεσθαι, καὶ
βαπτίζειν πάλιν ἐς γάλα γυναικὸς καὶ μύρον Αἰγύπτιον.*

Allegor. Homeric., quæ sub Heraclidis nomine feruntur, c. 69 (*ed. Schow, p. 710*).

*Ἐπειδήπερ ἐκ τῶν βαναύσων*¹ [*Βαύνων*] *διάπυρος ὁ τοῦ
σιδήρου μύδρος ἑλκυσθεὶς ὕδατι βαπτίζεται, καὶ τὸ φλογῶ-
δες ὑπὸ τῆς ἰδίας φύσεως ὕδατι κατασβεσθὲν ἀναπαύεται.*

Siquidem ignea ferri massa, fornicibus extracta, aquæ immergitur (*Gesner's translation*).

---

¹ *Valcknaer ad Ammon.* p. 215 : Eadem medicina Heraclito est facienda Allegor. Hom. p. 475, ἐκ τῶν βαναύσων (l. βαύνων), etc.

Si βαναύσων recte legitur, necesse est, Heraclidem βαναύσον de fornace dixisse. Sed probabilius est, cum Valck. ad Ammon. p. 215, emendandum esse βαίνων; nam βαῦνος ἡ κάμινος (*Schow*). So *Heyne* (*Epist. ad Schow*)

Example 72.

Plotinus,* *Ennead I. book 8, on Good and Evil, § 13.* Of the condition of the soul, in the corrupt and vicious, he says:

"She dies, therefore, as the soul may die; and death to her, while yet IMMERGED (BAPTIZED) in the body, is to be sunk in matter and to be filled therewith, and also when gone forth, to lie there still."

* A Greek philosopher, of the New-Platonic school, born 205 after Christ.

Example 73.

The same writer, Ennead VI. book 9, on the Good, or the One, § 8.

"But now, since a part of us is contained by the body, as if one has the feet in water but with the rest of the body stands out above, towering up by what is not IMMERGED (BAPTIZED) in the body we by this are attached, as to our own centre, with that which is as a centre of all."

Greek Text.

Plotini Ennead. I. lib. 8, 13 (*ed. Creutzer, Vol. I. p. 154–5; recogn. Kirchhoff, Vol. II. p. 400*).

Ἀποθνήσκει οὖν, ὡς ψυχὴ ἂν θάνοι· καὶ ὁ θάνατος αὐτῇ καὶ ἔτι ἐν τῷ σώματι βεβαπτισμένῃ, ἐν ὕλῃ ἐστὶ καταδῦναι καὶ πλησθῆναι αὐτῆς, καὶ ἐξελθούσῃ ἐκεῖ κεῖσθαι.

Ejusd. Ennead. VI. lib. 9, 8 (*ed. Creutzer, Vol. II. p. 1403; recog. Kirchhoff, Vol. I. p. 89*).

Νῦν δὲ ἐπεὶ μέρος ἡμῶν κατέχεται ὑπὸ τοῦ σώματος, οἷον εἴ τις τοὺς πόδας ἔχει ἐν ὕδατι, τῷ δ' ἄλλῳ σώματι ὑπερέχοι,[1] τῷ δὴ μὴ βαπτισθέντι τῷ σώματι ὑπέραντες,[2] τούτῳ συνάπτομεν κατὰ τὸ ἑαυτῶν κέντρον τῷ οἷον πάντων κέντρῳ.

[1] Or, ὑπερέχει
[2] Or, ὑπεράραντες

Example 74.

Argonautic Expedition,* *line 512.*

"But when Titan IMMERSED (BAPTIZED) HIMSELF into the Ocean-stream."

---

* Written early in the Christian era, probably in the fourth century.

Example 75.

Alexander* *of Aphrodisias, Medical and Physical Problems, II. 38.* In answer to the question, why fevers, etc., are more hard to cure in brutes than in men, he says:

"Because they have their nature and perceptive faculty IMMERSED (BAPTIZED) in the depth of the body, and not diverted to outward things by what pertains to the rational soul, as is the case in men."

---

* A Greek writer on philosophy and medicine, beginning of the third century after Christ; but by some (with less reason) supposed to be *Alexander of Tralles,* in the sixth century.

Greek Text.

Orphei Argonaut., 512 (*ed. Hermann*).

Ἀλλ' ὅτ' ἐς Ὠκεανοῖο ῥόον βαπτίζετο Τιτήν.

Alexandri Aphrodis. Probl. med. et phys. II. 38 (*Ideler, Physic. et Medic. Gr. min. Vol. I. p. 12*).

Ὅτι τὴν φύσιν ἔχουσι καὶ τὴν αἰσθετικὴν δύναμιν βεβαπτισμένην ἐν τῷ βάθει τοῦ σώματος, καὶ [οὐκ] περιελκομένην ὑπὸ τῶν λογιστικῆς ψυχῆς ἐπὶ τὰ ἐκτός, καθάπερ ἐπὶ ἀνθρώπων ἔχει.

Attributed by some, but without sufficient grounds,[1] to Alexander Trallianus.

---

[1] Seitdem sie aber *Griechisch* bekannt gemacht ist, hat man gefunden, dass man alle Ursache habe, der Angabe der Manuscripte Glauben beizumessen, und dem Restaurator der Aristotelischen Philosophie auch unter den Aerzten eine Stelle einzuräumen (*Schoell, Geschichte der Griechischen Literatur, deutsche Ausgabe, Vol. II. p.* 793).

EXAMPLE 76.

The same Work, I. 28. In answering the question, why many foolish persons have offspring who are very wise, and *vice versa*, he says of the former:

"They have the soul very much IMMERSED (BAPTIZED) in the body;* and on this account the seminal germ, partaking in greatest measure of the rational and physical power, causes their offspring to be more wise."

---

* Compare Example 71, and the statement, in regard to the rational nature of man, in Example 54.

EXAMPLE 77.

Chrysostom, Select Discourses*, XXIX. on Clemency*, etc. Speaking of David's clemency toward Saul, when he had him in his power in the cave (1 Sam. 24 : 3–7), he says:

"Sawest thou the nets of David stretched, and the prey intercepted therein, and the huntsman standing, and all exhorting to PLUNGE (BAPTIZE) the sword into the enemy's breast?

---

* See the remark on Example 45.

GREEK TEXT.

Ejusdem I. 28.

Ἔχουσι τὴν ψυχὴν ἄγαν βεβαπτισμένην τῷ σώματι, καὶ διὰ τοῦτο τὸ σπέρμα πλείστης μετέχον δυνάμεως λογιστικῆς καὶ φυσικῆς τὰ ὑπ' αὐτοῦ τικτόμενα φρονιμώτερα ποιεῖ.

Chrysostomi Homil. select. XXIX. de Mansuet., etc. (*ed. Montf. Vol. XII. p.* 647).

Εἶδες τοῦ Δαυὶδ τὰ δίκτυα τεταμένα, καὶ τὸ θήραμα ἐναπειλημμένον, καὶ τὸν κυναγέτην ἑστῶτα, καὶ πάντας ἐγκελευομένους Βαπτίσαι τὸ ξίφος εἰς τὸ τοῦ πολεμίου στῆθος;

Example 78.

The same writer, Expos. of Ps. VII. § 14. Speaking of Absalom and David, he says:

"For he, indeed, desired to PLUNGE (BAPTIZE) his right hand* in his father's neck; but the father, even in such a case, exhorted the soldiers to spare him."

---

* The armed right hand, by a common figure for the weapon held in it.

Examples 79 and 80.

Basil (the Great), On Baptism, book I. ch. 2, 10.* Commenting on the Apostle's words, Rom. 6 : 3, he says:

"We were immersed [baptized], says he, in order that from it we might learn this: that as wool IMMERSED (BAPTIZED) in a dye is changed as to its color; or rather (using John the Baptist as a guide, when he prophesied of the Lord, 'He will immerse [baptize] you in the Holy Spirit and fire'), ... let us say this: that as steel, IMMERSED (BAPTIZED) in the fire kindled up by spirit

---

* A distinguished Greek writer of the Christian Church, born 330 after Christ.

Greek Text.

Ejusdem Expos. in Ps. VII. § 14.

Αὐτὸς μὲν γὰρ ἐπεθύμει τὴν δεξιὰν τῷ λαιμῷ βαπτίσαι τῷ πατρικῷ· ὁ δὲ πατὴρ καὶ οὕτω φείσασθαι αὐτοῦ παρῄνει τοῖς στρατιώταις.

Basilii Magni, de Baptismo lib. I. c. 2, 10 (*ed. Garnier, Vol. II. p. 656*).

Ἐβαπτίσθημεν, φησὶν, ἵν᾽ ἐκ τούτου ἐκεῖνο παιδευθῶμεν, ὅτι ὥσπερ τὸ ἔριον βαπτισθὲν ἐν βάμματι μεταποιεῖται κατὰ τὸ χρῶμα· μᾶλλον δὲ, ἵνα τῷ βαπτιστῇ Ἰωάννῃ προφητεύσαντι περὶ τοῦ κυρίου, ὅτι αὐτὸς ὑμᾶς βαπτίσει ἐν πνεύματι ἁγίῳ καὶ πυρί, ὁδηγῷ χρησάμενοι, ... τοῦτο εἴπωμεν· ὅτι ὥσπερ ὁ σίδηρος βαπτιζόμενος ἐν τῷ πυρὶ ἀναζωπυρουμένῳ ὑπὸ πνεύματος, εὐγνωστότερος μὲν γίνε-

IN THE LITERAL, PHYSICAL SENSE. 39

(wind), becomes more easy to test whether it has in itself any fault, and more ready for being refined; ... so it follows and is necessary, that he who is immersed [baptized] in fire (that is, in the word of instruction, which convicts of the evil of sin and shows the grace of justification) should hate and abhor unrighteousness, as it is written, and should desire to be cleansed through faith in the power of the blood of our Lord Jesus Christ."

EXAMPLE 81.

Heliodorus,* Æthiopics (Story of Theagenes and Chariclea), book I. ch. 30.

"And every form of war was enacted and witnessed; the natives sustaining the conflict with zeal and with all their force; the others, having greatly the advantage both in number and in the unexpectedness of the attack, and slaying some on land,

---

* See the remark on Example 39.

GREEK TEXT.

ται, εἴ τινα ἔχει ἐν ἑαυτῷ κακίαν, ἑτοιμότερος δὲ πρὸς τὸ καθαρισθῆναι· ... οὕτως ἀκόλουθον καὶ ἀναγκαῖον τὸν βαπτισθέντα ἐν τῷ πυρί, τουτέστιν ἐν τῷ λόγῳ τῆς διδασκαλίας, ἐλέγχοντι μὲν τῶν ἁμαρτημάτων τὴν κακίαν, φανεροῦντι δὲ τῶν δικαιωμάτων τὴν χάριν, μισῆσαι μὲν καὶ βδελύξασθαι τὴν ἀδικίαν, καθὼς γέγραπται· εἰς ἐπιθυμίαν δὲ ἐλθεῖν τοῦ καθαρισθῆναι διὰ τῆς πίστεως ἐν δυνάμει τοῦ αἵματος τοῦ κυρίου ἡμῶν Ἰησοῦ Χριστοῦ.

Heliodori Æthiopicorum lib. I. 30 (ed. *Coray*, p. 47; ed. *Bekker*, p. 35).

Καὶ πολέμου πᾶν εἶδος καὶ ἐνηργεῖτο καὶ ἐξηκούετο, τῶν μὲν ἐγχωρίων προθυμίᾳ καὶ ῥώμῃ πάσῃ τὴν μάχην ὑφισταμένων, τῶν δὲ, τῷ τε πλήθει καὶ τῆς ἐφόδου τῷ ἀπροσδοκήτῳ πλεῖστον ὑπερφερόντων, καὶ τοὺς μὲν ἐπὶ

and PLUNGING (BAPTIZING) others, with their boats and huts, into the lake.

EXAMPLE 82.

Achilles Tatius; Story of Clitophon and Leucippe, book II. ch. 14.*
"And there is a fountain of gold there. They PLUNGE (BAPTIZE) into the water, therefore, a pole smeared with pitch, and open the barriers of the stream. And the pole is to the gold what the hook is to the fish, for it catches it; and the pitch is a bait for the prey."

* See the remark on Example 54.

EXAMPLE 83.

The same Work, book III. ch. 21. Speaking of the short sword used by jugglers and stage-players, so constructed that, when a blow is given, the blade is driven back into the hilt and no harm is done, the narrator says:
"And they who behold suppose that the steel is PLUNGED (BAPTIZED) down the body; but it runs back into the hollow of the hilt."

GREEK TEXT.

γῆς ἀναιρούντων, τοὺς δὲ εἰς τὴν λίμνην αὐτοῖς σκάφεσι καὶ αὐτοῖς οἰκήμασι βαπτιζόντων.

Achillis Tatii de Leucippes et Clitophontis Amoribus, lib. II. c. 14 *(ed. Jacobs, p. 38).*

Καὶ ἔστιν ἐκεῖ χρυσίου πηγή. Κοντὸν οὖν εἰς τὸ ὕδωρ βαπτίζουσι, πίσσῃ πεφαρμαγμένον, καὶ ἀνοίγουσι τοῦ ποταμοῦ τὰ κλεῖθρα. Ὁ δὲ κοντὸς πρὸς τὸν χρυσὸν οἷον πρὸς τὸν ἰχθὺν ἄγκιστρον γίνεται, ἀγρεύει γὰρ αὐτόν· ἡ δὲ πίσσα δέλεαρ γίνεται τῆς ἄγρας.

Ejusdem lib. III. c. 21 *(p. 77).*

Καὶ οἱ μὲν ὁρῶντες δοκοῦσι βαπτίζεσθαι τὸν σίδηρον κατὰ τοῦ σώματος, ὁ δὲ εἰς τὸν χηραμὸν τῆς κώπης ἀνέδραμε.

IN THE LITERAL, PHYSICAL SENSE.

EXAMPLE 84.

Julian,* *Ode on Cupid.*
"As I was once twining a garland, I found Cupid in the roses; and holding by the wings I IMMERSED (BAPTIZED) him into wine, and took and drank him; and now, within my members, he tickles with his wings."

* In the first half of the sixth century after Christ.

EXAMPLE 85.

Simplicius,* *Commentary on the Manual of Epictetus, ch. 38, 10.* Contrasting beauty, as it appears in imperfect material forms, with absolute and perfect beauty in the soul, he says:
"Beauty, in bodies, is in flesh and sinews, and things that make up the body, of animals for example; beautifying them,

* Of the seventh century after Christ.

GREEK TEXT.

Juliani Ægyptii, in Amorem (*Anthol. Gr. Tom. II. p. 493; Anacr. ed. Fischer, p. 223*).

Στέφος πλέκων ποθ' εὗρον
ἐν τοῖς ῥόδοις Ἔρωτα·
καὶ τῶν πτερῶν κατασχὼν
ἐβάπτισ' εἰς τὸν οἶνον,
λαβὼν δ' ἔπιον αὐτόν·
καὶ νῦν ἔσω μελῶν μου
πτεροῖσι γαργαλίζει.

Simplicii Comment. in Epict. Enchirid. c. XXXVIII. 10 (*ed. Schweigh. Vol. IV. p. 366*).

Τὸ ἐν σώμασι καλὸν, ἐν σαρξίν ἐστι, καὶ νεύροις, καὶ τοῖς τὸ σῶμα συμπληροῦσιν, εἰ τύχοι, τῶν ζώων· καλλύ-

indeed, as much as possible, but also itself partaking of their deformity and IMMERSED (BAPTIZED) into it."

EXAMPLE 86.

Æsopic Fables; fable of the Man and the Fox.*
"A certain man, having a grudge against a fox for some mischief done by her, after getting her into his power contrived a long time how to punish her; and DIPPING (BAPTIZING) tow in oil, he bound it to her tail and set fire to it."

* Writer and date unknown.

GREEK TEXT.

νον μὲν, ὡς δυνατὸν, ἐκεῖνα· μεταλαμβάνον δὲ καὶ αὐτὸ τῆς ἐκείνων ἀσχημοσύνης, καὶ βεβαπτισμένον εἰς αὐτήν.

Παραλληλοι˙ μυθοι· Ανθρωπος και Αλωπηξ (ed. Coray, Fab. 163).

᾿Ανήρ τις, ἐχθραίνων ἀλώπεκι διά τινα ταύτης ῥᾳδιουργίαν, ἐπὶ πολὺ ταύτην μετα τὸ κατασχεῖν τιμωρῆσαι ἐμηχανήσατο, καὶ στυπεῖον ἐλαίῳ βαπτίσας, τῇ κέρκῳ ταύτης προσδήσας, ὑφῆψε πυρί.

§ 2.

IN THE TROPICAL OR FIGURATIVE SENSE.

1. To plunge, to immerse, to whelm (as in ingulfing floods), in calamities, in ruin, in troubles, in cares, in poverty, in debts, in stupor, in sleep, in ignorance, in pollution, etc.

EXAMPLE 87.

Dion Cassius,* *Roman History, book XXXVIII. ch.* 27. Philiscus, consoling Cicero in his exile, says of his triumphant adversaries, now exposed to the hazards of the unsettled times:
"For, as being borne along in a troubled and unsettled state of affairs, they differ little, or rather not at all, from those who are driven by storm at sea, but [are borne] up and down, now this way now that way; and if they commit any even the slightest mistake, are totally SUBMERGED (BAPTIZED)."

* See the remark on Example 31.

GREEK TEXT.

Dionis Cassii Historiæ Romanæ lib. XXXVIII. c. 27 (*ed. Sturz*).

῎Ατε γὰρ ἐν τεταραγμένοις καὶ ἀκαταστάτοις πράγμασι φερόμενοι, μικρὸν μᾶλλον δὲ οὐδὲν τῶν χειμαζομένων διαφέρουσιν, ἀλλ' ἄνω τε καὶ κάτω, ποτὲ μὲν δεῦρο, ποτὲ δὲ ἐκεῖσε· κἂν ἄρα τι καὶ τὸ βραχύτατον σφαλῶσι, παντελῶς βαπτίζονται.

Example 88.

Libanius,* *Epistle XXV.* Referring to the earthquake, in wnich two of his friends had perished, he says:
"And I myself am one of those SUBMERGED (BAPTIZED) by that great wave."

---
* A Greek philosopher and rhetorician, born 315 after Christ.

Example 89.

The same writer, Life of himself. Speaking of the prudent conduct of the chief magistrate, during a scarcity of bread in the city, he says:
"He did indeed exhort the body of bakers to be more just, but did not think it expedient to employ forcible measures, fearing a general desertion; whereby the city would immediately have been WHELMED (BAPTIZED), as a ship when the seamen have abandoned it."

Example 90.

Gregory of Nazianzus,* *Discourse XL. 11.* Urging his hearers not to defer their baptism, till they should be burdened with more sins to be forgiven, he says:

---
* Born about 330 after Christ.

Greek Text.

Libanii Sophistæ Epist. XXV. (*ed. Wolf, p. 11*).

Καὶ αὐτός εἰμι τῶν βεβαπτισμένων ὑπὸ τοῦ μεγάλου κύματος ἐκείνου.

Ejusdem de Vita sua (*ed. Morell, Vol. II. p. 64*).

Παρεκάλει μὲν τὸ τῶν σιτοποιῶν ἔθνος εἶναι δικαιοτέρους. ἀνάγκας δὲ οὐκ ᾤετο δεῖν ἐπάγειν, δεδιὼς τὴν ἐπὶ πλεῖον ἀπόδρασιν· ᾧ ἂν εὐθὺς ἐβαπτίζετο τὸ ἄστυ, καθάπερ ναῦς ἐκλιπόντων τῶν ναυτῶν.

"Nor let us take more lading than we are able to carry; that we may not be IMMERGED (BAPTIZED), vessel and men, and make shipwreck of the grace, losing all because we hoped for more."

EXAMPLE 91.

Chrysostom,* *Discourses on Lazarus, I. 10.* Recounting the several traits in the character and conduct of the rich man, which were so many aggravations of the miseries of Lazarus, he says:
"But now, living in wickedness, and arrived at the last stage of vice, and exhibiting such inhumanity, . . . and passing by him as a stone without shame and without pity, and after all these things enjoying such abundance; consider how probable it was, that he WHELMED (BAPTIZED) the soul of the poor man as with successive waves."

---

* See the remark on Example 45.

===

GREEK TEXT.

Gregorii Nazianz. Orat. XL. 11 (*stud. Monach. Benedict. Vol. I. p. 698*).

Μηδὲ φορτισθῶμεν πλέον ἢ δυνάμεθα φέρειν, ἵνα μὴ αὐτάνδρῳ τῇ νηὶ βαπτισθῶμεν, καὶ τὸ χάρισμα ναυαγή· σωμεν, ἀνθ' ὧν τὸ πλεῖον ἠλπίσαμεν τὸ πᾶν ἀπολέσαντες.

Chrysostomi de Lazaro Conc. I. 10 (*ed. Montf. Vol. I. p. 721*).

Νυνὶ δὲ καὶ πονηρίᾳ συζῶν, καὶ πρὸς ἔσχατον κακίας ἐληλακὼς, καὶ τοσαύτην ἀπανθρωπίαν ἐπιδεικνύμενος, . . . καὶ ὥσπερ λίθον αὐτὸν παρατρέχων ἀναισχύντως καὶ ἀνιλέως, καὶ μετὰ ταῦτα πάντα τοσαύτης ἀπολαύων εὐπορίας· ἐννόησον πῶς εἰκὸς ἦν, ὥσπερ ἐπαλλήλοις κύμασι βαπτίζειν αὐτὸν τοῦ πένητος τὴν ψυχήν.

Example 92.

Chariton of Aphrodisias,[*] *Story of the loves of Chærea and Cal lirrhoe, book II. ch. 4.* Speaking of Dyonisius, and of his efforts to subdue his passion for Calirrhoe, he says:
"Then, therefore, might be seen the conflict of reason and passion. For, although WHELMED (BAPTIZED) by desire, the generous man endeavored to resist; and emerged as from a wave, saying to himself: 'Art thou not ashamed, Dyonisius, a man the first of Ionia for virtue and repute!'"

---

[*] Author of the Greek romance here quoted, probably near the end of the fourth century after Christ.

Example 93.

The same Work, book III. ch. 4. On another occasion, speaking of the violence of Dyonisius' passion for Callirrhoe, he says:
"But Dyonisius, a man of culture, was seized indeed by a tempest, and was WHELMED (BAPTIZED) as to the soul; but yet he struggled to emerge from the passion, as from a mighty wave."

GREEK TEXT.

Charitonis Aphrodis. de Chærea et Callirrhoe amator. Narrat. lib. II. ch. 4 (*ed. D'Orville, p. 28*).

Τότ' οὖν ἰδεῖν ἀγῶνα λογισμοῦ καὶ πάθους. καίτοι γὰρ βαπτιζόμενος ὑπὸ τῆς ἐπιθυμίας γενναῖος ἀνὴρ ἐπειρᾶτο ἀντέχεσθαι. καθάπερ δὲ ἐκ κύματος ἀνέκυπτε λέγων πρὸς ἑαυτόν· οὐκ αἰσχύνῃ, Διονύσιε, ἀνὴρ ὁ πρῶτος τῆς Ἰωνίας ἕνεκεν ἀρετῆς τε καὶ δόξης·;[1]

Ejusdem lib. III. c. 2 (*ed. D'Orville, p. 42*).

Διονύσιος δέ, ἀνὴρ πεπαιδευμένος, κατείληπτο μὲν ὑπὸ χειμῶνος, καὶ τὴν ψυχὴν ἐβαπτίζετο· ὅμως δὲ ἀνακύπτειν ἐβιάζετο, καθάπερ ἐκ τρικυμίας, τοῦ πάθους.

---

[1] Fortis enim vir, quamvis a libidine mersitatus, contra tamen tenere nitebatur, et, ut e fluctibus emergens, ipse sic ad se (*Reiske*).

IN THE TROPICAL OR FIGURATIVE SENSE. 47

EXAMPLE 94.

The same Work, book III. ch. 4. Describing the vessel of the pirates, who had plundered of its gold and jewels the tomb of Callirrhoe (prematurely buried), and finding her alive had sold her into slavery, and were now pursued by the vengeance of the gods, he says:

"For I saw a vessel, wandering in fair weather, filled with its own tempest, and WHELMED (BAPTIZED) in a calm."

The whole statement is figurative; representing, under the image of *its own tempest* (one within itself) and *foundering in a calm*, the desperate condition of the vessel and crew, abandoned to the elements and wandering without control, all on board but one having perished with thirst.

EXAMPLE 95.

Basil (the Great),* Discourse XIV. Against Drunkards, § 4. He says of the intoxicated:

"More pitiable than those who are tempest-tossed in the deep, whom waves receiving one from another, and over-WHELMING (BAPTIZING), do not suffer to rise out of the surge; so also the

---

* See the remark on Examples 75 and 76.

Overwhelm, in the sense "*to immerse and bear down*" (Webster, No. 2, and Worcester).

GREEK TEXT.

Ejusdem lib. III. c. 4 (*ed. D'Orville, p. 49*).

Πλοῖον γὰρ ἐθεασάμην ἐν εὐδίᾳ πλανώμενον, ἰδίου χειμῶνος γέμον, καὶ βαπτιζόμενον ἐν γαλήνῃ.

Basilii Magni Hom. XIV. in Ebriosos, 4 (*ed. Garnier, Vol. II. p. 125*).

Ἐλεεινότεροι τῶν ἐν πελάγει χειμαζομένων, οὓς ἄλλα ἐξ ἄλλων διαδεχόμενα καὶ ἐπιβαπτίζοντα¹ κύματα ἀναφέ-

---

[1] Compare the use of this compound in the next example, and the remarks on it in the following note.

souls of these are driven about beneath the waves, being WHELMED (BAPTIZED) with wine."

EXAMPLE 96.

Josephus*, *Jewish War, book I. ch. 27, 1.* Relating the occurrence that led to the mock trial and condemnation of Herod's persecuted sons, he says:
"This, as a final blast, over-WHELMED (BAPTIZED) the tempest-tossed youths."

---

* See the remark on Example 53.
Overwhelm, as in the preceding example. The metaphor is derived from the effect of a sudden blast, bearing down upon (over) the shattered vessel, and whelming it in the deep.

EXAMPLE 97.

The same Work, book III. ch. 7, 15. The people of Jerusalem, expostulating with Josephus on his purpose to abandon the besieged city and its inhabitants to their fate, say to him:
"And that it did not become him, either to fly from enemies,

GREEK TEXT.

ρειν οὐκ ἐπιτρέπει τοῦ κλύδωνος· οὕτω δὴ καὶ τούτων αἱ ψυχαὶ ὑποβρύχιοι φέρονται βεβαπτισμέναι τῷ οἴνῳ.

Josephi de Bello Jud. lib. I. c. 27, 1 (*ed. Oberthür*).

Τοῦθ' ὥσπερ τελευταία θύελλα χειμαζομένους τοὺς νεανίσκους ἐπεβάπτισε.¹

Ejusdem lib. III. c. 7, 15.

Πρέπειν δὲ αὐτῷ μήτε φεύγειν τοὺς ἐχθροὺς, μήτε

---

¹ Ἐπ-εβάπτισε, strictly, *over-whelmed* (coming *down upon* whelmed, as in the deep). The rendering, *to submerge repeatedly* (*wiederholt untertauchen*, Rost und Palm. griech. Hdwbch.), *to immerge repeatedly* (*wiederholt eintauchen*, Pape, griechisch-deutsches Hdwbch.), *to dip, drench, again* or *in addition* (Liddell and Scott, Greek Lex.), is not pertinent here; for the effect of the '*final*' and overwhelming blast is meant, not the repetition of something before experienced.

or to abandon friends; nor to leap off, as from a ship overtaken by a storm, into which he had entered in fair weather; that he would himself over-WHELM (BAPTIZE) the city, as no one would longer dare to make resistance to the enemy, when he was gone through whom their courage was sustained."

EXAMPLE 98.

The same Work, book IV. ch. 3, 3. Speaking of the evils inflicted by the band of robber-chiefs who found their way into the city of Jerusalem during the siege, he says:

"Who, even apart from the sedition, afterwards WHELMED (BAPTIZED) the city."

This natural and expressive image of trouble and distress occurs often in the Old Testament. For example, Ps. 69 : 2, "I am come into deep waters, where the floods overflow me;" VV. 14, 15, "Let me be delivered ... out of the deep waters, let not the waterflood overflow me;" Ps. 18 : 16, 17, "He drew me out of many waters, he delivered me from my strong enemy." Job's afflictions are expressed under the same image (ch. 22 : 11): "The flood of waters covers thee." Compare Ps. 124 : 4, 5; 144 : 7; 32 : 6; Ezek. 26 : 19.

EXAMPLE 99.

Himerius,* Selection XV. § 3. He says of Themistocles:

---

* See the remark on Example 40.

===

GREEK TEXT.

ἐγκαταλείψειν τοὺς φίλους, μηδὲ ἀποπηδᾶν, ὥσπερ χειμαζομένης νεὼς, εἰς ἣν ἐν γαλήνῃ παρῆλθεν. ἐπιβαπτίσειν γὰρ αὐτὸν τὴν πόλιν, μηδενὸς ἔτι τολμῶντος τοῖς πολεμίοις ἀνθίστασθαι, δι' ὃν ἀναθαρροῖεν οἰχομένου.

Ejusdem lib. IV. c. 3, 3 (*ed. Oberthür*).

Οἳ δὴ καὶ δίχα τῆς στάσεως ὕστερον ἐβάπτισαν τὴν πόλιν.

"He was great at Salamis; for there, fighting, he WHELMED (BAPTIZED) all Asia."*

* The power of Asia was broken by the destruction of its fleet at sea, and hence the propriety of the figure.

EXAMPLE 100.

Libanius,* *Declamation XX.* On the same subject (and apostrophizing Themistocles, in the speech represented as spoken by his father), he says:
"The crowning achievement was Salamis; where thou didst WHELM (BAPTIZE) Asia."

* See the remark on Example 88.

EXAMPLE 101.

The same writer, Epistle 310, to Siderius.
"But he who bears with difficulty what he is now bearing, would be WHELMED (BAPTIZED) by a slight addition."

GREEK TEXT.

Heimerii Sophistæ Eclog. XV. § 3 (*ed. Wernsdorf*).

Μέγας ἐπὶ Σαλαμῖνα· ἐβάπτισε γὰρ ὅλην ἐκεῖ τὴν Ἀσίαν μαχόμενος.¹

Libanii Declamat. XX (*ed. Wolf, p. 521*).

Ὁ τῶν ἔργων κολοφών, ἡ Σαλαμίς, περὶ ἣν τὴν Ἀσίαν ἐβάπτισας.²

Ejusdem Epist. 310 (*ed. Wolf, p. 150*).

Ὁ δὲ μόλις ἃ νῦν φέρει φέρων ὑπὸ μικρᾶς ἂν βαπτισθείη προσθήκης.³

¹ Ibi enim totam Asiam pugnando demersit (*Wernsdorf*).—Compare: patriam demersam extuli (*Cic. pro Sulla*, 31).
² Operum apex Salamis, circa quam Asiam mersisti (*Wolf*).
³ Ille a levissima etiam accessione facile submergetur (*Id.*).

EXAMPLE 102.

The same writer, Epistle 962, to Gessius.
"For this is he who found the wretched Cimon WHELMED (BAPTIZED), and did not neglect him when abandoned."

EXAMPLE 103.

Plutarch,* On the good Genius of Socrates, XXIII.
"Such is the manner of the good Genius; that we, WHELMED (BAPTIZED) by worldly affairs, . . . should ourselves struggle out, and should persevere, endeavoring by our own resolution to save ourselves and gain the haven."

---

* See the remark on Example 64.

EXAMPLE 104.

Chrysostom,* Expos. of Ps. 114 (116), § 3. Speaking of the believer's governing principle, and of his prospects, he says:

---

* See the remark on Example 45.

GREEK TEXT.

Ejusdem Epist. 962 (*ed. Wolf, p. 449*).

Οὗτός ἐστιν ὁ βαπτιζόμενον εὑρὼν τὸν ἄθλιον Κίμωνα,¹ καὶ προδεδομένον οὐ περιιδών.

Plutarchi de Genio Socratis XXIII (*ed. Wyttenb. Vol. III. p. 393*).

Οὕτως τοῦ δαιμονίου ὁ τρόπος·² ἡμᾶς βαπτιζομένους ὑπὸ τῶν πραγμάτων . . . αὐτοὺς ἐξαμιλλᾶσθαι, καὶ μακροθυμεῖν, δι' οἰκείας πειραμένους ἀρετῆς σώζεσθαι, καὶ τυγχάνειν λιμένος.

---

¹ Hic ille est, qui miserum Cimonem calamitatibus oppressum vidit (*Wolf*).

² Sententia quidem universe facilis ad explendum, ut Anon. T. V. οὕτως, ᾧ ἔνι, τοῦ δαιμονίου ὁ τρόπος. ἰᾷ μὲν γὰρ ἡμᾶς—.Non recepi, ut e conjectura, non e libro, profectum (*Wyttenb.*).

"For he who is controlled by that love, and sustained by the hope of that good, is WHELMED (BAPTIZED) by none of the present evils."

Example 105.

The same writer, on 1 Cor. Discourse VIII.
"For if we were pained for sins, ... nothing else would grieve us, this pain expelling all sadness; so that with confession we should gain also another thing, not to be WHELMED (BAPTIZED) by the troubles of the present life, nor to be puffed up by prosperity."

Example 106.

The same writer, Expos. of Ps. 141 (142), § 2. Commenting on the words, 'I cried unto thee, O Lord, I said, thou art my hope,' etc., he says:
"The evils did not WHELM (BAPTIZE) him, but rather gave him wings."

Greek Text.

Chrysostomi Expos. in Ps. 114, § 3 *(ed. Montf. Vol. V. p. 307).*

Ὁ γὰρ ἐκείνῳ τῷ ἔρωτι κατεχόμενος, καὶ ταῖς ἐλπίσι τῶν ἀγαθῶν τρεφόμενος ἐκείνων, οὐδενὶ τῶν παρόντων βαπτίζεται δεινῶν.

Ejusdem in Epist. I. ad Cor. Hom. VIII *(Vol. X. p. 72).*

Καὶ γὰρ εἰ ἠλγοῦμεν ἐπὶ τοῖς ἁμαρτήμασιν, ... οὐδὲν ἂν ἄλλο ἡμᾶς ἐλύπεσε, τῆς ὀδύνης ταύτης πᾶσαν ἀθυμίαν παρωθουμένης. ὥστε καὶ ἕτερον ἂν ἐκερδαίνομεν μετὰ τῆς ἐξομολογήσεως, τὸ μὴ βαπτίζεσθαι τοῖς λυπηροῖς τοῦ παρόντος βίου, μηδὲ φυσᾶσθαι τοῖς λαμπροῖς.

Ejusdem Expos. in Ps. 141, § 2 *(Vol. V. p. 445).*

Οὐκ ἐβάπτισεν αὐτὸν τὰ δεινά, ἀλλὰ μᾶλλον ἐπτέρωσε.

Example 107.

The same writer, Expos. of Ps. 111 (112), § 4.

"For it is impossible that a soul, abounding in mercy, should ever be WHELMED (BAPTIZED) by the annoyances of passion."

Example 108.

Heliodorus,* Æthiopics (Story of Theagenes and Chariclea), book II. ch. 3.

"And Cnemon, perceiving that he was wholly absorbed in grief, and WHELMED (BAPTIZED) in the calamity, and fearing lest he may do himself some harm, secretly takes away the sword."

* See the remark on Example 39.

Example 109.

The same Work, book IV. ch. 20.

"For Charicles, indeed, it shall be lawful to weep, both now and hereafter; but let not us be WHELMED (BAPTIZED) with him in his grief, nor let us heedlessly be borne away by his tears, as by floods, and throw away the favorable occasion."

Greek Text.

Ejusdem Expos. in Ps. 111, § 4 (*Vol. V. p. 283*).

Καὶ γὰρ ἀμήχανον ψυχὴν πλουτοῦσαν ἐλεημοσύνῃ, ὑπὸ ἀηδίας παθῶν βαπτισθῆναί ποτε.

Heliodori Æthiopicorum lib. II. c. 3 (*ed. Bekker*).

Ὁ δὲ Κνήμων ὅλον ὄντα πρὸς τῷ πάθει καταμαθὼν καὶ τῇ συμφορᾷ βεβαπτισμενον, δεδιώς τε μή τι κακὸν ἑαυτὸν ἐργάσηται, τὸ ξίφος ὑφαιρεῖ λάθρᾳ.

Ejusdem lib. IV. c. 20.

Χαρικλεῖ μὲν ἐξέσται νῦν τε καὶ μετὰ ταῦτα θρηνεῖν, ἡμεῖς δὲ μὴ συμβαπτιζώμεθα τῷ τοίτου πάθει, μηδὲ λάθωμεν ὥσπερ ῥεύμασι τοῖς τούτου δάκρυσιν ὑποφερόμενοι καὶ τὸν καιρὸν προϊέμενοι.

Example 110.

The same Work, book V. ch. 16.

"But for us your own wanderings, if you were willing, would best forward the entertainment, being pleasanter than any dancing and music; the relation of which, having often deferred it, as you know, because the occurrences still WHELMED (BAPTIZED) you, you could not reserve for a better occasion than the present."

Example 111.

Achilles Tatius,* Story of Leucippe and Clitophon, book III. ch. 10.
"What so great wrong have we done, as in a few days to be WHELMED (BAPTIZED) with such a multitude of evils?"

* See the remark on Example 54.

Example 112.

The same Work, book VII. ch. 2.
"Misfortunes assailing WHELM (BAPTIZE) us."

Greek Text.

Ejusdem lib. V. c. 16.

Ἡμῖν δὲ ἡ σὴ πλάνη κάλλιστα ἂν, εἰ βουληθείης, τὴν εὐωχίαν παραπέμποι, χοροῦ τε γινομένη καὶ αὐλοῦ παντὸς ἡδίων· ἣν πολλάκις μοι διελθεῖν, ὡς οἶσθα, ὑπερθέμενος, ἐπειδή σε τὰ συμβεβηκότα ἐβάπτιζεν, οὐκ ἔστιν ὅπως ἂν ἐς καιρὸν βελτίονα τοῦ παρόντος φυλάξειας.

Achillis Tatii de Leucippes et Clitophontis Amoribus, lib. III. c. 10 (*ed. Jacobs*).

Τί τηλικοῦτον ἠδικήσαμεν, ὡς ἐν ὀλίγοις ἡμέραις τοσούτῳ πλήθει βαπτισθῆναι κακῶν;

Ejusdem lib. VII. c. 2.

Ἐμπίπτουσαι¹ δὲ αἱ τύχαι βαπτίζουσιν ἡμᾶς.

---

¹ Ἐμπίπτειν proprie dicitur de tempestate ingruente (*Jacobs, Annott.* p. 881).

IN THE TROPICAL OR FIGURATIVE SENSE. 55

EXAMPLE 113.

The same writer, book VI. ch. 19. Speaking of love, contending with and subdued by anger in the same bosom, he says:

"And he, WHELMED (BAPTIZED) by anger, sinks; and desiring to escape into his own realm is no longer free, but is compelled to hate the object beloved."

EXAMPLE 114.

Libanius,* Funeral Discourse on the Emperor Julian, ch. 148.

"For grief for him, WHELMING (BAPTIZING) the soul, and clouding the understanding, brings as it were a mist even upon the eyes, and we differ little from those who are now living in darkness."

* See the remark on Example 88.

EXAMPLE 115.

The same Discourse, ch. 71.

"And he showed the same forethought also concerning the

GREEK TEXT.

Ejusdem lib. VI. c. 19.

'Ο δὲ τῷ θυμῷ βεβαπτισμένος καταδύεται, καὶ εἰς τὴν ἰδίαν ἀρχὴν ἐκπηδῆσαι θελων οὐκέτι ἐστὶν ἐλεύθερος, ἀλλὰ μισεῖν ἀναγκάζεται τὸ φιλούμενον.

Libanii Parental. in Julianum Imperat. c. 148 (*Fabricii Biblioth. Gr. Vol. VII. p. 369*).

'Η γὰρ ἐπὶ τῷδε λύπη, βαπτίζουσα μὲν τὴν ψυχήν,[1] συνθολοῦσα δὲ τὴν γνώμην, ἀχλύν τινα καὶ τοῖς ὄμμασιν ἐπιφέρει, καὶ μικρόν τι διαφέρομεν τῶν ζώντων νῦν ἐν σκότῳ.

Ejusdem c. 71 (*p. 297*).

'Επεδείξατο δὲ τὴν αὐτὴν πρόνοιαν καὶ περὶ τὰς ἐν

[1] Animum submergens (*Version of Olearius*).

Councils in the cities, which formerly flourished both in numbers and wealth, afterwards were nothing. . . . And they, indeed [those who neglected their public duties, for their own interests and pleasures] slept, and indulged the body, and laughed at those who went not the same way with them; but the remaining part, being small, was WHELMED (BAPTIZED), and the service rendered to the people terminated in beggary."

EXAMPLE 116.

The same writer, On the Articles of Agreement (among the teachers of youth in the city).

"Especially if our public discourses had enjoyed an auspicious fortune, and it had been our lot to sail with favoring gales, as they who before us presided over the bands of the young; . . . but now, as you see, the business [of instructing the young] being WHELMED (BAPTIZED), and all the winds being set in motion against it," etc.

GREEK TEXT.

ταῖς πόλεσι βουλὰς, αἳ πάλαι μὲν πλήθεσί τε καὶ πλούτοις ἔθαλλον, ἔπειτα ἦσαν οὐδέν· . . . καὶ οἱ μὲν ἐκάθευδόν τε καὶ ἐχαρίζοντο τῷ σώματι, καὶ τῶν οὐ τὴν αὐτὴν αὐτοῖς ἐλθόντων κατεγέλων. τὸ δὲ ὑπολελειμμένον ὀλίγον ὂν ἐβαπτίζετο, καὶ τὸ λειτουργεῖν τοῖς πλείοσιν εἰς τὸ προσαιτεῖν ἐτελεύτα.

Ejusdem Orat. XLIII. περι των Συνθηκων (*ed. Reiske, Vol. II. p. 428*).

Μάλιστα μὲν οὖν εἰ καὶ χρηστῆς ἀπέλαυε τῆς τύχης τὰ τῶν ἡμετέρων λόγων, καὶ πλεῖν ἐξ οὐρίων ὑπῆρχεν, ὥσπερ τοῖς πρὸ ἡμῶν ταῖς τῶν νέων ἐφεστηκόσιν ἀγέλαις· . . . . . νῦν δέ, ὡς ὁρᾶτε, βαπτιζομένου τοῦ πράγματος,[1] καὶ πάντων ἐπ' αὐτὸ κεκινημένων τῶν πνευμάτων, κ. τ. λ.

---

[1] Juventutem literis imbuendi (*Reiske*).

IN THE TROPICAL OR FIGURATIVE SENSE.

EXAMPLE 117.

Themistius,* *Oration XX (Funeral Discourse on the death of his father).* Remarking, that philosophy forbade the indulgence of sorrow, he says:

"But whenever she observed me WHELMED (BAPTIZED) by grief, and moved to tears, she is angry, and threatens to do me some fearful and incurable evil."

---

* See the remark on Example 41.

EXAMPLE 118.

Josephus,* *Antiquities of the Jews, book X. ch. 9, 4.* Describing the murder of Gedaliah by his own guests at a banquet, after he had drunk to intoxication, he says:

"Seeing him in this condition, and PLUNGED (BAPTIZED) by drunkenness into stupor and sleep, Ishmael leaping up, with his ten friends, slays Gedaliah and those reclining with him at the banquet."

---

* See the remark on Example 64.

GREEK TEXT.

Themistii Sophistæ Orat. XX. *init.* (*ed. Dindorf, p. 233*).

Ἀλλ' ὁπότε αἴσθοιτο βαπτιζόμενόν τε ὑπὸ τῆς ὀδύνης, καὶ εἰς δάκρυα καταφερόμενον, χαλεπαίνει τε καὶ ἐπαπειλεῖ δεινά ἄττα με ἐργάσεσθαι καὶ ἀνήκεστα.

Josephi Antiq. Jud. lib. X. c. 9, 4 (*ed. Oberthür*).

Θεασάμενος δὲ οὕτως αὐτὸν ἔχοντα, καὶ βεβαπτισμένον εἰς ἀναισθησίαν καὶ ὕπνον ὑπὸ τῆς μέθης, ὁ Ἰσμαῆλος ἀναπηδήσας, μετὰ τῶν δέκα φίλων, ἀποσφάττει τὸν Γοδολίαν καὶ τοὺς σὺν αὐτῷ κατακειμένους ἐν τῷ συμποσίῳ.

Example 119.

Clement of Alexandria,* *The Educator,* book II. ch. 2.
"For drowsy is every one who is not watchful for wisdom, but is PLUNGED (BAPTIZED) by drunkenness into sleep."

---

* A distinguished Greek writer of the Christian Church, last quarter of the second, and first quarter of the third century after Christ.

Example 120.

Evenus of Paros,* *Epigram XV.* Bacchus (the use of wine), when too freely indulged in, he says:
"PLUNGES (BAPTIZES) in sleep, neighbor of death."

---

* About 250 before Christ.

Example 121.

Heliodorus,* *Æthiopics (Story of Theagenes and Chariclea),* book IV. ch. 17.

"When midnight had PLUNGED (BAPTIZED) the city in sleep, an

---

* See the remark on Example 39.

Greek Text.

Clementis Alexandr. Pædag. lib. II. c. 2 (*ed. Potter, Vol. I. p. 182*).

'Υπνώδης γὰρ πᾶς, ὁ μὴ εἰς σοφίαν ἐγγρηγορῶν, ἀλλὰ ὑπὸ μέθης βαπτιζόμενος εἰς ὕπνον.

Eveni Parii et al. Epigr. XV.[1] (*Anthol. Gr. I. p. 166, ed. Jacobs, I. p. 99; Bergk, Poet. Gr. Lyr. p. 447*).

Βαπτίζει δ' ὕπνῳ γείτονι τοῦ[2] θανάτου.

Heliodori Æthiopicorum lib. IV. c. 17 (*ed. Bekker*).

'Επειδὴ μέσαι νύκτες ὕπνῳ τὴν πόλιν ἐβάπτιζον,

---

[1] Veteris Eveni videtur, et fortasse Elegiæ particula (*Jacobs*).
[2] Τῷ θάνατου Pal. τοῦ θ. Planudes (*Schneidewin*).
[3] Compare: Invadunt urbem somno vinoque sepultam (*Virgil, Æn.* 2, 265).

IN THE TROPICAL OR FIGURATIVE SENSE.

armed band of revellers took possession of the dwelling of Chariclea."

EXAMPLE 122.

Chrysostom,* Admonition I. to Theodorus.

"Therefore I beseech thee, before thou art deeply WHELMED (BAPTIZED) by this intoxication, to return to soberness, and to arouse, and thrust off the satanic debauch."

* See the remark on Example 45.

EXAMPLE 123.

The same writer, Select Discourses, II., on Prayer.

"If blessed David, therefore, being a king, and WHELMED (BAPTIZED) with ten thousand cares, . . called upon God seven times a day; what apology and excuse should we have, being so much at leisure, and not continually beseeching him, and that too when we are to reap so great a gain!"

GREEK TEXT.

ἔνοπλος κῶμος τὴν οἴκησιν τῆς Χαρικλείας κατελαμβανεν.

Chrysostomi Parænesis prior ad Theod. lapsum (*ed. Montf. Vol. I. p. 27*).

Διὰ τοῦτο παρακαλῶ πρὶν ἢ σφόδρα ὑπὸ ταύτης βαπτισθῆναί σε τῆς μέθης, ἀνανῆψαι καὶ διεγερθῆναι, καὶ τὴν σατανικὴν κραιπάλην ἀπώσασθαι.

Ejusdem Eclog. de Oratione Hom. II. (*Vol. XII. p. 446*).

Εἰ οὖν ὁ μακάριος Δαυὶδ βασιλεὺς ὤν, καὶ μυρίαις βαπτιζόμενος φροντίσι, . . . ἑπτάκις τῆς ἡμέρας παρεκάλει τὸν Θεὸν, τίνα ἂν ἔχοιμεν ἀπολογίαν καὶ συγγνώμην ἡμεῖς, τοσαύτην σχολὴν ἄγοντες, καὶ μὴ συνεχῶς αὐτὸν ἱκετεύοντες, καὶ ταῦτα τοσοῦτον μέλλοντες καρποῦσθαι κέρδος;

Example 124.

Libanius,[*] *Memorial to the king, on the neglect and abuse of the imprisoned.* Answering the plea, that the magistrates were encumbered with official business, and had no time for attention to those imprisoned, or held for trial, he says:
" But you do not allege this want of leisure to those who give sumptuous banquets, nor that you could not spend so much of the day drinking at the table; . . . but if one asks your judgment of any of the greater matters, you are not at leisure but are OVERWHELMED (BAPTIZED), and the multitude of other affairs holds you in subjection; as if those affairs, of which you speak, give place to wine-cups, but grudge to some their safety!"

---

[*] See the remark on Example 82.

Example 125.

Discourse on Zeal and Piety,[*] § 1. Commenting on the words (Ps. 82 : 4), '*They walk on in darkness*,' the writer says:

---

[*] By an ancient Greek writer, near the age of Chrysostom, to whom it has been erroneously attributed.

Greek Text.

Libanii Orat. de Vinctis (*ed. Reiske, Vol. II. p. 456*).

Σὺ δὲ πρὸς μὲν τοὺς λαμπροὺς ἑστιάτορας τὴν ἀσχολίαν ταύτην οὐ λέγεις, οὐδ' ὡς οὐκ ἂν δύναιο πίνειν κατακείμενος τοσαῦτα μέρη τῆς ἡμέρας· . . . ἂν δέ τι τῶν μειζόνων τὴν σὴν ἀπαιτῇ γνώμην, οὐκ ἄγεις σχολὴν, ἀλλὰ βαπτίζῃ,[1] καί σε ὁ τῶν πραγμάτων τῶν ἄλλων ὄχλος ὑφ' αὑτῷ πεποίηται, ὥσπερ τῶν πραγμάτων ἐκείνων, ἃ λέγεις, τοῖς μὲν ἐκπώμασιν εἰκόντων, σωτηρίας δέ τισι φθονούντων.

---

[1] Scil. πόνοις καὶ μερίμναις (*Reiske*).

"Thus, then, the congregation IMMERSED (BAPTIZED) in ignorance, and unwilling to emerge* to the knowledge of the spiritual teaching, God calls night."

* This expression shows that he does not mean *imbued with* ignorance, but *whelmed, immersed in* it.

EXAMPLE 126.

Isidorus* of Pelusium; On the interpretation of Holy Scripture, book II. epist. 76 (on the words, '*Watch and pray*,' etc.).

"Most men, therefore, IMMERSED (BAPTIZED) in ignorance, have their minds incapacitated for consolation with reference to afflictions; but those, on the contrary, who are governed by sound reason, repel them all."

* A Greek writer of the Christian Church; died 450 after Christ.

EXAMPLE 127.

Clement of Alexandria,* Exhortation to Pagans, I. 3.

"But the foolish are stocks and stones; and yet more senseless even than stones is a man IMMERSED (BAPTIZED) in ignorance."

* See the remark on Example 119.

GREEK TEXT

De Zelo ac Piet. (*Chrysost. Op.*, ed. *Montf. Vol. VIII.* Spurior. p. 61).

Οὕτως οὖν τὴν συναγωγὴν ὁ Θεὸς τὴν ἀγνοίᾳ βεβαπτισμένην, καὶ μὴ βουλομένην ἀνανεῦσαι πρὸς τὴν γνῶσιν τῆς πνευματικῆς διδασκαλίας, νύκτα καλεῖ.

Isidori Pelusiotæ de Interp. div. Script. lib. II. epist. 76 (*ed. Ritterh. 1606*).

Οἱ μὲν οὖν πολλοὶ τῶν ἀνθρώπων, ἀμαθίᾳ βεβαπτισμένοι, πρὸς τὰς συμφορὰς ἔχουσι τὰς ψυχὰς ἀπαραμυθήτους· οἱ δὲ λογισμῷ σώφρονι κυβερνώμενοι ἀπωθοῦνται πάντας.

Clement. Alexandri, Cohort. ad Gentes, I. 3 (*ed. Potter, Vol. I. p. 4*).

Λίθοι δὲ καὶ ξύλα οἱ ἄφρονες· πρὸς δὲ καὶ λίθων ἀναισθητότερος ἄνθρωπος ἀγνοίᾳ βεβαπτισμένος.

Example 128.

The same writer, Stromata, book III. ch. 18. Asserting the sanctity of the marriage relation, he quotes the Apostle's words (1 Cor. 6 : 9, 10, '*Neither fornicators . . nor adulterers,*' etc.), and adds:

"And we indeed 'were washed,' who were among these but they who wash into this sensuality,* IMMERSE (BAPTIZE) from sobriety into fornication, teaching to indulge the pleasures and passions."

---

* He alludes here to the false teachers and corrupters of Christianity; who, instead of a doctrine that deters and cleanses from sin, taught the indulgence of it; and hence those immersed by them they 'washed' (as Clement expresses it) '*into* sensuality' instead of washing from it.

Example 129.

Chrysostom,* Discourse V. on Titus, § 3.
"How were we IMMERSED (BAPTIZED) in wickedness, so that we could not be cleansed, but needed regeneration!"

---

* See the remark on Example 45.

Greek Text.

Ejusdem Stromat. lib. III. c. 18 (*ed. Potter, Vol. I. p. 562*).

Καὶ ἡμεῖς μὲν ἀπελουσάμεθα, οἱ ἐν τούτοις γενόμενοι· οἱ δὲ εἰς ταύτην ἀπολούοντες τὴν ἀσέλγειαν, ἐκ σωφροσύνης εἰς πορνείαν βαπτίζουσι,¹ ταῖς ἡδοναῖς καὶ τοῖς πάθεσι χαρίζεσθαι δογματίζοντες.

Chrysostomi in Epist. ad Titum, Homil. V. 3 (*ed. Montf., Vol. XI. p. 761*).

Πῶς ἦμεν ἐν τῇ κακίᾳ βεβαπτισμένοι, ὡς μὴ δύνασθαι καθαρθῆναι, ἀλλ' ἀναγεννήσεως δεηθῆναι!

---

¹ Non solum autem ipsi damnantur, sed ii etiam, qui ab ipsis baptizati, eorum imitantur libidinem et venerem nefariam (*Herveti Comment. in loc.*).

Example 130.

The same writer, on Genesis, ch. 13, Discourse XXXIV. § 5.

Speaking of the spirit of true humility, requiring each to account others better than himself, he adds:

"And I say not this of us, who are WHELMED (BAPTIZED) with ten thousand sins; but even if one were conscious to himself of ten thousand just deeds, and should not account this of himself, that he is last of all, he would have no benefit of so many just deeds."

Example 131.

Justin Martyr,* Dialogue with a Jew, LXXXVI.

"As also us, WHELMED (BAPTIZED) with most grievous sins which we have done, our Christ, by being crucified upon the tree, and by water for cleansing, redeemed and made a house of prayer and adoration."

---

* A learned Greek writer of the Christian Church, born near the close of the first century after Christ.

Greek Text.

Ejusdem in cap. XIII. Gen. Hom. XXXIII. 5 (*Vol. IV. p. 339*).

Καὶ τοῦτο λέγω, οὐ περὶ ἡμῶν τῶν μυρίοις ἁμαρτήμασι βεβαπτισμένων· ἀλλὰ κἂν μυρία τις ᾖ κατορθώματα ἑαυτῷ συνειδὼς, μὴ τοῦτο δὲ λογίζοιτο καθ' ἑαυτὸν, ὅτι πάντων ἐστὶν ἔσχατος, οὐδὲν αὐτῷ ὄφελος ἂν γένοιτο τῶν τοσούτων κατορθωμάτων.

Justini Martyris Dial. cum Tryphone Judæo (*ed. Otto, Vol. I. P. ii. p. 300*).

Ὡς καὶ ἡμᾶς βεβαπτισμένους ταῖς βαρυτάταις ἁμαρτίαις, ἃς ἐπράξαμεν, διὰ τοῦ σταυρωθῆναι ἐπὶ τοῦ ξύλου καὶ δι' ὕδατος ἁγνίσαι ὁ Χριστὸς ἡμῶν ἐλυτρώσατο, καὶ οἶκον εὐχῆς καὶ προσκυνήσεως ἐποίησε.

Example 132.

Diodorus,* *the Sicilian, Historical Library, book I. ch. 73.* Speaking of the three divisions of the territory of Egypt, he says: "The second part the kings have received for public revenues; ... and on account of the abundant supply from these, they do not WHELM (BAPTIZE) the common people with taxes."

* See the remark on Example 13.

Example 133.

Plutarch.* *Life of Galba, XXI.* As Galba's reason for not making Otho his heir, he says:
"Knowing him to be dissolute and prodigal, and WHELMED (BAPTIZED) with debts amounting to fifty millions."

* See the remark on Example 64.

Example 134.

The same writer, On the education of children, XIII. As an example of misjudging parental fondness, he says:
"For being anxious that their children should speedily excel

Greek Text.

Diodori Siculi Biblioth. Hist. lib. I. c. 73 (*ed. Bekker*).

Τὴν δὲ δευτέραν μοῖραν οἱ βασιλεῖς παρειλήφασιν εἰς προσόδους· ... τοὺς δὲ ἰδιώτας διὰ τὴν ἐκ τούτων εὐπορίαν, οὐ βαπτίζουσι ταῖς εἰσφοραῖς.

Plutarchi Vit. Galbæ XXI (*ed. Reiske, Vol. V. p. 633*).

Ἀκόλαστον εἰδὼς καὶ πολυτελῆ, καὶ πεντακισχιλίων μυριάδων ὀφλήμασι βεβαπτισμένον.

Ejusdem de liberis educandis, XIII. (*ed. Wyttenb., Vol. I. p. 31*).

Σπεύδοντες γὰρ τοὺς παῖδας ἐν πᾶσι τάχιον πρωτεῦ-

IN THE TROPICAL OR FIGURATIVE SENSE. 65

in all things, they impose on them excessive labors. . . . For as plants are nourished by a moderate amount of water, but are choked by too much, in the same manner a soul grows by proportionate labors, but is OVERWHELMED (BAPTIZED) by such as are excessive."

EXAMPLE 135.

Plato,* *Euthydemus, or the Disputer, ch. VII.* · Speaking of young Cleinias, confounded with the sophistical questions, and subtilties of the professional disputants, he says :
"And I, perceiving that the youth was OVERWHELMED (BAPTIZED), wishing to give him a respite," etc.

* Born 429 before Christ.

EXAMPLE 136.

Philo,* *the Jew (an extract in Eusebius, Preparation for the Gospel, book VIII., at the end).*
"And one might show it also from this, that those who live

* Middle of the first century of the Christian era.

GREEK TEXT.

σαι, πόνους αὐτοῖς ὑπερμέτρους ἐπιβάλλουσιν. . . .
Ὥσπερ γὰρ τὰ φυτὰ τοῖς μὲν μετρίοις ὕδασι τρέφεται, τοῖς δὲ πολλοῖς πνίγεται, τὸν αὐτὸν τρόπον ψυχὴ τοῖς μὲν συμμέτροις αὔξεται πόνοις, τοῖς δ' ὑπερβάλλουσι βαπτίζεται.

Platonis Euthyd. c. VII, *(ed. Stallbaum, Vol. VI. p. 90).*

Καὶ ἐγὼ γνοὺς βαπτιζόμενον¹ τὸ μειράκιον, βουλόμενος ἀναπαῦσαι αὐτό, κ. τ. λ.

Philonis Jud. (Eusebii Præp. Ev. lib. VIII. *fin.*); *Op. ed. Mangey, II. p. 647.*

Τεκμηριώσαιτο δ' ἄν τις καὶ ἐκ τοῦ τοὺς μὲν νήφοντας

¹ Well expressed by Schleiermacher : Ich aber, da ich sah, wie der Knabe schon ganz zugedeckt war, wollte ihm einige Ruhe verschaffen.

E

soberly, and content with little, excel in understanding; but those, on the contrary, who are always glutted with drink and food, are least intelligent, as though the reason were WHELMED (BAPTIZED) by the things overlying it."

EXAMPLE 137.

Plotinus,* *Ennead I. book IV. On Happiness, § 9.*
"But when he does not continue [happy], WHELMED (BAPTIZED) either with diseases, or with arts of Magians?"

---

* See the remark on Example 72.

EXAMPLE 138.

Chrysostom,* *On Ps. 48 : 17 (49 : 16, 'Be not afraid,'* etc.).
"Such as was Job, neither WHELMED (BAPTIZED) by poverty, nor elated by riches."

---

* See the remark on Example 45.

EXAMPLE 139.

The same writer, Discourse on the trials and constancy of Job. Speaking of the patriarch's example, he says:

GREEK TEXT.

καὶ ὀλιγοδεῖς συνετωτέρους εἶναι, τοὺς δὲ ποτῶν ἀεὶ καὶ σιτίων ἐμπιπλαμένους ἥκιστα φρονίμους, ἅτε βαπτιζομένου τοῖς ἐπιοῦσι τοῦ λογισμοῦ.

Plotini Ennead. I. lib. IV. de Beatitudine, § 9 (*ed. Kirchhoff*, *Vol. II. p. 312*).

Ἀλλ' ὅταν μὴ παρακολουθῇ, βαπτισθεὶς ἢ νόσοις ἢ μάγων τέχναις;

Chrysostomi Expos. in Ps. XLVIII. (*ed. Montf., Vol. V. p. 507*).

Οἷος ἦν ὁ Ἰώβ, οὔτε ὑπὸ τῆς πενίας βαπτιζόμενος, οὔτε ὑπὸ τοῦ πλούτου ἐπαιρόμενος.

IN THE TROPICAL OR FIGURATIVE SENSE.

"And if thou art in affliction, fly to it for refuge; and if in wealth, receive thence the corrective; so as neither to be WHELMED (BAPTIZED) with poverty, nor puffed up with wealth."

EXAMPLE 140.

Theodoret,* *Eccles. Hist. book V. ch. 4.*
"That Diodorus whom I have before mentioned, who, in a most difficult tempestuous sea, preserved the ship of the church un-WHELMED (un-BAPTIZED), holy Meletius constituted pastor of Tarsus.

* Born 393 (made Bishôp of Cyrrhus 423) after Christ.

EXAMPLE 141.

Basil* (the Great), Discourse on the martyr Julitta, IV.
"As a pilot, skillful and undisturbed through much experience in sailing, preserving the soul erect and un-WHELMED (un-BAPTIZED), and high above every storm."

* See the remark on Examples 79, 80.

GREEK TEXT.

Ejusdem Hom. de Jobi patientia et virtute (*Vol. XII. p. 347*).

Κἂν ἐν ἀθυμίᾳ ᾖς, πρὸς αὐτὸν κατάφευγε· κἂν ἐν πλούτῳ, τὸ φάρμακον ἐντεῦθεν λάμβανε. ὥστε μήτε πτωχείᾳ βαπτισθῆναι, μήτε πλούτῳ φυσηθῆναι.

Theodoreti Eccles. Hist. lib. V. ch. 4 (*ed. Simond, Vol. III. p. 708*).

Ὁ δὲ θεῖος Μελέτιος Διόδωρον ἐκεῖνον, οὗ καὶ πρόσθεν ἐμνήσθην, τόν ἐν τῷ παγχαλέπῳ κλύδωνι ἀβάπτιστον τὸ τῆς ἐκκλησίας διασώσαντα σκάφος, Ταρσέων κατέστησε ποιμένα.

Basilii Magni Hom. in Martyrem Julittam, IV. (*ed. Garnier, Vol. II. p. 37*).

Ὥσπέρ τις κυβερνήτης σοφὸς καὶ ἀτάραχος ὑπὸ τῆς ἄγαν περὶ τὸν πλοῦν ἐμπειρίας, ὀρθὴν καὶ ἀβάπτιστον, καὶ παντὸς χειμῶνος ὑψηλοτέραν τὴν ψυχὴν διασώζων.

2. To overwhelm (figuratively) with an intoxicating liquor, or a stupefying drug, that takes full possession of one's powers, like a resistless flood; or (as the figure may sometimes be understood) to steep in, as by immersing in a liquid.[1]

EXAMPLE 142.

Philo* (the Jew), On a contemplative Life.

"And I know some, who, when they become slightly intoxicated, before they are completely OVERWHELMED (BAPTIZED) provide, by contribution and tickets,† a carousal for the morrow; regarding the hope of the future revel as part of the present festivity."

Compare Basil (Example 95): "So also the souls of these are driven about beneath the waves, being WHELMED (BAPTIZED) with wine."

* See the remark on Example 136.

† Those who took part in a common entertainment contributed each his share of the expense, or gave a *ticket* to be presented afterward for payment.

EXAMPLE 143.

Plutarch,* Banquet, book III. Question 8.

"For of the slightly intoxicated only the intellect is disturb-

* See the remark on Example 53.

[1] So the word *steep* ("from the same root as *dip*, with *s* prefixed," *Worcester's Dict.*) is used figuratively in English.

GREEK TEXT.

Philonis Judæi de Vita contempl. (*ed. Mangey, Vol. II. p. 478*).

Οἶδα δέ τινας, οἳ, ἐπειδὰν ἀκροθώρακες γένωνται, πρὶν τελέως βαπτισθῆναι, εἰς τὴν ὑστεραίαν πότον ἐξ ἐπιδόσεως καὶ συμβολῶν προευτρεπιζομένους· μέρος ὑπολαμβάνοντας τῆς ἐν χερσὶν εὐφροσύνης εἶναι τὴν περὶ τῆς εἰς τὸ μέλλον μέθης ἐλπίδα.

Plut. Symp. lib. III. Quaest. 8 (*ed. Wyttenb. Vol. III. p. 675*).

Τῶν γὰρ ἀκροθωράκων ἡ διάνοια μόνον τετάρακται, τὸ

ed; but the body is able to obey its impulses, being not yet OVERWHELMED (BAPTIZED)."

EXAMPLE 144.

The same Work, book VI. (Introd.). Timotheus, saying that those who sup with Plato (on simple and wholesome fare) enjoy themselves also on the following day, adds:
"For, truly, a great provision for a day of enjoyment is a happy temperament of the body, un-WHELMED (un-BAPTIZED) and unencumbered."

EXAMPLE 145.

The same writer, On the comparative skill of water and land animals, XXIII.
"So then, O Hercules, there is manifest stratagem, with guile; for the worthy man, himself sober as you see, purposely sets upon us while still affected with yesterday's debauch, and OVERWHELMED (BAPTIZED)."

EXAMPLE 146.

Plato,* Banquet, ch. IV. Complaining of the ill effects of an immoderate use of wine, the speaker says:

---

* See the remark on Example 135.

GREEK TEXT.

δὲ σῶμα ταῖς ὁρμαῖς ἐξυπηρετεῖν δύναται, μήπω βεβαπτισμένον.

Ejusdem lib. VI. Proœm. (*ed. Wyttenb. Vol. III. p. 816*).

Μέγα γὰρ ὡς ἀληθῶς εὐημερίας ἐφόδιον εὐκρασία σώματος ἀβαπτίστου καὶ ἐλαφροῦ.

Ejusd. de sollertia animal., XXIII. (*ed. Wyttenb. Vol. IV. p. 956*).

' Ἐνέδρα μὲν οὖν, ὦ Ἡρακλέων, σὺν δόλῳ καταφανής· κραιπαλῶσι γὰρ ἔτι τὸ χθιζὸν καὶ βεβαπτισμένοις νήφων, ὡς ὁρᾷς, ὁ γενναῖος ἐκ παρασκευῆς ἐπιτέθειται.

"For I myself am one of those who yesterday were OVERWHELMED (BAPTIZED)."

In this use, the Greek word corresponds to the English *drench*.* So *Shakesp. Macb. i.* 7 (speaking of the "spongy officers," plied "with wine and wassel"),

"When in swinish sleep
Their drenched natures lie."

* "Icelandic *dreckia*, to plunge in water.; Swedish *drånca*, same sense, also to drown" (*Wedgewood, Dict. of Eng. Etymology*).

EXAMPLE 147.

Athenæus,* *Philosopher's Banquet, book V. ch. 64.*
"You seem to me, O guests, to be strangely flooded with vehement words, and WHELMED (BAPTIZED) with undiluted wine.

'For a man taking draughts of wine, as a horse does of water, talks like a Scythian, not knowing even *koppa*;†
and he lies speechless, plunged in the cask.'"

---

* Beginning of the third century after Christ.
† A Greek numerical sign.

GREEK TEXT.

Platonis Sympos. c. IV. (*ed. Stallb. Vol. I. p. 25*).

Καὶ γὰρ αὐτός εἰμὶ τῶν χθὲς βεβαπτισμένων.¹

Athenæi Deipnosoph. lib. V. c. 64 (*ed. Dindorf, Vol. I. p. 481*).

Δοκεῖτέ μοι, ἄνδρες δαιτυμόνες, σφοδροῖς κατηντλῆ-
σθαι λόγοις παρὰ προσδοκίαν βεβαπτίσθαι τε τῷ ἀκράτῳ·

  Ἀνὴρ γὰρ ἕλκων οἶνον ὡς ὕδωρ ἵππος
  Σκυθιστὶ φωνεῖ, οὐδὲ κόππα γιγνώσκων·
  κεῖται δ' ἄναυδος ἐν πίθῳ κολυμβήσας.²

---

¹ Vino obrutorum (*Ast, Lex. Plat.*).
² Ἐν πίθῳ κολυμβήσας jocose dicitur, *qui se mero ingurgitavit, quasi qui ipsi dolio sese immersisset* (*Schweigh.*).

IN THE TROPICAL OR FIGURATIVE SENSE. 71

EXAMPLE 148.

Lucian,* Bacchus, VII. Speaking of the fabled fountain of Silenus, and its effects on the old men who drink of it, he says:
"When an old man drinks, and Silenus takes possession of him, immediately he is mute for some time, and seems like one heavy-headed and WHELMED (BAPTIZED)."

* See the remark on Example 28.

EXAMPLE 149.

Conon,* Narration L. Describing how Thebe destroyed her husband (Alexander, tyrant of Pheræ), to prevent his meditated murder of herself and her three brothers, he says:
"And Thebe, learning the purpose [of Alexander], gave daggers to the brothers, and urged them to be ready for the slaughter; and having WHELMED (BAPTIZED) Alexander with much wine and put him to sleep, she sends out the guards of the bed-chamber, under pretense of taking a bath, and called the brothers to the deed."

* About the beginning of the Christian era.

GREEK TEXT.

Luciani Bacchi VII. (*ed. Lehmann, Vol. VII. p. 298*).

Ἐπειδὰν πίῃ ὁ γέρων, καὶ κατάσχῃ αὐτὸν ὁ Σιληνὸς, αὐτίκα ἐπιπολὺ ἄφωνός ἐστι, καὶ καρηβαροῦντι καὶ βεβαπτισμένῳ ἔοικε.

Cononis Narrat. L. (*Script. poet. hist. Gr., ed. Westermann, p. 150*).

Θήβη δὲ τὸ βούλευμα μαθοῦσα, τοῖς μὲν ἀδελφοῖς ἐγχειρίδια δοῦσα παρασκευάζεσθαι πρὸς τὴν σφαγὴν παρεκάλει, οἴνῳ δὲ πολλῷ Ἀλέξανδρον βαπτίσασα καὶ κατευνάσασα ἐκπέμπει τοὺς τοῦ θαλάμου φύλακας προφάσει ὡς λουτροῖς χρησομένη, καὶ τοὺς ἀδελφοὺς ἐπὶ τὸ ἔργον ἐκάλει.

Example 150.

Aristophon* (*Athenæus, Philosopher's Banquet, book IX. ch. 44*).
The servant-girl, describing the effect of a cup of wine given by her master, says:
"They WHELMING (BAPTIZING) potently, he set me free."

The sense is well given in Younge's free translation:
  "And then, by steeping me completely in it,
      He set me free."

---

* A Greek comic writer, beginning of the third century after Christ.

Example 151.

Proclus,* *Chrestomathy, XVI.*
"And the IO-BACCHUS was sung at festivals and sacrifices of Bacchus, IMBATHED (BAPTIZED) with much wantonness."

So Milton uses the corresponding English word: "And the sweet odor of the returning gospel imbathe his soul with the fragrancy of heaven."

---

* Born 412 after Christ.

Greek Text.

Aristophon, Athen. Deipnosoph. lib. XI. c. 44 (*ed. Dindorf, Vol. II. p. 1057*).

Εἶτ' ἐλευθέραν ἀφῆκεν βαπτίσας ἐρρωμένως.

Procli Chrestom. XVI. (*ed. Gaisford, p. 384*).

Ἤιδετο δὲ ὁ ΙΟΒΑΚΧΟΣ ἐν ἑορταῖς καὶ θυσίαις Διονύσου, βεβαπτισμένος πολλῷ φρυάγματι.¹

---

¹ Leg. omnino φρυάγματι. Natum mendum, ut innumera alia in Græcis Latinisque auctoribus, ex depravata pronunciandi consuetudine, qua η et ι et υ eodem sono male efferuntur (*Schottus*).

§ 3.

ITS USE IN COMPOSITION WITH A PREPOSITION.

1. With the preposition *in*.

EXAMPLE 152.

Plutarch,* *Life of Sylla*, XXI. Account of the defeat of Archelaus' Asiatic troops, and the storming of his camp, by Sylla.

"And dying they filled the marshes with blood, and the lake with dead bodies; so that, until now, many barbaric bows, and helmets, and pieces of iron breastplates, and swords, are found IMMERSED (BAPTIZED) in the pools."

---

* See the remark on Example 53.

GREEK TEXT.

Plutarchi Vit. Syllæ XXI: (*ed. Schæffer*).

Καὶ κατέπλησαν ἀποθνήσκοντες αἵματος τὰ ἔλη, καὶ νεκρῶν τὴν λίμνην· ὥστε μέχρι νῦν πολλὰ βαρβαρικὰ τόξα, καὶ κράνη, καὶ θωράκων σπάσματα σιδηρῶν, καὶ μαχαίρας ἐμβαπτισμένας τοῖς τέλμασιν εὑρίσκεσθαι.

Example 153.

Nicander,* fragment of a work on husbandry, book II. Directions for preparing a turnip salad.

"Cut turnip-roots and the rind before it is withered, after gently cleansing it, into thin slices; and having dried them a little in the sun, sometimes just dip in boiling water, and IMMERSE (BAPTIZE) many [together] in sharp brine; and at other times, put into a vessel white new-wine with vinegar, half and half, and pickling them in it cover over with salt."

* Middle of the second century before Christ

Example 154.

Synesius,* Epistle LVII. After saying that his fondness, from childhood, for leisure and study, had not deterred him from serving his fellow-men, in private and public affairs, he adds:

"None of these has withdrawn me from philosophy, or cut me off from that blest leisure; for to do with compulsion, and

* Born about 378 after Christ; made Bishop of Ptolemais in the year 410.

Greek Text.

Nicandri Georg. II. (Athen. Deiphnosoph. lib. IV. c. XI. (*ed. Dindorf, Vol. I. p. 303*).

Τμῆγε δὲ γογγυλίδος ῥίζας καὶ ἀκαρφέα φλοιὸν,
ἦκα καθηράμενος, λεπτουργέας· ἠελίῳ δὲ
αὐήνας ἐπὶ τυτθὸν, ὅτ᾽ ἐν ζεστῷ¹ ἀποβάπτων
ὕδατι δριμείῃ πολέας ἐμβάπτισον ἄλμῃ·
ἄλλοτε δ᾽ αὖ λευκὸν γλεῦκος συστάμνισον ὄξει,
ἶσον ἴσῳ, τὰς δ᾽ ἐντὸς ἐπιστύψας ἁλὶ κρύψαις.

Synesii Epist. LVII. (*ed. Petav. p. 194*).

Τούτων οὐδὲν ἐμὲ φιλοσοφίας ἀφεῖλκεν, οὐδὲ τὴν εὐδαίμονά μοι σχολὴν ὑπετέμνετο. τὸ γὰρ ὠθισμῷ καὶ

¹ Possis et sic scribere, ὁτὲ 'ν ζεστῷ (*Schweigh.*).

with toil, and with pains, this is what wastes time, and IMMERSES (BAPTIZES) the soul in cares of business."

EXAMPLE 155.

The same writer; On Dreams. Speaking of the union of mind (pure intelligence) with the sensuous spirit in one being, and the debasement of the former by this union, he says:
"For, to mind, how should a stupid and unreasoning life be agreeable? But to the image,* on account of the then peculiar constitution of the spirit, the lower region is more congenial, for like takes pleasure in like; and if from the two there is made one by the conjunction, even the mind would be IMMERSED (BAPTIZED) in pleasure."

* The soul, separate from the body, with which the sensuous spirit becomes its connecting medium.

2. With the prep. *through,* expressing *transition, alternation;* hence what is *mutually* done, by two or more, to one another.

EXAMPLE 156.

Polyænus, Stratagems, book IV. ch.* 2, 6. The device by which Philip, King of Macedon, while exercising in the wrestling-

* About the middle of the second century after Christ.

GREEK TEXT.

μόχθῳ καὶ μόλις ποιεῖν, τοῦτό ἐστιν ὁ δαπανᾷ τὸν χρόνον, καὶ τὴν ψυχὴν ἐμβαπτίζει μερίμναις πραγμάτων.

Ejusdem de Insomniis (*p. 140*).

Νῷ γὰρ πῶς καλὸν βίος ἔμπληκτος καὶ ἀνόητος; τῷ δὲ εἰδώλῳ, διὰ τὴν ποιὰν τότε τοῦ πνεύματος σύστασιν, ἡ κάτω χώρα προσήκει· ὁμοίῳ γὰρ ὁ ὅμοιον ἥδεται. εἰ δὲ ἓν ἐξ ἀμφοῖν τῷ συνδυασμῷ γίνεται, καὶ ὁ νοῦς ἂν ἐμβαπτισθείη τῷ ἥδεσθαι.

school with Menegetes the pancratiast,* evaded the importunities of his soldiers, who had gathered round clamoring for their pay.

"Philip, not having it, came forward streaming with sweat, covered with dust, and smiling on them said : You say justly, fellow-soldiers ; but indeed, for this very purpose I am myself now anointed against the barbarian, in order that I may many times over repay you thanks. Saying this, and clapping his hands, he ran through the midst and threw himself into the swimming-bath ; and the Macedonians laughed. Philip did not give over DIPPING (BAPTIZING) IN A MATCH with the pancratiast, and sprinkling water in the face, until the soldiers wearied out dispersed."

This was the *dipping match*, or game of *dipping each other;* each party striving to prove his superior strength and agility by putting the other under water, and also by splashing it in his face ("*sprinkling water in the face*") till he was deprived of breath.

* The name for an expert in both wrestling and boxing.

Greek Text.

Polyæni Strategemat. lib. IV. c. ii. 6 (*ed. Coray*).

Οὐκ ἔχων ὁ Φίλιππος προσῆλθεν, ἱδρῶτι ῥεόμενος, κεκονιμένος, [καὶ] προσμειδιάσας αὐτοῖς, Δίκαια (ἔφη) λέγετε, ὦ συστρατιῶται, ἀλλά τοι κἀγὼ διὰ τοῦτο νῦν ἐπὶ τὸν βάρβαρον ἀλείφομαι, ὅπως ὑμῖν πολλαπλασίως ἀποτίσαιμι τὰς χάριτας. Ταῦτα εἰπών, καὶ ταῖν χεροῖν κροτῶν, διὰ μεσῶν δραμὼν, ἐς κολυμβήθραν ἐπέρριψεν [ἑαυτόν]. καὶ οἱ Μακεδόνες ἐγέλασαν. Ὁ Φίλιππος μέχρι τοσούτου διαβαπτιζόμενος[1] πρὸς τὸν παγκρατιαστὴν, καὶ κατὰ τοῦ προσώπου ῥαινόμενος, οὐκ ἀνῆκεν, ἔστ᾽ ἂν οἱ στρατιῶται καμόντες ἀπερρύησαν.

[1] Both the *prep*. and the *mid*. form express what is mutual and reciprocal. Compare the note on the following page.

Example 157.

Demosthenes,[*] *Against Aristogeiton, Oration I. 5.* Showing what class of persons Aristogeiton was accustomed to harrass, by false accusation and extortion, he says:

"Not the speakers [public orators], for these know how TO PLAY THE DIPPING (BAPTIZING) MATCH with him, but private persons and the inexperienced."

In this case the compound word is used metaphorically, and the sense is: For these know how to match him in foul language,—in the game of sousing one another.

---

[*] Born 385 before Christ. By some his authorship of this speech is doubted, but not on decisive grounds.

---

3. With the prep. *down,* hence *downward;* merely strengthening the expression of the simple idea.

Example 158.

Chrysostom,[*] *Discourse on Gluttony and Drunkenness (at the end).*
"For as a ship, that has become filled with water, is soon

---

[*] See the remark on Example 45.

Greek Text.

Demosth. in Aristog. I. 5. (*ed. Bekker, Vol. IV. p.* 874).

Οὐχὶ μὰ Δία τοὺς λέγοντας, οὗτοι μὲν γὰρ ἐπίστανται τούτῳ διαβαπτίζεσθαι,[²] ἀλλὰ τοὺς ἰδιώτας καὶ τοὺς ἀπείρους.

Chrysostomi Eclog. Hom. XII. de Ingluvie et Ebrietate (*ed. Montf., Vol. XII. p.* 516).

Καθάπερ γὰρ πλοῖον ὑπέραντλον γεγονὸς ταχέως κατα-

---

² *Διαβαπτίζω,* certatim immergo. Polyæn. 4, 2. 6. ... Metaph. conviciando certo, forma media ap. Demosth. p. 782, 26 : *Οὗτοι* [μὲν] *γὰρ ἐπίστανται τούτῳ διαβαπτίζεσθαι,* ubi var. *συνδιαβαπτίζεσθαι.* G. Dindorf (*Steph. Thes. nov. ed. Vol. II. col.* 1111).

SUBMERGED (BAPTIZED), and becomes deep under the waves; so also a man, when he gives himself up to gluttony and drunkenness, goes down the steep, and causes reason to be whelmed beneath the waves."

EXAMPLE 159.

Alexander of Aphrodisias,* Medical and Physical Problems, I. 16.
Why is it that some die of fright? Because the physical force, fleeing too much into the depth [of the body] along with the blood, at once WHELMS (BAPTIZES) and quenches the native and vital warmth at the heart, and brings on dissolution."

---

* See the remark on Example 75.

EXAMPLE 160.

The same Work, I. 17.
"Why is it that many die, of those who have drunk wine to excess? Because, again, the abundance of wine WHELMS (BAPTIZES) the physical and the vital power and warmth."

GREEK TEXT.

βαπτίζεται καὶ ὑποβρύχιον γίνεται· οὕτω καὶ ἄνθρωπος, ὅταν τῇ ἀδηφαγίᾳ καὶ μέθῃ ἑαυτὸν ἐκδῷ, κατὰ κρημνὸν ἄπεισι, καὶ ὑποβρύχιον ἐργάζεται τὸν λογισμόν.

Alexandri Aphrodis. Probl. med. et phys. I. 16 (*Ideler, Physic. et Medic. Gr. min. Vol. I. p. 9*).

Διὰ τί ἔνιοι φοβηθέντες ἀπέθανον; ὅτι φεύγουσα λίαν ἡ φυσικὴ δύναμις εἰς τὸ βάθος μετὰ τοῦ αἵματος τὸ ἔμφυτον θερμὸν καὶ ζωτικὸν τὸ παρὰ τῆς καρδίας γενόμενον ἀθρόως καταβαπτίζει καὶ σβέννυσι, καὶ φθορὰν ἐπάγει.

Ejusdem I. 17 (*ibid.*).

Διὰ τί πολλοὶ τῶν οἰνοφλυγησάντων ἀπέθανον; ὅτι πάλιν τὸ πλῆθος τοῦ οἴνου τὴν φυσικὴν καὶ τὴν ζωτικὴν δύναμιν καὶ θερμότητα καταβαπτίζει.

Example 161.

Alciphron's* *Epistles, book II. Ep. 3.* Menander to Glycera, showing why he declines King Ptolemy's invitation to his court in Egypt.

"Is it a great and wonderful thing to see the beautiful Nile? Is it not also a great thing to see the Euphrates? Is it not a great thing also to see the Danube? Are not also the Thermodon, the Tigris, the Halys, the Rhine, among the great things? If I am to see all the rivers, life to me will be WHELMED (BAPTIZED), not beholding Glycera."

---

* Probably, middle of the second century after Christ.

Example 162.

Achilles Tatius,* *Story of Leucippe and Clitophon, book I. ch. 3.*

"For that which, of a sudden, comes all at once and unexpected, shocks the soul, falling on it unawares, and WHELMS (BAPTIZES)."

---

* See the remark on Example 54.

Example 163.

The same Work, book II. ch. 31.

GREEK TEXT.

Alciphronis Rhet. Epist. lib. II. 3 (*ed. Wagner*).

Ἦ μέγα καὶ θαυμαστὸν ἰδεῖν τὸν καλὸν Νεῖλον; οὐ μέγα καὶ τὸν Εὐφράτην ἰδεῖν; οὐ μέγα καὶ τὸν Ἴστρον; οὐ τῶν μεγάλων καὶ ὁ Θερμώδων, ὁ Τίγρις, ὁ Ἅλυς, ὁ Ῥῆνος; Εἰ μέλλω πάντας τοὺς ποταμοὺς ὁρᾶν, καταβαπτισθήσεταί μοι τὸ ζῆν, μὴ βλέποντι Γλυκέραν.

Achillis Tatii de Leucippes et Clitophontis Amoribus, lib. I. c. 3 (*ed. Jacobs*).

Τὸ μὲν γὰρ ἐξαίφνης ἀθρόον καὶ ἀπροσδόκητον ἐκπλήσσει τὴν ψυχήν, ἄφνω προσπεσόν, καὶ κατεβάπτισε.

'And Satyrus had a remnant of the drug, with which he had put Conops to sleep. Of this, while serving us, he covertly pours a part into the last cup which he brought to Panthia; and she rising went into her bedchamber, and immediately fell asleep. But Leucippe had another chamber-servant; whom having WHELMED (BAPTIZED) with the same drug, Satyrus . . comes to the third door, to the door-keeper; and him he laid prostrate with the same draught."

EXAMPLE 164.

Origen,* *Comment. on John, ch. 11 : 45; on the words, 'Many believed on him.'*

"And whom would they not move to believe the preaching of Jesus (and, verily, as if out of death and putridity), of those who were altogether WHELMED (BAPTIZED) by wickedness," etc.

---

* Latter half of the second, and first half of the third century.

GREEK TEXT.

Ejusdem lib. II. c. 31.

Εἶχε δ' ὁ Σάτυρος τοῦ φαρμάκου λείψανον, ᾧ τὸν Κώνωπα ἦν κατακοιμίσας· τούτου διακονούμενος ἡμῖν ἐγχεῖ λαθὼν κατὰ τῆς κύλικος τῆς τελευταίας, ἣν τῇ Πανθίᾳ προσέφερεν. Ἡ δὲ ἀναστᾶσα ᾤχετο εἰς τὸν θάλαμον αὐτῆς, καὶ εὐθὺς ἐκάθευδεν. Εἶχε δὲ ἑτέραν ἡ Λευκίππη θαλαμηπόλον, ἣν τῷ αὐτῷ φαρμάκῳ καταβαπτίσας ὁ Σάτυρος . . ἐπὶ τὴν τρίτην θύραν ἔρχεται πρὸς τὸν θυρωρόν· κἀκεῖνον ἐβεβλήκει τῷ αὐτῷ πόματι.

Origenis Comment. in Joan. T. XXVIII. 9 (*ch. 11 : 45; ed. Garnier, Vol. IV. p. 380*).

Καὶ τίνα γε οὐκ ἂν κινήσαι πρὸς τὸ πιστεῦσαι τῷ τοῦ Ἰησοῦ κηρύγματι, καὶ ἀληθῶς ὡσπερεὶ ἐκ νεκρότητος καὶ δυσωδίας, τῶν πάνυ ὑπὸ τῆς κακίας καταβεβαπτισμένων, κ. τ. λ.

COMPOUNDED WITH A PREPOSITION. 81

EXAMPLE 165.

Basil* (*the Great*), *Discourse XIV., against Drunkards*, § 7.
"For wine WHELMS (BAPTIZES) the reason and the understanding. . . . And what ship without a pilot, borne by the waves as it may happen, is not more safe than the drunken man?"

* See the remark on Examples 79, 80.

EXAMPLE 166.

Eustathius* (*Eumathius*), *Story of Hysmenias and Hysmene book VI.*
"And sleeping I was troubled in spirit with the strangeness of the report, and as to my whole mind WHELMED (BAPTIZED) with the affliction."

* Probably, of the eleventh century after Christ.

EXAMPLE 167.

The same Work, book VII. Apostrophizing Hysmenias, who had been cast into the sea, by command of the pilot, to appease Neptune, Hysmene says (in the writer's peculiar manner):
"Thou, indeed, wast borne away by the swell and the rush

GREEK TEXT.

Basilii Magni Hom. XIV. in Ebriosos VII. (*ed. Garnier, Vol. II. p. 129*).

Τὸν μὲν γὰρ λογισμὸν καὶ τὸν νοῦν ὁ οἶνος καταβαπτίζει . . . ποῖον δὲ πλοῖον ἀκυβέρνητον, ὑπὸ τῶν κυμάτων ὡς ἂν τύχῃ φερόμενον, οὐκ ἀσφαλέστερόν ἐστι τοῦ μεθύοντος;

Eustathii (Eumathii) de Ismeniæ et Ismenes Amoribus, lib. VI. (*ed. Teucher, p. 234*).

Καὶ ἤμην ὑπνῶν τῷ παραδόξῳ τὴν ψυχὴν καταθορυβηθεὶς τοῦ ἀκούσματος, καὶ ὅλον τῇ θλίψει τὸν νοῦν καταβαπτισθείς.

Ejusdem lib. VII. (*p. 310*).

Σὺ μὲν ἀπήχθης. τῷ σάλῳ καὶ τῷ ῥοθίῳ τοῦ κύματος·

of the wave; but my spirit thou didst WHELM (BAPTIZE), surging round, with whole seas of wailings."

EXAMPLE 168.

The same Work, book VII. Neptune, says Hysmene, speaking of the storm which occasioned the sacrifice of Hysmenias,
"Empties all his fury on the sea, and strives to WHELM (BAPTIZE) the whole vessel with the waves."

GREEK TEXT.

ἐμοῦ δὲ κατεβάπτισας τὴν ψυχὴν ὅλαις θαλάσσαις κωκυτῶν περικλύζουσα.

Ejusdem lib. VII. *fin.* (*p. 320*).

Ὅλον θυμὸν κατὰ θαλάσσης κενοῖ, ὅλην τὴν ναῦν φιλονεικεῖ καταβαπτίσαι τοῖς κύμασι.

SECTION II.

Usage of the Greek Versions of the Old Testament.

EXAMPLE 169.

Version of the Seventy,* *4 Kings, ch. 5 : 14* (English Bible 2 Kings 5 : 14).
"And Naaman went down, and IMMERSED (BAPTIZED) HIMSELF in the Jordan, seven times."

The sense is correctly given in the common English Bible: '*And dipped himself seven times in the Jordan.*'

---

* Completed as early as the middle of the second century before Christ.

EXAMPLE 170.

Version of Aquila,* *Job, ch. 9 : 31* (English Bible, '*thou shalt plunge me in the ditch*').
"Even then thou wilt PLUNGE (BAPTIZE) me in corruption."

---

* First half of the second century after Christ.

===

GREEK TEXT.

Septuag. interpret. 4 Reg. c. 5 : 14 (*ed. Tischend.*).

Καὶ κατέβη Ναιμὰν καὶ ἐβαπτίσατο ἐν τῷ Ἰορδάνῃ ἑπτάκις.

Hexapl. Orig. Cap. IX. Job (*ed. Montf. Vol. I. p. 409*).

31. Α. καὶ τότε ἐν διαφθορᾷ βαπτίσεις με.

Example 171.

Version of Symmachus,* *Ps. 68 : 3* (Eng. Bible, Ps. 69 : 2, '*I sink in deep mire*').
"I am PLUNGED (BAPTIZED) into bottomless depths."

---

* Last half of the second century after Christ.

Example 172.

Version (or gloss) of an ancient writer, now unknown, Ps. 9 : 16 (Eng. Bible, Ps. 9 : 15, '*are sunk down*').
"ARE IMMERSED."

Example 173.

Version of the Seventy,* *Is. 21 : 4.*
"Iniquity WHELMS me."

---

* Compare the remark on Example 169.

Example 174.

The same version; Judith, ch. 12 : 5–9.
"And the attendants of Holofernes brought her into the tent,

===

GREEK TEXT.

Hexapl. Orig. Ps. LXVIII. (*ed. Montf. Vol. I. p. 572*).

3. Σ. ἐβαπτίσθην εἰς ἀπεράντους καταδύσεις.[1]

Vet. Interpret. Græc. Fragm. Ps. IX. (*ed. Drusius, p. 882*).

16. וּטְבְּעוּ, ἐβαπτίσθησαν.[2]

Septuag. interpret. Es. XXI. 4 (*ed. Tischend.*).

Ἡ ἀνομία με βαπτίζει.

Septuag. interpret. Judith, c. 12 : 5–9 (*ed. Tischend.*).

Καὶ ἠγάγοσαν αὐτὴν οἱ θεράποντες Ὀλοφέρνου εἰς

---

[1] Demersus sum in infinitas voragines (*Montf.*).
[2] Demersæ sunt (*Hieron.*).

and she slept until midnight. - And she arose at the morning watch, ⁶ and sent to Holofernes, saying: Let my Lord give command, to allow thy handmaid to go forth for prayer; ⁷ and Holofernes commanded the body-guards not to hinder her. And she remained in the camp three days; and went forth by night* into the valley of Bethulia, and IMMERSED (BAPTIZED) HERSELF, in the camp at the fountain.† ⁸ And when she came up, she

Compare, in ch. 6 : 11, '*the fountains that were under Bethulia;*' ch. 7, '*and* [Holofernes and' his horsemen] *viewed the passages up to the city, and came to the fountains of their waters, and took them;*' v. 17, '*and they* [the Ammonites and Assyrians] *pitched in the valley, and took the waters, and the fountains of the children of Israel.*'
There was evidently no lack of water for the immersion of the body, after the Jewish manner; namely by walking into the water to the proper depth, and then sinking down till the whole body was immersed.

---

* Accompanied by her maid, as stated in ch. 13 : 3.

† One of the oldest Greek manuscripts (no. 58), and the two oldest versions (the Syriac and Latin) read, '*immersed (baptized) herself in the fountain of water*' (omitting, '*in the camp*'). According to the common Greek text, this was done '*at the fountain;*' to which she went, because she had there the means of immersing herself. Any other use of water, for purification, could have been made in her tent.

Greek Text.

τὴν σκηνήν, καὶ ὕπνωσε μέχρι μεσούσης τῆς νυκτός· καὶ ἀνέστη πρὸς τὴν ἑωθινὴν φυλακήν, ⁶ καὶ ἀπέστειλε πρὸς Ὀλοφέρνην λέγουσα Ἐπιταξάτω δὴ ὁ κύριός μου ἐᾶσαι τὴν δούλην σου ἐπὶ προσευχὴν ἐξελθεῖν. ⁷ καὶ προσέταξεν Ὀλοφέρνης τοῖς σωματοφύλαξι μὴ διακωλύειν αὐτήν· καὶ παρέμεινεν ἐν τῇ παρεμβολῇ ἡμέρας τρεῖς, καὶ ἐξεπορεύετο κατὰ νύκτα εἰς τὴν φάραγγα Βετυλοία, καὶ ἐβαπτίζετο ἐν τῇ παρεμβολῇ ἐπὶ τῆς πηγῆς τοῦ ὕδατος.¹

---

¹ Ἐν τῇ παρεμβολῇ 2°] 58 (*ed. Holmes et Parsons*). Ἐπὶ τῆς πηγῆς] . . *ἐν τῇ πηγῇ* 58 (*ibid.*). Et baptizabat se in fonte aquæ (*Vet. Lat. ed Sabatier*). ܘܥܡܕܐ ܗܘܐ ܒܡܒܘܥܐ (*Bibl. Polyglott., ed. Walton*).

besought the Lord God of Israel to direct her way, for the raising up of the sons of his people. ⁹ And entering in pure, she remained in the tent, till one brought her food at evening."

EXAMPLE 175.

The same version, Wisdom of Sirach, ch. 34 : 27 (Eng. Bible, Ecclesiasticus, 34 : 25).

"IMMERSING (BAPTIZING) HIMSELF from a dead body, and touching it again, what is he profited by his bathing?"

In this construction (*immerse from*), the writer puts the *means* for the *effect*; immersion of the body being the *means* (symbolically) by which one was *freed* from the pollution of contact with the dead.* This brevity of expression is so common an idiom in the sacred writings (and in the early imitations of them) that it has become a recognized figure of speech.† For example, 2 Cor. 11 : 3, '*so your minds should be corrupted from the simplicity that is in Christ;*' 'corrupted from,' that is, turned from by being corrupted,—the means put for the effect.

---

* '*Sprinkled from an evil conscience*' is the correct translation of Heb. 10 : 22, where also the writer puts *means* for *effect*; for the metaphorical application of the phrase here presupposes the literal use of the same form, and we must give the literal meaning, unless we would sink the writer's metaphor.

† Compare Winer's Grammar of the New Test., § 66, 2 (Masson's translation, § 66, 2, *d*, p. 643, Am. edition).

GREEK TEXT.

⁸ καὶ ὡς ἀνέβη,¹ ἐδέετο τοῦ κυρίου θεοῦ Ἰσραὴλ κατευθῦναι τὴν ὁδὸν αὐτῆς εἰς ἀνάστεμα τῶν υἱῶν τοῦ λαοῦ αὐτοῦ. ⁹ καὶ εἰσπορευομένη καθαρὰ παρέμενε τῇ σκηνῇ, μέχρις οὗ προσηνέγκατο τὴν τροφὴν αὐτῆς πρὸς ἑσπέραν.

Ejusdem lib. Siracidœ c. 34 : 27 (*ed. Tischend.*).

Βαπτιζόμενος ἀπὸ νεκροῦ καὶ πάλιν ἁπτόμενος αὐτοῦ, τί ὠφέλησε τῷ λουτρῷ αὐτοῦ;

---

¹ Ἀνέβη nämlich ἐκ τοῦ ὕδατος (*Fritzsche*, Exeget. Handb. zu den Apokr. d. alt. Test., *in loc.*).

SECTION III.

Summary of the lexical and grammatical uses of baptizein.

1. Lexical use.

1. From the preceding examples it appears, that the ground-idea expressed by this word is, *to put into or under water* (or other penetrable substance), so as entirely *to immerse* or *submerge;* that this act is always expressed in the literal application of the word, and is the basis of its metaphorical uses. This ground-idea is expressed in English, in the various connections where the word occurs, by the terms (synonymous in this ground-element) *to immerse, immerge, submerge, to dip, to plunge, to imbathe, to whelm.*

2. These examples are drawn from writers in almost every department of literature and science; from poets, rhetoricians, philosophers, critics, historians, geographers; from writers on husbandry, on medicine, on natural history, on grammar, on theology; from almost every form and style of composition, romances, epistles, orations, fables, odes, epigrams, sermons, narratives; from writers of various nations and religions, Pagan, Jew, and Christian, belonging to many different countries, and through a long succession of ages.

3. In all, the word has retained its ground-meaning, without change. From the earliest age of Greek literature down to its close (a period of about two thousand years), not an example has been found, in which the word has any other meaning.

There is no instance, in which it signifies to make a partial application of water by *affusion* or *sprinkling*, or *to cleanse, to purify*, apart from the literal act of immersion as the *means* of cleansing or purifying.*

4. The object immersed or submerged is represented as being plunged, or as sinking down, into the ingulfing fluid or other substance; or the immersing element overflows and thus ingulfs the object. The former is the more common case. The latter occurs in Example 4, where rocks, overflowed by the tide when at the flood, are said not to be IMMERSED at ebb-tide; Ex. 13, where the violent current of a river, swollen by heavy rains, is said to have SUBMERGED many attempting to swim through it; Example 14, where animals are said to be SUBMERGED by the overflowing of the Nile; Example 19, the mariners attempting to row out of the harbor to sea, against the storm and the heavy swell, a lofty surge dashes over their little vessel and SUBMERGES it. In the metaphorical application of the word, both cases are recognized as the ground of the usage.

5. The immersing substance is usually *water*, that being the element in which the act most commonly takes place. Other substances mentioned are: *wine*, Ex. 84; *a dye* (for coloring) Exs. 79 and 80; *blood*, Ex. 67, comp. Ex. 42; *breast-milk* and *ointment*, Ex. 70; *oil*, Ex. 86; *fire*, Exs. 79 and 80; *brine*, Ex. 153; *mud* and *slime*, at the bottom of standing pools, Exs. 59, and 152; the human *breast*, Ex. 77; the *neck*, Exs. 68, 78; the human *body*, Exs. 72, 75, 76.

6. The word *immerse*, as well as its synonyms *immerge*, etc., expresses the full import of the Greek word BAPTIZEIN. The idea of *emersion* is not included in the meaning of the Greek

---

* When *part* of an object is said to be immersed, the word is applied to that part alone, and the rest of the object is expressly excepted from its application. Thus, in Ex. 6, the *oaken part* (of the fish-spear) is said to be IMMERSED, "and the rest is buoyed up;" in Ex. 7, the body is said to be "IMMERSED as far as to the breasts," all above being expressly excepted; so Exs. 11 and 38, in one of which the body from the waist upward, and in the other the head, is excepted.

word. It means, simply, to put into or under water (or other substance), without determining whether the object immersed sinks to the bottom, or floats in the liquid, or is immediately taken out. This is determined, not by the word itself, but by the nature of the case, and by the design of the act in each particular case. A living being, put under water without intending to drown him, is of course to be immediately withdrawn from it; and this is to be understood, wherever the word is used with reference to such a case. But the Greek word is also used where a living being is put under water for the purpose of drowning, and of course is left to perish in the immersing element. All this is evident from the following examples.

Example 28, "IMMERSING (BAPTIZING) so that he should not be able to come up again;" Ex. 27, "as you would not wish, sailing in a large and polished and richly gilded ship, to be SUBMERGED (BAPTIZED);" Ex. 41, "nor [knows] the pilot whether he saves, in the voyage, one whom it were better to SUBMERGE (BAPTIZE);" Ex. 43, "desiring to swim through, they were IMMERSED (BAPTIZED) by their full armour;" Ex. 48, "having SUBMERGED (BAPTIZED) his ship with much merchandise, then blames the sea for having ingulfed it full laden;" Ex. 51, "and the dolphin, angry at such a falsehood, IMMERSING (BAPTIZING) killed him;" Ex. 16, "pressing him down and IMMERSING (BAPTIZING) him while swimming, . . . they did not desist till they had entirely suffocated him;" Ex. 17, "being IMMERSED (BAPTIZED) in a swimming-bath, by the Gauls, he dies;" Ex. 44, "and stretching out a hand to others, [would] save them, as if drawing up persons SUBMERGED (BAPTIZED);" Ex. 52, "the ship being in danger of BECOMING IMMERGED (BAPTIZED), he threw out all the lading into the sea;" Ex. 72, "and death to her [the soul] while yet IMMERGED (BAPTIZED) in the body," etc.; Ex. 73, "towering up by what is not IMMERGED (BAPTIZED) in the body;" Ex. 75, "they have their nature and perceptive faculty IMMERSED (BAPTIZED) in the depth of the body;" Ex. 76, "they have the soul very much IMMERSED (BAPTIZED) in the depth of the body;" Ex. 81, "slaying some on land, and PLUNGING (BAPTIZING) others with their boats and huts into the lake;" Ex. 84, "I IMMERSED (BAPTIZED) him into wine, and took and drank him;" Ex. 85, "but also itself partaking of their deformity, and IMMERSED (BAPTIZED) into it.

7. The word is used of the most familiar acts and occurrences of common life; as, IMMERSING (BAPTIZING) wool in a dye, to color it (Exs. 79 and 80); steel in fire, to heat it for tempering (*ibidem*); heated iron (steel) in water to temper it (Ex. 71); an object in a liquid, in order to drink it (Ex. 84); a person in the waves, in sport or revenge (Exs. 26 and 60); a ship in the sea, by overloading it (Ex. 48); an animal in the water, to drown it (Ex. 51); tow in oil, for burning (Ex. 86); salt in water, to dissolve it (Ex. 50); a pole into the bed of a river, to reach something at the bottom (Ex. 82); a bladder in water, by forcing it under (Ex. 24); the hollow hand in water, to fill it (Ex. 57); the hand in blood, to besmear it (Ex. 67); a branch in a liquid, in order to sprinkle it about (Ex. 69); a medical preparation (a pessary of cantharides) in breast-milk and ointment, to allay the irritation (Ex. 70); a sword into an enemy's breast (Ex. 77); sliced turnips in brine, for a salad (Ex. 153); etc.

8. The ground-idea is preserved in the several metaphorical uses of the word. This is evident from many examples.

Thus, of certain persons liable at any moment to be plunged in ruin, it is said (Ex. 87): "they differ little .. from those who are driven by storm at sea; ... and if they commit any even the slightest mistake, are totally SUBMERGED (BAPTIZED);" of one overwhelmed with sorrows by the calamity in which a friend had perished (Ex. 88): "SUBMERGED (BAPTIZED) by that great wave;" of one under the influence of an overmastering passion (Ex. 92): "although WHELMED (BAPTIZED) by desire, the generous man endeavored to resist, and emerged as from a wave;" of a similar case (Ex. 93): "but Dyonisius .. was seized indeed by a tempest, and was WHELMED (BAPTIZED) as to the soul; but yet he struggled to emerge from the passion, as from a mighty wave;" of an enterprise, ruined by untoward events (Ex. 116): "the business [of instructing the young] being WHELMED (BAPTIZED) and all the winds being set in motion against it;" of a people lying in ignorance (Ex. 125): "the congregation IMMERSED (BAPTIZED) in ignorance, and unwilling to emerge to the knowledge of the spiritual teaching;" of the mind oppressed and stupified by intemperance in eating and drinking (Ex. 136):

"as though the reason were WHELMED (BAPTIZED) by the things overlying it;" (with a negation) of one self-collected in difficulties and dangers (Ex. 141): "preserving the soul erect and un-WHELMED (un-BAPTIZED), and high above every storm;" of persons under the power of intoxicating drinks (Ex. 95): "so also the souls of these [the intoxicated] are driven about beneath the waves, being WHELMED (BAPTIZED) with wine;" Ex. 147, "flooded with vehement words, and WHELMED (BAPTIZED) with undiluted wine" (where one who is so overborne and subdued by the power of wine, is represented as "*plunged in the cask*").

The idea of a total submergence lies at the basis of these metaphorical uses. Any thing short of this, such as the mere sprinkling or pouring of water on an object, viewed as the ground of these metaphorical senses, would be simply absurd.

9. In Christian Greek literature, the word retained its distinctive meaning, and continued to be freely used both in the literal and metaphorical sense (Exs. 39, 44, 45–47, 58, 77, 78, 79 and 80, 81, 90, 91, 95, 104–107, 119, 121–123, 125–131, 138–141, 154, 155, 158, 164, 165).

10. In the metaphorical sense it is often used absolutely, meaning *to whelm in* (or *with*) *ruin, troubles, calamities, sufferings, sorrows, business, perplexity, intoxication.* See Exs. 98–102, 115, 116, 124, 135, 142–146, 148, 150. That, in this absolute use, the literal image on which the usage is founded was not lost from view, is evident from Ex. 124: "you are not at leisure but are OVERWHELMED, and the multitude of other affairs holds you in subjection" (more literally, '*has brought you under itself;*' with which compare Ex. 95).

2. Grammatical construction.

The word is construed, in connection with the immersing substance, as follows:

1. With the prep. *into* before the name of the element into which an object is PLUNGED or IMMERSED, expressing fully the act of *passing* from one element into another.

Ex. 61, "(around) every thing that is IMMERSED into it;' Ex. 64, "PLUNGE thyself into the sea;" Ex. 65, "PLUNGING himself into the lake Copais;" Ex. 67, "DIPPING his hand into the blood;" Ex. 68, "he PLUNGED the whole sword into his own neck;" Ex. 70, "again IMMERSE into breast-milk and Egyptian ointment;" Ex. 74, "IMMERSED HIMSELF into the Ocean-stream;" Ex. 77, "TO PLUNGE the sword into the enemy's breast;" Ex. 81, "and PLUNGING others with their boats and huts into the lake;" Ex. 82, "they PLUNGE into the water, therefore, a pole smeared with pitch;" Ex. 84, "I IMMERSED him into wine;" Ex. 85, "and IMMERSED into it;" (metaphorically) Ex. 118, "PLUNGED by drunkenness into stupor and sleep;" Ex. 119, "PLUNGED by drunkenness into sleep;" Ex. 128, "IMMERSE from sobriety into fornication."

2. With the prep. *in*, denoting *locality*, or the element *in* or *within* which the act takes place.

Ex. 59, "IMMERSED and sinking in the pools;" Ex. 72, "to

GREEK TEXT.

Ex. 61, (περι—) παντὶ τῷ βαπτισθέντι εἰς αὐτό. Ex. 64, βαπτίσον σεαυτὸν εἰς θάλασσαν. Ex. 65, ἑαυτὸν βαπτίζων εἰς τὴν Κωπαΐδα λίμνην. Ex. 67, εἰς τὸ αἷμα τὴν χεῖρα βαπτίσας. Ex. 68, ὅλον εἰς τὴν ἑαυτοῦ σφαγὴν ἐβάπτισε τὸ ξίφος. Ex. 70, βαπτίζειν πάλιν ἐς γάλα γυναικὸς, κ. τ. λ. Ex. 74, ἐς Ὠκεανοῖο ῥόον βαπτίζετο. Ex. 77, βαπτίσαι τὸ ξίφος εἰς τὸ τοῦ πολεμίου στῆθος. Ex. 81, τοὺς δὲ εἰς τὴν λίμνην . . . βαπτιζόντων. Ex. 82, κοντὸν οὖν εἰς τὸ ὕδωρ βαπτίζουσι πίσσῃ πεφαρμαγμένον. Ex. 84, ἐβάπτισ' εἰς τὸν οἶνον. Ex. 85, καὶ βεβαπτισμένον εἰς αὐτήν. Ex. 118, βεβαπτισμένον εἰς ἀναισθησίαν καὶ ὕπνον ὑπὸ τῆς μέθης. Ex. 119, ὑπὸ μέθης βαπτιζόμενος εἰς ὕπνον. Ex. 128, ἐκ σωφροσύνης εἰς πορνείαν βαπτίζουσι.

Ex. 59, βαπτιζόμενοι καὶ καταδύνοντες ἐν τοῖς τέλμα-

her, while yet IMMERGED in the body;" Ex. 75, "IMMERSED in the depth of the body;" Exs. 79, 80, "as wool IMMERSED in a dye;" *Ibid.*, "as steel IMMERSED in the fire;" (metaphorically) Ex. 129, "IMMERSED in wickedness;" (compounded with *in*) Ex. 152, "IMMERSED in the pools;" Ex. 153, "IMMERSE in brine;" and metaphorically, Ex. 154, "IMMERSES the soul in cares of business;" Ex. 155, "even the mind would be IMMERSED in pleasure."

3. Also with the simple *dative* as a *local* case, denoting *locality*, viz. the element in which, or where, the act is performed.

Ex. 60, "in waves of the sea IMMERSING;" Ex. 71, "IS PLUNGED in water;" Ex. 73, "towering up by what is not IMMERGED in the body;" Ex. 76, "IMMERSED in the body;" Ex. 78, "TO PLUNGE his right hand in his father's neck;" Ex. 86, "and DIPPING tow in oil;" (figuratively) Ex. 120, "PLUNGES in[1] sleep;" Ex. 121,

[1] That this is the true construction here, is rendered most probable by comparison with Exs. 118 and 119, "PLUNGED by drunkenness into stupor and sleep."

Greek Text.

σιν. Ex. 72, αὐτῇ καὶ ἔτι ἐν τῷ σώματι βεβαπτισμένῃ. Ex. 75, βεβαπτισμένην ἐν τῷ βάθει τοῦ σώματος. Exs. 79. 80, ὥσπερ τὸ ἔριον βαπτισθέν ἐν βάμματι. *Ibid.* ὥσπερ ὁ σίδηρος βαπτιζόμενος ἐν τῷ πυρί. Ex. 129, ἐν τῇ κακίᾳ βεβαπτισμένοι. Ex. 152, ἐμβαπτισμένας τοῖς τέλμασιν. Ex. 153, ἐμβάπτισον ἄλμῃ. Ex. 154, τὴν ψυχὴν ἐμβαπτίζει μερίμναις πραγμάτων. Ex. 155, καὶ ὁ νοῦς ἂν ἐμβαπτισθείη τῷ ἥδεσθαι.

Ex. 60, κύμασι πόντου βαπτίζων. Ex. 71, ὕδατι βαπτίζεται. Ex. 73, τῷ δὴ μὴ βαπτισθέντι τῷ σώματι ὑπεράντες. Ex. 76, βεβαπτισμένην τῷ σώματι. Ex. 78, τὴν δεξιὰν τῷ λαιμῷ βαπτίσαι τῷ πατρικῷ. Ex. 86, καὶ στυπεῖον ἐλαίῳ βαπτίσας. Ex. 120, βαπτίζει δ᾽ ὕπνῳ.

"had PLUNGED the city in¹ sleep;" Ex. 125, "IMMERSED in² ignorance."

This construction (confined mostly to poetry) is required in some examples, and is the probable one in others. One man immerses another *in* (not *with*) waves of the sea; a heated mass of iron (steel) is plunged or immersed *in* (not *with*) water, to cool it; what is inclosed in the human body is immersed *in* (not *with*) it; a weapon is plunged *in* (not *with*) the neck.

4. In the metaphorical sense of *whelming, overwhelming* (submerging, as with an overflowing flood), the *passive* is construed with the usual expression of the efficient cause, and both the *active* and *passive* with the dative of *means* or *instrument* (*by*, or *with*).

Compare the literal use in Exs. 4 and 19, and the figurative use in Ex. 106; and especially Exs. 136, "WHELMED by the things overlying it," and 168, "(Neptune) strives to WHELM the whole vessel with the waves."

Ex. 88, "SUBMERGED by that great wave;" Ex. 92, "WHELMED by desire;" Ex. 103, "WHELMED by worldly affairs;" Ex. 107, "be WHELMED by the annoyances of passion;" Ex. 117, "WHELMED by grief;" Ex. 122, "before thou art deeply WHELMED by this

---

¹ See the note on the preceding page.

² Not *imbued with*, as is evident from the following expression '*emerge to.*' The choice is between the two conceptions '*whelmed with*' (as an overflowing flood), and '*immersed in*' (sunk in ignorance). The latter conception is the most natural and probable one; so in Exs. 126, 127.

GREEK TEXT.

Ex. 121, ὕπνῳ τὴν πόλιν ἐβάπτιζον. Ex. 125, ἀγνοίᾳ βεβαπτισμένην.

Ex. 88, βεβαπτισμένων ὑπὸ τοῦ μεγάλου κύματος ἐκείνου. Ex. 92, βαπτιζόμενος ὑπὸ τῆς ἐπιθυμίας. Ex. 103, βαπτιζομένους ὑπὸ τῶν πραγμάτων. Ex. 107, ὑπὸ ἀηδίας παθῶν βαπτισθῆναι. Ex. 117, βαπτιζόμενόν τε ὑπὸ τῆς ὀδύνης. Ex. 122, πρὶν ἢ σφόδρα ὑπὸ ταύτης βαπτισθῆ-

intoxication;" Ex. 138, "neither WHELMED by poverty, nor elated by riches;" Ex. 164, "WHELMED by wickedness."

Ex. 91, "to WHELM as with successive waves;" Ex. 132, "they do not WHELM the common people with taxes;" Ex. 149, "and having WHELMED Alexander with much wine" (compare Ex. 95); Ex. 163, "whom having WHELMED with the same drug;" Ex. 168, "didst WHELM ... with whole seas of wailings."

Ex. 104, "is WHELMED by none of the present evils;" Ex. 105, "to be WHELMED by the troubles of the present life;" Ex. 111, "to be WHELMED with such a multitude of evils;" Ex. 123, "WHELMED with ten thousand cares;" Ex. 133, "WHELMED with debts" (and many others).

5. Rarely with the prep. *down* (*down into*, i. e. below the

Greek Text.

ναί σε τῆς μέθης. Ex. 138, οὔτε ὑπὸ τῆς πενίας βαπτιζόμενος, οὔτε ὑπὸ τοῦ πλούτου ἐπαιρόμενος. Ex. 164, ὑπὸ τῆς κακίας καταβεβαπτισμένων.

Ex. 91, ὥσπερ ἐπαλλήλοις κύμασι βαπτίζειν. Ex. 132, τοὺς δὲ ἰδιώτας .. οὐ βαπτίζουσι ταῖς εἰσφοραῖς. Ex. 149, οἴνῳ δὲ πολλῷ 'Αλέξανδρον βαπτίσασα. Ex. 163, ἣν τῷ αὐτῷ φαρμάκῳ καταβαπτίσας. Ex. 168, κατεβάπτισας .. ὅλαις θαλάσσαις κωκυτῶν.

Ex. 104, οὐδενὶ τῶν παρόντων βαπτίζεται δεινῶν. Ex. 105, βαπτίζεσθαι τοῖς λυπηροῖς τοῦ παρόντος βίου. Ex. 111, τοσούτῳ πλήθει βαπτισθῆναι κακῶν. Ex. 123, μυρίαις βαπτιζόμενος φροντίσι. Ex. 133, ὀφλήμασι βεβαπτισμένον.

external surface). Ex. 83₁ "PLUNGED down the body;" Ex. 63, "un-DIPPED [down] in water."

GREEK TEXT.

Ex. 83, βαπτίζεσθαι . . . κατὰ τοῦ σώματος.¹ Ex. 63 (with acc.), ἀβάπτιστόν τε καθ᾽ ὕδωρ.

---

¹ And with the genitive alone, Ex. 62, ἀβάπτιστός εἰμι . . . ἅλμαι; also (in some editions) Ex. 74, ὅτε γ᾽ Ὠκεάνοιο ῥόον (ed. Schneid.). Comp. Bernh. Gr. Synt. Kap. 3, 47, a, p. 168.

SECTION IV.

Application of these Results to the New Testament.

---

1. We have thus taken a full survey of the use of this word among those who spoke the Greek language, and to whom the New Testament was directly addressed, in numerous examples from their own writings, composed before and during the age of Christ and his apostles, and for a long time after; showing its unvarying signification through all this time, and its grammatical construction in connection with the name of the element, in which the act it expresses took place.

Let us now open the New Testament, and observe how the following passages must have been read and understood, by those whose manner of using this word has been shown in the foregoing examples.

Matt. 3 : 6. "And were IMMERSED (BAPTIZED) in the Jordan by him."*

Matt. 3 : 11. "I indeed IMMERSE (BAPTIZE) you in water. . . . He will IMMERSE (BAPTIZE) you in holy spirit and fire."*
Compare the writer's note on Matt. 3 : 11.

Mark 1 : 5. "And were all IMMERSED (BAPTIZED) in the river Jordan by him."*

---

* See Ex. 169, "IMMERSED (BAPTIZED) HIMSELF in the Jordan" (Eng. Bible, dipped himself . . in the Jordan'), and the examples referred to in Section III. 2, 2, (on p. 92).

G

Mark 1 : 8. "I indeed IMMERSED (BAPTIZED) you in water; but he will IMMERSE (BAPTIZE) you in holy spirit."*

Compare the writer's note, just referred to, on Matt. 3 : 11.

Mark 1 : 9. "Jesus came from Nazareth of Galilee, and was IMMERSED (BAPTIZED) by John into the Jordan."†

The reader of the New Testament in the Greek language, to whom this was his mother tongue, could be at no loss to know what was done in these cases; or what was required to be done by the command in Matt. 28 : 19, and similar passages.

2. The accompanying circumstances accord with this unvarying meaning of the word. For example, John at first resorted to the river Jordan, as a convenient place for IMMERSING (BAPTIZING) the multitudes who came to him. Ænon was afterwards selected for this purpose, and for the express reason, "because there was much water there, and they came and were IMMERSED (BAPTIZED)" (John 3 : 23). In the most circumstantial account given in the New Testament of the administration of the rite (the immersion of the eunuch by Philip, Acts 8 : 38), it is said that "they went down both into the water;" and that after the rite was performed, "they came up out of the water."‡

3. The other acts, with which it is compared in the New Testament, accord with and require this meaning. It is represented as a *burial;* Rom. 6 : 4, "we are buried with him by the IMMERSION (BAPTISM);" Col. 2 : 12, "buried with him by (prop. in) the IMMERSION (BAPTISM)."§ It is spoken of as having been

---

* See the note on the preceding page.

† See Ex. 171, "I am PLUNGED (BAPTIZED) into bottomless depths," and the examples referred to in Section III. 2, 1, (on pp. 91, 92.).

‡ It has been erroneously supposed, that the same thing is stated in Matt. 3 : 16, and Mark 1 : 10. But the prep. *from* ($\dot{a}\pi\dot{o}$) is there used; and the proper rendering is, 'up from the water.' But here (in Acts) the prep. is $\dot{\epsilon}\kappa$, *out from*, *out of;* and the only possible rendering is, 'came up out of the water,' into which (as just before said) they had gone down.

§ The language is here so explicit, and the reference so obvious, that all Chris-

typefied, when the Israelites "were under the cloud, and passed through the sea," "IMMERSED (BAPTIZED) in the cloud and in the sea" (1 Cor. 10 : 1, 2).*

4. This unvarying sense of the word is expressly distinguished from the application of water to some portion of the body, denoted by other words. In Mark 7 : 3, 4, it is said that the Pharisees "eat not" (i. e., never eat) "except they wash their hands," these being always liable to ceremonial defilement; and that when they come from a public place, as the market (the whole body having been exposed), "except they IMMERSE (BAPTIZE) THEMSELVES, they eat not." In the former case, the writer uses the appropriate word (NIPTEIN) for washing any portion of the body; as the *face* (Matt. 6 : 17), the *hands* (Matt. 15 : 2), the *feet* (John 13 : 5). In the latter case he uses, in distinction from it, the word BAPTIZEIN, which by constant usage expressed an entire submersion of the object spoken of. As there is here no limitation ("they IMMERSE THEMSELVES"), the whole body of course is meant.†

5. With this usage accords also the metaphorical sense of *overwhelming suffering*, found in Mark 10 : 38, 39, "can ye undergo the IMMERSION (BAPTISM) that I must undergo,"‡ and in Luke 12 : 50, "I have an IMMERSION (BAPTISM) to undergo;"‡ a sense founded on the idea of total submergence, as in floods of sor-

---

tian antiquity understood by it an allusion to the symbolic significance of the rite of immersion. (See examples in Section V. 1.) Almost all modern scholars are of the same opinion. The few attempts to set aside this obvious view have made little impression, and require no refutation.

* Compare the explanation of this given by the Greek interpreter *Theophylact*, Section V. Example 196.

† In Luke 11 : 38, there is no intimation that this was *always* practiced before dinner. On the contrary, the full and minute statement in Mark 7 : 3, 4, forbids this supposition, and Luke 11 : 38 must be understood accordingly. It was the case mentioned in v. 4 of Mark's statement, the Saviour having come from a crowd.

‡ As these passages are correctly rendered by Dr. Campbell (President of Marischal College, Aberdeen), "The four Gospels translated," etc.

row.* The same metaphorical sense, according to many interpreters, is found in 1 Cor. 15 : 29.

6. The *grammatical construction* accords also with the constant usage of Greek writers, and with the only recognized meaning of the word. Namely:

1. With the prep. *into*, expressing the act of *passing* from one element (the air) into another (water). Compare the *Summary* of the usage of Greek writers, *Section III. 2, 1*. For example: Mark 1 : 9, "WAS IMMERSED (BAPTIZED) by John into the Jordan."

2. With the prep. *in*, denoting *locality*, or the element *in* or *within* which the act is performed (*Summary, Section III. 2, 2*).

For example: Mark 1 : 5, "were all IMMERSED (BAPTIZED) in the river Jordan; Matt. 3 : 11, "I indeed IMMERSE (BAPTIZE) you in water; Mark 1 : 8, "I IMMERSED (BAPTIZED) you in water;" *ibid.*, "but he will IMMERSE (BAPTIZE) you in holy spirit;"* John 1 : 26, "I IMMERSE (BAPTIZE) in water;" v. 31, "I came IMMERSING (BAPTIZING) in water;" v. 33, "he who sent me to IMMERSE (BAPTIZE) in water;" same verse, "this is he who IMMERSES (BAPTIZES) in holy spirit."†

3. With the *dative* alone, either as a *local* case, '*in water*' e. g., (*Summary, Section V. 2, 3*), or as the *instrumental dative*, to distinguish the *element* used for immersing in one case from that employed in another.‡ The simple dative occurs, in the New Testament, only where the material or element used for immersing is to be thus distinguished. In all these instances, the distinction is between the element of *water*, and *the Holy Spirit* (or, *holy spirit*); and as the latter could less properly be conceived as the mere instrument of an act, it is in every such case construed with the local preposition *in*. (See Luke 3 : 16, Acts 1 : 5, 11 : 16.) This is the only explanation of the use

---

* Compare the remark on Ex. 98, and the *Summary* in Section III. 1, 8.
† See the remark on p. 97.
‡ Dr. Hackett (on Acts 1 : 5) : "ὕδατι, *with water* as the element by which, ἐν πνεύματι ἁγίῳ, *in the Holy Spirit*, as the element in which the baptism is performed." (*Commentary on the original text of the Acts of the Apostles*, 2d edition, p. 37.)

both of the simple dative, and of the dative with the preposition, in the same connection and relation.

7. The Greek word BAPTIZEIN expresses nothing more than the act of IMMERSION, the religious significance of which is derived from the circumstances connected with it. Thus when, in obedience to the command in Matt. 28 : 19, this act is performed on the assenting believer, in the name of the Father, and of the Son, and of the Holy Spirit, it by this becomes the Christian rite; and this distinguishes it from all other acts of life, and gives it a sacred relation and a sacred significance. But in Mark 7 : 4 ('except they immerse themselves'), and in Luke 11 : 38 ('that he had not immersed himself'), the act expressed by the same word is a superstitious Pharisaic ceremony, condemned by our Lord himself; and in Heb. 9 : 10, the mere ceremonial immersions of the Jews are meant. The act designated by the word, in all these cases, is the same; the relation in which it is performed constitutes the only distinction. In the Christian rite, being performed with a conscious reference to the burial and resurrection of Christ, the act associates with itself, in the mind of the believer, the religious ideas and obligations symbolized by it in virtue of this reference. It is also a recognition of the pollution of sin, and of the sanctifying agency of the spirit, as symbolized by the cleansing power of the element of water. But the word BAPTIZEIN did not, in itself, express *an immersion in the name of the Father, of the Son, and of the Holy Spirit;* nor an immersion with reference to the burial and resurrection of Christ, or to the sanctifying agency of the Spirit. Wherever it is used of the Christian rite, in the New Testament, this reference is clear from the connection; and only through this connection does it suggest the peculiar Christian ideas associated with it.

SECTION V.

Usage of the Church Fathers.

I.

Where they use this word (or the cognate noun) of the Christian rite, or describe the rite in other words.

What the Church Fathers, who wrote while the Greek was a living language, and to whom it was the mother tongue, understood to be the meaning of this word in the New Testament, will be seen from the following examples, to which many others of the same tenor might be added.

EXAMPLE 176.

Cyrill,[*] *Bishop of Jerusalem, Instruction III., On Baptism, xii.*
"For as Jesus assuming the sins of the world died, that having slain sin he might raise thee up in righteousness; so

---

[*] Born about 315 after Christ; made Bishop of Jerusalem in 350.

===

GREEK TEXT.

Cyrilli Hierosol. Catechesis III. de Baptismo, xii. (*ed. Touttée, p. 45*).

"Ὥσπερ γὰρ Ἰησοῦς τὰς οἰκουμενικὰς ἁμαρτίας ἀναλαβὼν ἀπέθανεν, ἵνα θανατώσας τὴν ἁμαρτίαν ἀναστήσῃ σε ἐν δικαιοσύνῃ· οὕτω καὶ σὺ καταβὰς εἰς τὸ ὕδωρ. καὶ

also thou, going down into the water, and in a manner buried in the waters as he in the rock, art raised again, walking in newness of life."

EXAMPLE 177.

The same writer, Initiation II., On the ceremonies of Baptism.
"O strange and wonderful transaction! Not truly did we die, nor were we truly buried, nor truly crucified did we rise again; but the imitation was in a similitude, while the salvation was in truth. Christ was really crucified, and really was buried, and truly rose again; and all these things have been graciously imparted to us, that sharing his sufferings in imitation, we might in truth obtain salvation."

EXAMPLE 178.

The same writer, Initiation II. 4.
"After these things, ye were led by the hand to the sacred font of the divine IMMERSION (BAPTISM), as Christ from the cross

GREEK TEXT.

τρόπον τινὰ ἐν τοῖς ὕδασι ταφεὶς, ὥσπερ ἐκεῖνος ἐν τῇ πέτρᾳ, ἐγείρῃ πάλιν ἐν καινότητι ζωῆς περιπατῶν.

Ejusdem Mystag. II. de Baptismi Caeremoniis (*ed. Touttée, p. 313*).

Ὦ ξένου καὶ παραδόξου πράγματος. οὐκ ἀληθῶς ἀπεθάνομεν, οὐδ' ἀληθῶς ἐτάφημεν, οὐδ' ἀληθῶς σταυρωθέντες ἀνέστημεν· ἀλλ' ἐν εἰκόνι ἡ μίμησις, ἐν ἀληθείᾳ δὲ ἡ σωτηρία. Χριστὸς ὄντως ἐσταυρώθη, καὶ ὄντως ἐτάφη, καὶ ἀληθῶς ἀνέστη· καὶ πάντα ἡμῖν ταῦτα κεχάρισται, ἵνα τῇ μιμήσει τῶν παθημάτων αὐτοῦ κοινωνήσαντες, ἀληθείᾳ τὴν σωτηρίαν κερδήσωμεν.

Ejusdem Mystag. II. 4 (*ed. Touttée, p. 312*).

Μετὰ ταῦτα, ἐπὶ τὴν ἁγίαν τοῦ θείου βαπτίσματος ἐχειραγωγεῖσθε κολυμβήθραν, ὡς ὁ Χριστὸς ἀπὸ τοῦ

to the prepared tomb. And each was asked, if he believes in the name of the Father, and of the Son, and of the Holy Spirit. And ye professed the saving profession, and sunk down thrice into the water, and again came up. And there, by a symbol, shadowing forth the burial of Christ," etc.

Example 179.

The same writer (in the same passage, eight lines below).
"And in the same ye died and were born; and that saving water became to you a grave and a mother."

Example 180.

The same writer, Instruction VIII., On the Holy Spirit II. 14.
"For the Lord saith: 'Ye shall be IMMERSED (BAPTIZED) in the Holy Spirit not many days after this.' Not in part the grace; but all-sufficing the power! For as he who sinks down in the

---

Greek Text.

σταυροῦ ἐπὶ τὸ προκείμενον μνῆμα. Καὶ ἠρωτᾶτο ἕκαστος εἰ πιστεύει εἰς τὸ ὄνομα τοῦ πατρός, καὶ τοῦ υἱοῦ, καὶ τοῦ ἁγίου Πνεύματος. καὶ ὡμολογήσατε τὴν σωτήριον ὁμολογίαν, καὶ κατεδύετε τρίτον εἰς τὸ ὕδωρ, καὶ πάλιν ἀνεδύετε· καὶ ἐνταῦθα, διὰ συμβόλου τὴν τριήμερον τοῦ Χριστοῦ αἰνιττόμενοι ταφήν, κ. τ. λ.

Ejusdem (*ibidem*).

Καὶ ἐν τῷ αὐτῷ ἀπεθνήσκετε καὶ ἐγεννᾶσθε· καὶ τὸ σωτήριον ἐκεῖνο ὕδωρ καὶ τάφος ὑμῖν ἐγίνετο καὶ μήτηρ.

Ejusdem Catechesis XVII. (de Spiritu Sancto II.) 14 (*p. 271*).

Λέγει γὰρ ὁ Κύριος· Ὑμεῖς βαπτισθήσεσθε ἐν πνεύματι ἁγίῳ οὐ μετὰ πολλὰς ταύτας ἡμέρας. οὐ μερικὴ ἡ χάρις, ἀλλὰ αὐτοτελὴς ἡ δύναμις. ὥσπερ γὰρ ὁ ἐνδύνων

waters and is IMMERSED (BAPTIZED), is surrounded on all sides by the waters, so also they were completely IMMERSED (BAPTIZED) by the Spirit."

EXAMPLE 181.

Basil* (the Great), On the Holy Spirit, ch. XV. 35.
"Imitating the burial of Christ by the IMMERSION (BAPTISM); for the bodies of those IMMERSED (BAPTIZED) are as it were buried in the water."

* Born about 330 after Christ; made Bishop of Cæsarea in 370.

EXAMPLE 182.

The same writer (in the same passage, a few lines below).
"The water presents the image of death, receiving the body as in a tomb."

EXAMPLE 183.

The same writer, On Baptism, book I. ch. 1, 4.
"Which we seem to have covenanted by the IMMERSION (BAPTISM)

GREEK TEXT.

ἐν τοῖς ὕδασι καὶ βαπτιζόμενος, πανταχόθεν ὑπὸ τῶν ὑδάτων περιβάλλεται· οὕτω καὶ ὑπὸ τοῦ πνεύματος ἐβαπτίσθησαν ὁλοτελῶς.

Basil. Mag. de Spirit. Sanct., c. XV. 35 (*ed. Garnier, Vol. III. p. 29*).

Μιμούμενοι τὴν ταφὴν τοῦ Χριστοῦ διὰ τοῦ βαπτίσματος. οἱονεὶ γὰρ ἐνθάπτεται τῷ ὕδατι τῶν βαπτιζομένων τὰ σώματα.

Ejusdem (*ibidem*).

Τὸ μὲν ὕδωρ τοῦ θανάτου τὴν εἰκόνα παρέχει, ὥσπερ ἐν ταφῇ τὸ σῶμα παραδεχόμενον.

Ejusd., de Baptismo, lib. I. c. 1, 4, *extr.* (*ed. Garnier, Vol. II. p. 628*).

Ὅπερ συντεθεῖσθαι δοκοῦμεν διὰ τοῦ ἐν τῷ ὕδατι

in water, professing to have been crucified with, to have died with, to have been buried with, and so forth, as it is written."

Example 184.

Chrysostom,* Comment. on 1 Cor. Discourse XL. 1.

. "For to be IMMERSED (BAPTIZED), and to sink down, then to emerge, is a symbol of the descent into the underworld, and of the ascent from thence. Therefore Paul calls the IMMERSION (BAPTISM) the burial, saying: 'We were buried, therefore, with him by the IMMERSION (BAPTISM) into death.'"

---

* Born about 347 after Christ; made Bishop and Patriarch of Constantinople in 398.

Example 185.

The same writer, On the Gospel of John, Discourse XXV.

"Divine symbols are therein celebrated, burial and deadness, and resurrection and life. And all these take place together; for when we sink our heads down in the water as in a kind of tomb, the old man is buried, and sinking down beneath is

---

Greek Text.

βαπτίσματος, ὁμολογοῦντες συνεσταυρῶσθαι, συντεθνηκέναι, συντεθάφθαι, καὶ τὰ ἐξῆς, καθὼς γέγραπται.

Chrysost. in Epist. ad I Cor. Hom. XL. 1 (*ed. Montf. Vol. X. p. 379*).

Τὸ γὰρ βαπτίζεσθαι καὶ καταδύεσθαι, εἶτα ἀνανεύειν, τῆς εἰς ᾅδου καταβάσεώς ἐστι σύμβολον καὶ τῆς ἐκεῖθεν ἀνόδου. διὸ τὸν τάφον τὸ βάπτισμα ὁ Παῦλος καλεῖ λέγων, συνετάφημεν οὖν αὐτῷ διὰ τοῦ βαπτίσματος εἰς τὸν θάνατον.

Chrysost. in Joannem Hom. XXV. (*ed. Montf. Vol. VIII. p. 146*).

Θεῖα τελεῖται ἐν αὐτῷ σύμβολα· τάφος καὶ νέκρωσις, καὶ ἀνάστασις καὶ ζωὴ, καὶ ταῦτα ὁμοῦ γίνεται πάντα. καθάπερ γὰρ ἐν τινὶ τάφῳ τῷ ὕδατι καταδυόντων ἡμῶν τὰς κεφαλὰς, ὁ παλαιὸς ἄνθρωπος θάπτεται, καὶ καταδὺς

all concealed at once; then, when we emerge, the new man comes up again."

EXAMPLE 186.

The same writer, On the Epistle to the Romans, Discourse XI. on ch. VI. 5.

"For as his body, buried in the earth, bore for fruit the salvation of the world; so also ours, buried in the IMMERSION (BAPTISM), bore for fruit righteousness, sanctification, sonship, ten thousand benefits, and will bear also the final gift of the resurrection. Since, therefore, we indeed in water, but he in earth, and we in respect to sin, but he in respect to the body was buried, on this account he did not say, 'planted together in death,' but 'in the likeness of death.'"

EXAMPLE 187.

Athanasius,* Discourse on the Holy Passover, 5.

---

* Born near the close of the third or beginning of the fourth century; made Bishop of Alexandria in the year 328.

GREEK TEXT.

κάτω κρύπτεται ὅλος καθάπαξ· εἶτα ἀνανευόντων ἡμῶν, ὁ καινὸς ἄνεισι πάλιν.

Chrysostomi in Epist. ad Rom. Hom. XI. in c. VI. 5 (*ed. Montf.,* Vol. IX. p. 530).

Καθάπερ γὰρ τὸ σῶμα αὐτοῦ ταφὲν ἐν τῇ γῇ καρπὸν τῆς οἰκουμένης τὴν σωτηρίαν ἤνεγκεν· οὕτω καὶ τὸ ἡμέτερον ταφὲν ἐν τῷ βαπτίσματι, καρπὸν ἤνεγκε τὴν δικαιοσύνην, τὸν ἁγιασμόν, τὴν υἱοθεσίαν, τὰ μυρία ἀγαθά· οἴσει δὲ καὶ τὸ τῆς ἀναστάσεως ὕστερον δῶρον. ἐπεὶ οὖν ἡμεῖς μὲν ἐν ὕδατι, αὐτὸς δὲ ἐν γῇ, καὶ ἡμεῖς μὲν κατὰ τὸν τῆς ἁμαρτίας λόγον, ἐκεῖνος δὲ κατὰ τὸν τοῦ σώματος ἐτάφη, διὰ τοῦτο οὐκ εἶπε, σύμφυτοι τῷ θανάτῳ, ἀλλὰ τῷ ὁμοιώματι τοῦ θανάτου.

"In these benefits thou wast IMMERSED (BAPTIZED), O newly-enlightened; the initiation into the grace, O newly-enlightened, has become to thee an earnest of resurrection; thou hast the IMMERSION (BAPTISM) as a surety of the abode in heaven. Thou didst imitate, in the sinking down, the burial of the Master; but thou didst rise again from thence, before works witnessing the works of the resurrection.

EXAMPLE 188.

The same writer, Questions on the Psalms, Prop. 92.

"For that the child sinks down thrice in the font, and comes up, this shows the death, and the resurrection on the third day, of Christ."

EXAMPLE 189.

Gregory* of Nazianzus; Discourse XL., on the holy Baptism.

"Let us, therefore, be buried with Christ by the IMMERSION

* Born about 330 after Christ.

GREEK TEXT.

Athanasii Serm. in Sanctum Pascha, 5, (*ed. monach. ord. S. Bened. Tom. II. p. 457*).

Ἐν τούτοις ἐβαπτίσθης τοῖς ἀγαθοῖς νεοφώτιστε, ἀρραβών σοι γέγονεν ἀναστάσεως, νεοφώτιστε, ἡ τῆς χάριτος μύησις· ἐνέχυρον τῆς ἐν οὐρανῷ διαίτης ἔχεις τὸ βάπτισμα. ἐμιμήσω τῇ καταδύσει τοῦ δεσπότου τὸν τάφον· ἀλλὰ ἀνέδυς πάλιν ἐκεῖθεν, τὰ τῆς ἀναστάσεως ἔργα πρὸ τῶν ἔργων θεώμενος.

Ejusdem Quaest. in Psalmos Prop. XCII. (*Tom. II. p. 327*).

Τὸ γὰρ καταδῦσαι τὸ παιδίον ἐν τῇ κολυμβήθρᾳ τρίτον καὶ ἀναδῦσαι, τοῦτο δηλοῖ τὸν θάνατον καὶ τὴν τριήμερον ἀνάστασιν τοῦ Χριστοῦ.

Greg. Naz. Orat. XL. in sanct. baptisma (*ed. Prunæus, Vol. I. p. 642*).

Συνταφῶμεν οὖν Χριστῷ διὰ τοῦ βαπτίσματος, ἵνα καὶ

(BAPTISM), that we may also rise with him; let us go down with him, that we may also be exalted with him; let us come up with him, that we may also be glorified with him."

EXAMPLE 190.

John of Damascus,* On the orthodox Faith, book IV. ch. 9, on Faith and Baptism.

"For the IMMERSION (BAPTISM) shows the Lord's death. We are indeed buried with the Lord by the IMMERSION (BAPTISM), as says the holy apostle."

---

* Born about the end of the seventh century.

EXAMPLE 191.

The same writer; Parallels, book III. tit. iv., on Baptism, etc.

"Israel, if he had not passed through the sea, would not have been delivered from Pharaoh; and thou, if thou pass not through the water, wilt not be delivered from the bitter tyranny of the Devil."

GREEK TEXT.

συναναστῶμεν· συγκατέλθωμεν, ἵνα καὶ συνυψωθῶμεν· συνανέλθωμεν, ἵνα καὶ συνδοξασθῶμεν.

Joannis Damasceni de fide orthodoxa, lib. IV. c. 9, de fide et baptismo (*ed. Le Quien, Vol. 1. p. 259*).

Τὸ γὰρ βάπτισμα τὸν τοῦ κυρίου θάνατον δηλοῖ. συνθαπτόμεθα γοῦν τῷ κυρίῳ διὰ τοῦ βαπτίσματος, ὥς φησιν ὁ θεῖος ἀπόστολος.

Ejusdem Parallel. Lib. III. Tit. iv. de Bapt. et sacr. lavacri praedicat. (*Vol. II. p. 387*).

Ὁ Ἰσραὴλ, εἰ μὴ παρῆλθε τὴν θάλασσαν, οὐκ ἂν ἐχωρίσθη τοῦ φαραώ· καὶ σὺ ἐὰν μὴ παρέλθῃς διὰ τοῦ ὕδατος, οὐ χωρίσθησῃ τῆς πικρᾶς τυραννίδος τοῦ διαβόλου.

Example 192.

Theophylact,* *Comment. on Nahum, ch. I.*

"For one IMMERSION (BAPTISM) is spoken of, as also one faith, because of the doctrine respecting the initiation, being one in all the Church, which has been taught to IMMERSE (BAPTIZE) with invocation of the Trinity, and to symbolize the Lord's death and resurrection by the threefold sinking down and coming up."

* Archbishop of Achrida, about 1070; gives the views of the old Greek interpreters.

Example 193.

The same writer, On the Acts of the Apostles, ch. 1 : 5. Commenting on the words, 'ye shall be IMMERSED (BAPTIZED) in the Holy Spirit, he says:

"The word BE IMMERSED (BE BAPTIZED), signifies the abundance, and as it were the riches of the participation of the Holy Spirit; as also, in that perceived by the senses, he in a manner has who is IMMERSED (BAPTIZED) in water, bathing the whole body, while he who simply receives water is not wholly wetted on all places."

Greek Text.

Theophylacti Comment. in Naum cap. I. (*Opera, ed. de Rubeis et Finetti, Venet. 1763, Vol. IV. p. 221*).

Ἐν μὲν γὰρ εἴρηται βάπτισμα, ὥσπερ καὶ πίστις μία, διὰ τὸ ἐπὶ τῇ τελετῇ δηλαδὴ δόγμα, ἐν ὂν ἐν πάσῃ Ἐκκλησίᾳ, τῇ παραλαβούσῃ βαπτίζειν τῇ τῆς Τριάδος ἐπικλήσει, καὶ τυποῦν τὸν τοῦ κυρίου θάνατον καὶ τὴν ἀνάστασιν τῇ τρισσῇ καταδύσει καὶ ἀναδύσει.

Ejusdem in Acta Apost. c. I. 5 (*Vol. III. p. 10*).

Ἡ βαπτισθῆναι λέξις, τὴν δαψίλειαν, καὶ οἱονεὶ τὸν πλοῦτον τῆς μετουσίας τοῦ ἁγίου πνεύματος σημαίνει· ὡς καὶ ἐπὶ τοῦ αἰσθητοῦ ἔχει τι ὁ βαπτιζόμενος ἐν ὕδατι, ὅλον τὸ σῶμα βρέχων, τοῦ λαμβάνοντος ἁπλῶς ὕδωρ οὐ πάντως ὑγραινομένου ἐξ ὅλων τῶν τόπων.

Example 194.

The same writer, Comment. on the Epistle to the Heb. ch. 6 : 2.
Commenting on the words, 'resurrection from the dead,' he says:
"For this takes place also in the IMMERSION (BAPTISM), through the figure of the coming up."

Example 195.

The same writer, On Rom. 6 : 5, 6.
"For our old man, that is, wickedness, was crucified with, that is, in like manner with the body of Christ, was buried in the IMMERSION (BAPTISM), that the body of sin might be destroyed."

Example 196.

The same writer, Comment. on 1 Cor. 9 : 2. Explaining the words, 'were all baptized unto Moses in the cloud and in the sea,' he says:
"That is, they shared with Moses both the shadow beneath the cloud, and the passage through the sea; for seeing him first pass through, they also themselves braved the waters. As also

---

GREEK TEXT.

Ejusdem in Epist. ad Hebr. c. VI. 2 (*Vol. II. p. 682*).

Ἀναστάσεώς τε νεκρῶν.) Τοῦτο γὰρ καὶ ἐν τῷ βαπτίσματι γίνεται διὰ τοῦ σχήματος τῆς ἀναδύσεως.

Ejusdem Comment. in Epist. ad Rom. c. VI. 5, 6. (*Vol. II. p. 42*).

Καὶ γὰρ ὁ παλαιὸς ἡμῶν ἄνθρωπος, τουτέστιν, ἡ κακία, συνεσταυρώθη, τουτέστιν, ὁμοίως τῷ σώματι τοῦ Χριστοῦ, ἐν τῷ βαπτίσματι ἐτάφη, ἵνα καταργηθῇ τὸ σῶμα τῆς ἁμαρτίας.

Ejusdem Comment. in I Epist. ad Cor. c. IX. 2 (*Vol. II. p. 177*).

Καὶ πάντες εἰς τὸν Μωσῆν ἐβαπτίσθησαν ἐν τῇ νεφέλῃ, καὶ ἐν τῇ θαλάσσῃ.) Τουτέστι, τῷ Μωσῇ ἐκοινώνησαν τῆς τε ὑπὸ τὴν νεφέλην σκιᾶς, καὶ τοῦ διόδου

in our case; Christ having first died and risen, we also are ourselves IMMERSED (BAPTIZED), imitating death by the sinking down, and resurrection by the coming up. 'They were IMMERSED (BAPTIZED) unto Moses,' therefore, instead of: they had him as a founder of the type of the IMMERSION (BAPTISM); for the being under the cloud, and the passing through the sea, were a type of the IMMERSION (BAPTISM)."

EXAMPLE 197.

The same writer, On the Epistle to the Romans, ch. 9 : 8. Commenting on the words, 'for at this time I will return, and Sarah shall have a son,' he says:

"Therefore, the word of God formed and begat Isaac; so also upon us God's children, in the font as in a womb, are uttered words of God, and they form us anew."

GREEK TEXT.

τῆς θαλάσσης. ἰδόντες γὰρ αὐτὸν πρῶτον διαβάντα, κατετόλμησαν καὶ αὐτοὶ τῶν ὑδάτων. Ὥσπερ καὶ ἐφ' ἡμῶν, πρῶτον τοῦ Χριστοῦ ἀποθανόντος καὶ ἀναστάντος, βαπτιζόμεθα καὶ αὐτοί, μιμούμενοι τὸν θάνατον διὰ τῆς καταδύσεως, καὶ τὴν ἀνάστασιν διὰ τοῦ ἀναδύσεως. Εἰς τὸν Μωσῆν οὖν ἐβαπτίζοντο, ἀντὶ τοῦ, αὐτὸν ἀρχηγὸν ἔσχον τοῦ τύπου τοῦ βαπτίσματος· τύπος γὰρ βαπτίσματος ἦν, τό τε ὑπὸ τὴν νεφέλην εἶναι, καὶ τὸ τὴν θάλασσαν διελθεῖν.

Ejusdem Comment. in Epist. ad Rom. c. IX. 8. (*Vol. II. p. 68*).

Τὸ οὖν ῥῆμα τοῦ θεοῦ διέπλασε τὸν Ἰσαὰκ καὶ ἐγέννησεν. Οὕτω δὴ καὶ ἐφ' ἡμῶν τῶν τέκνων τοῦ θεοῦ, ἐν τῇ κολυμβήθρᾳ ὡς ἐν μήτρᾳ, ῥήματα θεῖα ἐπιλέγονται, κἀκεῖνα ἡμᾶς ἀναπλάττουσιν.

Example 198.

The same writer, On Heb. 10 : 26.
"For our IMMERSION (BAPTISM) images the death of Christ; as, therefore, that was one, so also this is one."

Example 199.

The same writer, On Matt. 3 : 11.
"'He will IMMERSE (BAPTIZE) you in the Holy Spirit.'" That is, he will deluge you, ungrudgingly, with the graces of the Spirit."

Example 200.

The same writer, Comment. on Luke 24 : 45-53.
"For as he, having died, rose the third day, so also we, being typically buried in the water, then come up incorrupt as to our souls, and receiving the pledges of the incorruption of the body.

GREEK TEXT.

Ejusdem Comment. in Epist. ad Heb. c. X. v. 26 (*Vol. II. p. 726*).

Τὸ γὰρ βάπτισμα ἡμῶν τὸν θάνατον εἰκονίζει τοῦ Χριστοῦ· ὥσπερ οὖν ἐκεῖνος εἶς, οὕτω καὶ τοῦτο ἕν.

Ejusdem in Matt. Comment. c. III. v. 11 (*Vol. I. p. 18*).

Αὐτὸς ὑμᾶς βαπτίσει ἐν πνεύματι ἁγίῳ.) Τουτέστι, κατακλύσει ὑμᾶς ἀφθόνως ταῖς τοῦ πνεύματος χάρισιν.

Ejusdem Comment. in Luc. c. XXIV. vv. 45-53 (*Vol I. p. 497*).

Ὥσπερ γὰρ ἐκεῖνος θανὼν τριήμερος ἀνέστη, οὕτω καὶ ἡμεῖς ἐνθαπτόμενοι τυπικῶς τῷ ὕδατι, εἶτα ἀναδύνομεν ἄφθαρτοι τὰς ψυχάς, καὶ τῆς τοῦ σώματος ἀφθαρσίας τοὺς ἀρραβῶνας δεχόμενοι.

Example 201.

The same writer; On John ch. 3 : 14.
"For the cross and the death [thereon] are a cause to us of the grace through the IMMERSION (BAPTISM); if at least, being IMMERSED (BAPTIZED), we image forth the death of the Lord."

Example 202.

The same writer; on John 3 : 4, 5.
"For symbols of a burial and a resurrection, and an image [of them], are celebrated in this water; the thrice sinking down, symbols of the three days burial; then the man comes up, as did the Lord, bearing more bright and shining the garment of immortality, and having sunk the corruption in the water."

Example 203.

Hippolytus;* Discourse on the holy Theophany, ii.
"For thou hast just heard, how Jesus came to John, and was

---

* A bishop (probably of Rome), near the beginning of the third century.

Greek Text.

Ejusdem Comment. in Joannem, c. III. v. 14 (*Vol. I. p. 542*).

'Ο γὰρ σταυρὸς καὶ ὁ θάνατος αἴτιος ἡμῖν τῆς διὰ τοῦ βαπτίσματος χάριτος, εἴγε βαπτιζόμενοι, τὸν θάνατον τοῦ κυρίου εἰκονίζομεν.

Ejusdem in Joannem Comment. c. III. vv. 4, 5 (*p. 540*).

Ταφῆς γὰρ καὶ ἀναστάσεως σύμβολα καὶ εἰκὼν ἐν τῷ ὕδατι τούτῳ τελεῖται. αἱ τρεῖς καταδύσεις τῆς τριημέρου ταφῆς σύμβολα· εἶτα ἀναδύνει ὁ ἄνθρωπος ὥσπερ ὁ Κύριος, λαμπρότερον καὶ φαιδρότερον τὸ τῆς ἀφθαρσίας ἔνδυμα φορῶν, καὶ τὴν φθορὰν ἐγκαταβυθίσας τῷ ὕδατι.

Hippolyti Romani Orat. in sanct. Theoph. ii. (*ed. de Lagarde, p. 37*).

"Ηκουες γὰρ ἀρτίως πῶς ἐλθὼν ὁ 'Ιησοῦς πρὸς τὸν

IMMERSED (BAPTIZED) by him in the Jordan. O wonderful transactions! How was the boundless 'river, that makes glad the city of God,' bathed in a little water; the incomprehensible fountain that sends forth life to all men, and has no end, covered by scanty and transitory waters!"

GREEK TEXT.

'Ιωάννην ἐν τῷ 'Ιορδάνῃ ἐβαπτίσθη ὑπ' αὐτοῦ. ὦ παραδόξων πραγμάτων. πῶς ὁ᾽ ἀπερίγραπτος "ποταμὸς ὁ εὐφραίνων τὴν πόλιν τοῦ θεοῦ" ἐν ὀλίγῳ ὕδατι ἐλούετο, ἡ ἀκατάληπτος πηγὴ ἡ ζωὴν βλαστάνουσα πᾶσιν ἀνθρώποις καὶ τέλος μὴ ἔχουσα ὑπὸ πενιχρῶν καὶ προσκαίρων ὑδάτων ἐκαλύπτετο.

Examples from the Christian Fathers, who wrote in the Latin language.

EXAMPLE 204.

Tertullian;* *On the Resurrection of the Body*, ch. 47. Quoting Rom. 6 : 3, he says:

"Know ye not, that so many of us as were immersed into Christ Jesus, were immersed into his death?"

---

* Born about the middle of the second century; a presbyter at Carthage.

EXAMPLE 205.

The same passage (a few lines below).
"For by an image we die in baptism; but we truly rise in the flesh, as did also Christ."

EXAMPLE 206.

The same writer; Against Praxeas, ch. 26. Speaking of the Saviour's command, in Matt. 28 : 19, he says:
"And last of all, commanding that they should immerse into the Father, and the Son, and the Holy Spirit."

===

LATIN TEXT.

Tertulliani de Resurrectione Carnis, c. XLVII. (*ed. Oehler, Vol. II. p. 528*).

An ignoratis quod quicunque in Christum Jesum tincti sumus, in mortem ejus tincti sumus?

Ibidem.

Per simulacrum enim morimur in baptismate, sed per veritatem resurgimus in carne, sicut et Christus.

Ejusdem adversus Praxean, c. XXVI. (*Vol. II. p. 690*).

Et novissime mandans ut tinguerent in patrem et filium et spiritum sanctum.

Example 207.

The same writer; On the Soldier's Crown, ch. 3.
"Then we are three times immersed, answering somewhat more than the Lord prescribed in the Gospel."

Example 208.

The same writer; On Public Shows, ch. 4.
"When, entering into the water, we profess the Christian faith, in words of his own law."

* Example 209.

The same writer; On Baptism, ch. VII.
"As of baptism itself there is a bodily act, that we are immersed in water, a spiritual effect, that we are freed from sins."

Example 210.

Ambrose;* On the Sacraments, book II. ch. 7.
"Thou wast asked: Dost thou believe in God the Father almighty? Thou saidst, I believe; and thou didst sink down, that is, wast buried."

* Bishop of Milan; born about 340.

Latin Text.

Ejusdem de Corona Militis, c. iii. (*Vol. I. p. 421*).

Dehinc ter mergitamur, amplius aliquid respondentes quam Dominus in evangelio determinavit.

Ejusdem de Spectaculis, c. IV. (*Vol. I. p. 24*).

Cum aquam ingressi christianam fidem in legis suae verba profitemur.

Ejusdem de Baptismo, c. VII. (*Vol. I. p. 626*).

Quomodo et ipsius baptismi carnalis actus, quod in aqua mergimur, spiritalis effectus, quod delictis liberamur.

Ambrosii de Sacram. lib. II. c. vii. (*ed. monach. ord. S. Bened. Vol. II. col. 359*).

Interrogatus es: Credis in Deum Patrem omnipotentem? Dixisti: Credo; et mersisti, hoc est, sepultus es.

Example 211.

The same Work, book III. ch. I. 1.

Yesterday we discoursed respecting the font, whose appearance is, as it were, a form of sepulchre; into which, believing in the Father, and the Son, and the Holy Spirit, we are received and submerged, and rise, that is, are restored to life."

Example 212.

The same Work, book III. ch. I. 2.

"What then is a resurrection, except when we rise again from death to life? So then also in baptism, since there is a similitude of death, without doubt, whilst thou dost sink down and rise again, there is a similitude of the resurrection."

Example 213.

The same Work, book II. ch. 6, 19. On baptism, (in allusion to the words, '*dust thou art*,' etc.)

Hear then; for that in this age also the bond of the Devil might be loosed, it has been found how a living man might die, and living rise again. What is '*living*'? This is the living

---

Latin Text.

Ejusdem lib. III. c. I. 1 (*Vol. II. col. 361*).

Hesterno die de fonte disputavimus, cujus species veluti quaedam sepulchri forma est; in quem, credentes in Patrem et Filium et Spiritum sanctum, recipimur et demergimur et surgimus, hoc est, resuscitamur.

Ejusdem lib. III. c. I. 2 (*Vol. II. col. 361*).

Ergo resurrectio quid est, nisi quando de morte ad vitam resurgimus? Sic ergo et in baptismate, quoniam similitudo mortis est, sine dubio dum mergis et resurgis, similitudo fit resurrectionis.

Ejusdem lib. II. c. vi. 19 (*Vol. II. col. 359*).

Audi ergo; nam ut in hoc quoque saeculo nexus diaboli solveretur, inventum est quomodo homo vivus moreretur, et vivus resurgeret. Quid est vivus? Hoc est vita corporis vivens, cum

life of the body, when it came to the font, and was immersed into the font. What is water, except of earth? The divine sentence is satisfied, therefore, without the stupor of death. In that thou sinkest down [art immersed], that sentence is discharged, 'earth thou art, and into earth shalt thou go.' The sentence being fulfilled, there is room for the blessing, and for the divine remedy. Water then is of earth; but the capability of our life did not allow that we should be covered with earth, and rise again from the earth. Moreover, earth does not cleanse, but water cleanses; therefore the font is as a sepulchre."

EXAMPLE 214.

The same Work, book II. ch. vii. 23.

"That as Christ died, so also thou mayest taste of death; as Christ died to sin, and lives to God, so also thou mayest be dead to the former allurements of sins, through the sacrament of baptism, and rise through the grace of Christ. It is therefore a death, but not in the verity of corporeal death, but in a similitude; for when thou sinkest down, thou dost take on a similitude of death and burial."

LATIN TEXT.

veniret ad fontem, et mergeretur in fontem. Quid est aqua, nisi de terra? Satisfit ergo sententiae coelesti sine mortis stupore. Quod mergis, solvitur sententia illa: *terra es, et in terram ibis;* impletâ sententiâ, locus est beneficio remedioque coelesti. Ergo aqua de terra, possibilitas autem vitae nostrae non admittebat ut terra operiremur, et de terra resurgeremus. Deinde non terra lavat, sed aqua lavat; ideo fons quasi sepultura est.

Ejusdem lib. II. c. vii, 23. (*Vol. II. col. 360*).

Ut quomodo Christus mortuus est, sic et tu mortem degustes: quomodo Christus mortuus est peccato, et Deo vivit; ita et tu superioribus illecebris peccatorum mortuus sis per baptismatis sacramentum, et surrexeris per gratiam Christi. Mors ergo est, sed non in mortis corporalis veritate, sed in similitudine; cum enim mergis, mortis suscipis et sepulturae similitudinem.

Example 215.

Jerome,* Comment. on the Epist. to the Ephesians, book II. ch. 4 (on ch. 4 : 5).
"And thrice we are immersed, that there may appear one sacrament of the Trinity."

---
* Born in the year 331.

Example 216.

Alcuin;* Epistle XC. to the brethren at Lyons.
"To us it seems indeed, according to our feeble judgment, that as the inner man is formed anew after the image of his Maker, in the faith of the holy Trinity, so the outer man should be washed with a trine immersion; that what the Spirit invisibly works in the soul, that the priest may visibly imitate in water."

---
* Born 735; founder of christian education and schools in France, under Charlemagne.

Example 217.

The same Epistle. Speaking of the christian rite of baptism, he says:
"That you may know the things signified by this most sacred

LATIN TEXT.
Hieronymi Comment. in epist. ad Eph. lib. II. c. iv.
(*ed. Vallarsius, Vol. VII. p. 610*).

Et ter. mergimur, ut Trinitatis unum appareat sacramentum.

Alcuini Epist. XC. ad Fratres Lugdunenses (*ed. Migne, Vol. I. col. 291*).

Nobis vero juxta parvitatem ingenioli nostri videtur, ut sicut interior homo in fide sanctae Trinitatis ad imaginem sui conditoris reformandus est, ita et exterior trina mersione abluendus esse: ut quod invisibiliter Spiritus operatur in anima, hoc visibiliter sacerdos imitetur in aqua.

Ejusdem (*col. 292*).

Ut vero cognoscatis hujus sacratissimi mysterii significationes,

mystery, according to the understanding of the holy Fathers and the statutes of the Church, I will show to your love the same sacraments, with the catholic interpretation."

After a full description and explanation of the preliminary ceremonies, he adds:

"And so, in the name of the holy Trinity, he is baptized with a trine submersion."

---

* LATIN TEXT.

juxta sanctorum Patrum intelligentiam et statuta ecclesiastica, vestrae charitati eadem sacramenta catholica interpretatione ostendam.

Ibidem.

Et sic in nomine sanctae Trinitatis trina submersione baptizatur.

II.

Where the christian rite, or what is implied in it, is applied for purposes of illustration or comparison.

The Christian Fathers, in their expositions of the Scriptures, are fond of tracing allusions to this rite in the language of the Old Testament. Of this practice, one specimen must suffice.

EXAMPLE 218.

Basil (the Great); Discourse on Ps. 28 (Ps. 29 : 3).*
" 'The Lord dwells in the flood.' A flood is an inundation of water, concealing all that lies beneath, and cleansing all that was before polluted. The grace of the IMMERSION (BAPTISM), therefore, he calls a flood; so that the soul, washed from sins, and cleansed from the old man, is henceforth fitted for a habitation of God in the spirit."

---

* See the remark on Example 181.

The idea of *cleansing*, associated with the christian rite of immersion in water, naturally suggested comparison with the Jewish rites of purification, especially by water; and hence the Christian Fathers treat these ritual purifications as types, foreshadowing the grace (mark the word!) to be imparted through the christian rite.

GREEK TEXT.

Basilii Magni Hom. in Ps. XXVIII. (*ed. Garnier, Vol. I. p. 123*).

Κύριος τὸν κατακλυσμὸν κατοικεῖ.) κατακλυσμὸς ὕδατός ἐστιν ἐπίκλυσις ἐξαφανίζοντος πᾶν τὸ ὑποκείμενον, καὶ καθαρίζοντος ἅπαν τὸ προερρυπομένον. τὴν οὖν τοῦ βαπτίσματος χάριν κατακλυσμὸν ὀνομάζει. ὥστε τὴν ἀποπλυναμένην τὰ ἁμαρτήματα ψυχὴν, καὶ ἀποκαθηραμένην τὸν παλαιὸν ἄνθρωπον, ἐπιτηδείαν εἶναι λοιπὸν πρὸς κατοικητήριον τοῦ θεοῦ ἐν πνεύματι.

OF THE CHRISTIAN RITE. 123

EXAMPLE 219.

Cyrill,* Archbishop of Alexandria; on Isaiah, book I. Discourse i. (on ch. 1 : 16).

Speaking of the point just before stated by him, viz. that "men are justified, not by works of law, but through faith and the IMMERSION (BAPTISM)," he says:

"And this the ancient law figured to them as in shadows, and preached before the grace which is through the holy IMMERSION (BAPTISM)."

---

* Born towards the close of the fourth century; made Patriarch of Alexandria in 412.

EXAMPLE 220.

Theophylact;* Comment. on John ch. 5 : 1–4.

"For since an IMMERSION (BAPTISM) was to be given, having much efficacy, and quickening souls, God prefigures the IMMERSION (BAPTISM) in the Jewish rites; and gives them also water cleansing away pollutions, not properly being but accounted such, as those from the touching of a dead body or of a leper, or other such like things."

---

* See the remark on Example 192.

GREEK TEXT.

Cyrilli Archiep. Alex. in Es. lib. I. Orat. i. (*ed. Auberti, Vol. II. p. 17*).

Τοῦτο καὶ ὁ πάλαι νόμος αὐτοῖς ὡς ἐν σκιαῖς διετύπου, καὶ προανεκήρυττε τὴν χάριν τὴν διὰ τοῦ ἁγίου βαπτίσματος.

Theophylacti in Joannem Comment. cap. V. 1–4 (*Vol. I. pp. 567–8*).

Ἐπεὶ γὰρ ἔμελλε βάπτισμα δίδοσθαι πολλὴν ἔχον δύναμιν, καὶ ζωοποιοῦν τὰς ψυχάς, προζωγραφεῖ Θεὸς τὸ βάπτισμα ἐν τοῖς Ἰουδαϊκοῖς, καὶ δίδωσι μὲν καὶ ὕδωρ αὐτοῖς καθαῖρον μολυσμοὺς οὐ κυρίως ὄντας, ἀλλὰ δοκοῦντας, οἷον τοὺς ἀπὸ τοῦ ἅψασθαι νεκροῦ, ἢ λεπροῦ, καὶ τῶν τοιούτων ἑτέρων·

EXAMPLE 221.

Cyrill (just quoted), *Comment. on Isaiah, book I. Disc. iii. (on ch. 4 : 4).* Explaining the words, 'by the spirit of burning,' he says:

"But the spirit of burning we call the grace in the holy IMMERSION (BAPTISM), produced in us not without the Spirit. For we have been IMMERSED (BAPTIZED) not in mere water; but neither with the ashes of a heifer have we been sprinkled, for the cleansing of the flesh alone, as says the blessed Paul; but in the Holy Spirit, and a fire that is divine and mentally discerned, destroying the filth of the vileness in us, and consuming away the pollution of sin."

With this example should be connected the following:

EXAMPLE 222.

The same writer; On worshipping in spirit and in truth, book XII.
"For we are IMMERSED (BAPTIZED), not into fire perceptible by the senses, but in the Holy Spirit, like fire consuming away the pollution in souls."

GREEK TEXT.

Cyrilli Archiep. Alex. Comment. in Is. lib. I. Orat. III. (*Vol. II. p. 76*).

Καύσεως δὲ πνεῦμα φαμὲν τὴν ἐπὶ τῷ ἁγίῳ βαπτίσματι χάριν οὐ δίχα πνεύματος ἐν ἡμῖν γινομένην. βεβαπτίσμεθα μὲν γὰρ οὐκ ἐν ὕδατι γυμνῷ, ἀλλ' οὐδὲ σποδῷ δαμάλεως ἐρραντίσμεθα δὲ πρὸς μόνην τὴν τῆς σαρκὸς καθαρότητα, καθά φησιν ὁ μακάριος Παῦλος, ἀλλ' ἐν πνεύματι ἁγίῳ, καὶ πυρὶ τῷ θείῳ καὶ νοητῷ, τοὺς τῆς ἐν ἡμῖν φαυλότητος δαπανῶντι ῥύπους, καὶ τὸν τῆς ἁμαρτίας ἐκτήκοντι μολυσμόν.

Ejusdem de Adorat. in Spiritu et Verit. lib. XII. (*Vol. I. p. 436*).

Βεβαπτίσμεθα γὰρ οὐκ εἰς πῦρ αἰσθητὸν, ἀλλ' ἐν ἁγίῳ Πνεύματι, πυρὸς δίκην ἐκτήκοντι τὴν ἐν ψυχαῖς μολυσμόν.

EXAMPLE 223.

The same writer; Comment. on John, book XII. (on ch. 19 : 34).

"With a spear they pierce his side, and it poured forth blood mixed with water; as though God, for us, made that which was done an image and a kind of first-fruits of the mystic blessing, and of the holy IMMERSION (BAPTISM); for Christ's verily, and from Christ, is the holy IMMERSION (BAPTISM), and the virtue of the mystic blessing arose for us out of the holy flesh."

The allusion here is to the two elements of expiation and cleansing, blood and water. These, gushing forth *from* the Saviour's side, were an image, and a kind of first-fruits (an earnest, or assurance) of the holy IMMERSION, through which the mystic blessing (of pardon and sanctification) was to be imparted, and all whose virtue proceeded from his consecrated body.

The grounds for using the element of water are explained; as in the two following examples.

EXAMPLE 224.

Cyrill,* Bishop of Jerusalem, Instruction III. on Baptism, v.

"But if one desires to know why through water, and not through another of the elements, the grace is given, let him

* See the remark on Example 176.

GREEK TEXT.

Ejusdem Com. in Joannem lib. XII. (*Vol. IV. p. 1074*).

Λόγχῃ διανίττουσι τὴν πλευρὰν, ἡ δὲ μεμιγμένον ὕδατι τὸ αἷμα διέβλυσε, τῆς μυστικῆς εὐλογίας, καὶ τοῦ ἁγίου βαπτίσματος, εἰκόνα καὶ ἀπαρχὴν ὥσπέρ τινα τιθέντος ἡμῖν τοῦ Θεοῦ τὸ γεγενημένον. Χριστοῦ γὰρ ὄντως ἐστὶ καὶ παρὰ Χριστοῦ τὸ ἅγιον βάπτισμα, καὶ τῆς μυστικῆς εὐλογίας ἡ δύναμις ἐκ τῆς ἁγίας ἡμῖν ἀνέφυ σαρκός.

Cyrilli Archiep. Hierosol. Cateches. III. de Baptismo V. (*ed. Touttée, p. 41*).

Εἰ δέ τις ποθεῖ γνῶναι, διὰ τί δι' ὕδατος, καὶ μὴ δι' ἑτέρου τῶν στοιχείων, ἡ χάρις δίδοται, τὰς θείας γραφὰς

take up the divine Scriptures and he will find. For water is a great thing, and the noblest of the four elements of the world that appear."

EXAMPLE 225.

John of Damascus, On Faith and Baptism (On the orthodox Faith, book IV. ch. 9). See the remark on Example 190.

"For from the beginning, the Spirit of God moved upon the waters; and of old the Scripture testifies to water, that it is cleansing. In Noah's age God deluged the sin of the world by water. By water every one unclean, according to the law, is cleansed, even the garments themselves being washed with water. . . . And almost all things, according to the law, are cleansed with water. For the things seen are symbols of those apprehended by the mind."

A few lines below, he says of the Saviour's baptism:

"He [Christ] is IMMERSED (BAPTIZED), not as himself needing

GREEK TEXT.

ἀναλαβὼν εὑρήσει. Μέγα γάρ τι τὸ ὕδωρ, καὶ τῶν τεσσάρων τοῦ κόσμου στοιχείων τῶν φαινομένων τὸ κάλλιστον.

Joannis Damasceni de fide orthodoxa, lib. IV. c. 9 (*p. 260*).

'Απ' ἀρχῆς γὰρ πνεῦμα θεοῦ τοῖς ὕδασιν ἐπεφέρετο καὶ ἄνωθεν ἡ γραφὴ μαρτυρεῖ τῷ ὕδατι, ὡς ἐστι καθαρτήριον. ἐπὶ Νῶε δι' ὕδατος ὁ θεὸς τὴν κοσμικὴν ἁμαρτίαν κατέκλυσε. δι' ὕδατος πᾶς ἀκάθαρτος κατὰ τὸν νόμον καθαίρεται, καὶ αὐτῶν τῶν ἱματίων πλυνομένων τῷ ὕδατι. . . . Καὶ σχεδὸν ἅπαντα κατὰ τὸν νόμον ὕδατι καθαρίζεται· τὰ γὰρ ὁρατὰ σύμβολα τῶν νοουμένων εἰσίν.

(*Ibidem*).

Βαπτίζεται δὲ οὐχ ὡς αὐτὸς χρῄζων καθάρσεως, ἀλλὰ

cleansing, but appropriating my cleansing, that he may whelm sin, and bury all the old Adam in the water."

The exhortations to personal holiness in the Old Testament, founded on the Jewish ritual purifications (as in Isaiah 1 : 16–20), they apply to the christian rite as being first fulfilled in the grace therein imparted.

EXAMPLE 226.

Hippolytus ;* Discourse on the holy Theophany, x. After quoting Is. 1 : 16–19, he says:

"Thou sawest, beloved, how the prophet foretold the cleansing of the holy IMMERSION (BAPTISM). For he who goes down with faith into the bath of regeneration, is arrayed against the evil one, and on the side of Christ; he denies the enemy, and confesses Christ to be God; he puts off bondage, and puts on sonship; he comes up from the IMMERSION (BAPTISM), bright as the sun, flashing forth the rays of righteousness. But greatest of all, he comes up a son of God, and a fellow-heir with Christ."

* See the remark on Example 203.

GREEK TEXT.

τὴν ἐμὴν οἰκειούμενος κάθαρσιν, ... ἵνα κλύσῃ τὴν ἁμαρτίαν, καὶ πάντα τὸν παλαιὸν Ἀδὰμ ἐνθάψῃ τῷ ὕδατι.

Hippolyti Romani Orat. in Sanct. Theoph. X. (*ed. de Lagarde p. 42*).

Εἶδες, ἀγαπητέ πῶς προεῖπεν ὁ προφήτης τὸ τοῦ βαπτίσματος καθάρσιον. ὁ γὰρ καταβαίνων μετὰ πίστεως εἰς τὸ τῆς ἀναγεννήσεως λουτρὸν διατάσσεται τῷ πονηρῷ, συντάσσεται δὲ τῷ Χριστῷ. ἀπαρνεῖται τὸν ἐχθρόν, ὁμολογεῖ δὲ τὸ θεὸν εἶναι τὸν Χριστόν. ἀποδίεται τὴν δουλείαν, ἐνδύεται δὲ τὴν υἱοθεσίαν, ἀνέρχεται ἀπὸ τοῦ βαπτίσματος λαμπρὸς ὡς ὁ ἥλιος, ἀπαστράπτων τὰς τῆς δικαιοσύνης ἀκτῖνας. τὸ δὲ μέγιστον, ἄνεισιν υἱὸς θεοῦ καὶ συγκληρονόμος Χριστοῦ.

Example 227.

Justin Martyr; Dialogue with a Jew, xiv.* After saying
"Through the bathing, therefore, of repentance and of the
knowledge of God, which has been instituted for the iniquity
of God's people, (as Isaiah cries), we believed, and we make
known that this is that IMMERSION (BAPTISM) which he proclaimed,
which alone is able to cleanse those who repent, that this is
the water of life. What cisterns ye have dug out for yourselves are broken, and are useless to you;" he adds:
"For what is the benefit of that IMMERSION (BAPTISM), which
makes bright the flesh and the body only? Be IMMERSED (BAPTIZED)
as to the soul, from anger and from covetousness, from envy,
from hatred; and behold the body is clean."

* See the remark on Example 131.

They distinguish between the mere outward form of the rite, and the inward
work wrought in the soul.

Example 228.

Cyrill, Bishop of Jerusalem; Preface to the Instructions.*
"Simon also, the Magian, once came to the bath. He was
IMMERSED (BAPTIZED), but he was not enlightened; and the body

* See the remark on Example 176.

Greek Text.

Justini Martyris Dial. cum Tryphone, XIV. (*ed. Otto, Vol. I. P. ii.
p. 48*).

Τί γὰρ ὄφελος ἐκείνου τοῦ βαπτίσματος, ὁ τὴν σάρκα
καὶ μόνον τὸ σῶμα φαιδρύνει; Βαπτίσθητε τὴν ψυχὴν
ἀπὸ ὀργῆς καὶ ἀπὸ πλεονεξίας, ἀπὸ φθόνου, ἀπὸ μίσους·
καὶ ἰδοὺ τὸ σῶμα καθαρόν ἐστι.

Cyrilli archiep. Hierosol. Praef. Cateches. (*ed. Milles, p. 2*).

Προσῆλθέ ποτε καὶ Σίμων τῷ λουτρῷ ὁ μάγος· ἐβαπτίσθη, ἀλλ' οὐκ ἐφωτίσθη· καὶ τὸ μὲν σῶμα ἔβαψεν ὕδατι,

indeed he dipped in water, but the heart he did not enlighten by the Spirit. And the body went down indeed, and came up; but the soul was not buried with Christ, nor was raised with him."

From the idea of cleansing, associated with immersion in water, they call Christ's expiatory death an IMMERSION (BAPTISM), not only as an expression of overwhelming suffering (Mark 10 : 38, 39, Luke 12 : 50), but also because by it he cleansed from sin. So in the following example, in which both allusions are distinctly recognized.

* EXAMPLE 229. *

Chrysostom;* on the petition of the sons of Zebedee, V. (On the words, 'Can ye drink,' etc.).
"Here calling his cross and death a cup and an IMMERSION (BAPTISM) ; a cup, because he drank it with pleasure ; an IMMERSION (BAPTISM), because by it he cleansed the world. And not because of this only, but also because of the facility of the resurrection. For as he who is IMMERSED (BAPTIZED) with water, rises again with great ease, not at all hindered by the nature of the waters ;

* See the remark on Example 184.

GREEK TEXT.

τὴν δὲ καρδίαν οὐκ ἐφώτισε Πνεύματι· καὶ κατέβη μὲν τὸ σῶμα, καὶ ἀνέβη· ἡ δὲ ψυχὴ οὐ συνετάφη Χρίστῳ, οὐδὲ συνεγέρθη.

Chrysostomi de Petit. fil. Zebed. VII. (*ed. Montf. Vol I. p. 521*).

Ποτήριον ἐνταῦθα καὶ βάπτισμα καλῶν τὸν σταυρὸν τὸν ἑαυτοῦ, καὶ τὸν θάνατον· ποτήριον μὲν, ἐπειδὴ μεθ' ἡδονῆς αὐτὸν ἐπῄει, βάπτισμα δὲ, ὅτι δι' αὐτοῦ τὴν οἰκουμένην ἐκάθηρεν· οὐ διὰ τοῦτο δὲ μόνον, ἀλλὰ καὶ διὰ τὴν εὐκολίαν τῆς ἀναστάσεως· ὥσπερ γὰρ ὁ βαπτιζόμενος ὕδατι, μετὰ πολλῆς ἀνίσταται τῆς εὐκολίας, οὐδὲν ὑπὸ τῆς φύσεως τῶν ὑδάτων κωλυόμενος, οὕτω καὶ αὐτὸς εἰς

so also he, having gone down into death, with greater ease came up; for this cause he calls it an IMMERSION (BAPTISM). But what he says is to this effect: 'Can ye be slain, and die?' For now is the time for these, deaths, perils, and toils."

In like manner, they use this word of the sufferings shared with Christ by his followers, which they called an IMMERSION (in suffering) "by blood," and "by martyrdom;" ascribing to this figurative *immersion in suffering* the same cleansing efficacy, as to the literal immersion in water.

EXAMPLE 230.

The same writer; Discourse ii, on Saint Lucian, the Martyr.

"And wonder not, if I call the witness [the martyrdom] an IMMERSION (BAPTISM). For here, also, the Spirit hovers over with great fullness, and there is a taking away of sins, and a cleansing of the soul wonderful and strange; and as they who are immersed are bathed with water, so are they who witness [who are martyrs], with their own blood."

EXAMPLE 231.

John of Damascus;* On the orthodox faith, book iv. c. 9, on faith and baptism.

* See the remark on Example 190.

GREEK TEXT.

θάνατον καταβὰς, μετὰ πλείονος ἀνέβη τῆς εὐκολίας· διὰ τοῦτο βάπτισμα αὐτὸ καλεῖ. ὃ δὲ λέγει τοιοῦτόν ἐστι· δύνασθε σφαγῆναι, καὶ ἀποθανεῖν; τούτων γὰρ ὃ καιρὸς νῦν, θανάτων, καὶ κινδύνων, καὶ πόνων.

Ejusdem Hom. in S. Lucianum Martyrem, II. (*Vol. II. p. 520*).

Καὶ μὴ θαυμάσητε, εἰ βάπτισμα τὸ μαρτύριον ἐκάλεσα, καὶ γὰρ ἐνταῦθα τὸ πνεῦμα μετὰ πολλῆς ἐφίπταται τῆς δαψιλείας, καὶ ἁμαρτημάτων ἀναίρεσις, καὶ ψυχῆς γίνεται καθαρμὸς θαυμαστός τις καὶ παράδοξος· καὶ ὥσπερ οἱ βαπτιζόμενοι τοῖς ὕδασιν, οὕτως οἱ μαρτυροῦντες τῷ ἰδίῳ λούονται αἵματι.

"Seventh, that which is by blood and martyrdom, with which Christ himself for us was IMMERSED (BAPTIZED), as exceedingly august and blessed, such as is defiled by no subsequent pollutions."

EXAMPLE 232.

Hilary,*Bishop of Poictiers, on Ps. 118 (119), letter III. 5.

"There is reserved, therefore, so far as we may judge, a cleansing of that perfected purity, even after the waters of baptism; [viz.] that which sanctifies us by the coming of the Holy Spirit; that which refines us with the fire of judgment; that which through the infliction of death will purge from the carrion stain and fellowship; that which by the suffering of martyrdom will wash away with devoted and faithful blood."

In the same figurative sense, they use it of whatever was supposed to have an atoning or expiatory virtue, as penitence and tears. So in the two following examples; in the first of which, the literal immersion in water is expressly distinguished from this figurative application of it.

EXAMPLE 233.

Athanasius;† Questions, LXXII. (to Prince Antiochus).

"For it is proper to know, that, in like manner with the

* Born about the end of the third century.   † See the remark on Ex. 187.

GREEK AND LATIN TEXT.

Joannis Damásceni de Fide orthodoxa, lib. IV. c. 9, de fide et baptismo (*ed. Lequien, Vol. I. p. 266*).

Ἕβδομον, τὸ δι' αἵματος καὶ μαρτυρίου ὃ καὶ αὐτὸς ὁ Χριστὸς ὑπὲρ ἡμῶν ἐβαπτίσατο, ὡς λίαν αἰδέσμον καὶ μακάριον, ὅσον δευτέροις οὐ μολύνεται ῥύποις.

Hilarii Pictavorum episc. Tract. in CXVIII. Psal. lit. iii. (*ed. monach. ord. S. Bened. col. 259*).

Est ergo, quantum licet existimare, perfectae illius emundatio puritatis etiam post baptismi aquas reposita: quae nos sancti Spiritus sanctificet adventu, quae judicii igni nos decoquat, quae per mortis injuriam a labe morticinae et societate purgabit, quae martyrii passione devota ac fideli sanguine abluet.

Athanasii Quaest. ad Antioch. LXXIII. (*ed. monach. ord. S. Bened. Vol. II. p. 286*).

Δεῖ γὰρ εἰδέναι, ὅτι ὁμοίως τοῦ βαπτίσματος ἡ τῶν

IMMERSION (BAPTISM), the fountain of tears cleanses man. Wherefore many, having defiled the holy IMMERSION (BAPTISM) by offences, were cleansed by tears and declared just."

Of course, the 'fountain of tears' does not represent the baptismal *rite;* for, from this it is expressly distinguished. It is, therefore, an IMMERSION only in a figurative sense, as having, through the same imparted grace, the same cleansing effect as the literal IMMERSION in water. In this figurative sense the word is used in the following extract.

EXAMPLE 234.

The same writer; in the same passage.

"Three IMMERSIONS (BAPTISMS), purgative of all sin whatever, God has bestowed on the nature of men. I mean, that of water; and again, that by the witness of one's own blood; and thirdly, that by tears, in which also the harlot was cleansed."

This word became, necessarily, a technical designation of the christian rite; but without losing its proper literal significance, as has already been shown by many of the foregoing extracts, and as may be seen in the two following examples.

EXAMPLE 235.

Apostolic Canons; *Can. L.*

"If any bishop, or presbyter, shall not perform three IMMERSIONS

---

* As early as the fifth century.

GREEK TEXT.

δακρύων πηγὴ καθαρίζει τὸν ἄνθρωπον· διόπερ πολλοὶ διὰ πταισμάτων μολύναντες τὸ ἅγιον βάπτισμα, διὰ δακρύων ἐκαθαρίσθησαν καὶ δίκαιοι ἀπεδείχθησαν.

Ejusdem (*Ibidem*).

Τρία βαπτίσματα καθαρτικὰ πάσης οἵας δήποτε ἁμαρτίας ὁ θεὸς τῇ φύσει τῶν ἀνθρώπων ἐδωρήσατε· λέγω δὲ τὸ ὕδατος, καὶ πάλιν τὸ διὰ μαρτυρίου τοῦ ἰδίου αἵματος, καὶ τρίτον τὸ διὰ δακρύων, εἰς ὅπερ καὶ ἡ πόρνη ἐκαθαρίσθη.

Canones Sanct. Apostolorum; can. L. (*Pandect. Can. Apost. ct.*, ed. Beverige, Vol. 1. p. 33).

Εἴ τις ἐπίσκοπος ἢ πρεσβύτερος μὴ τρία βαπτίσματα

(BAPTISMS) for one initiation,* but one IMMERSION (BAPTISM), that given into the death of the Lord, let him be deposed."

* So this rite was called, as being the *initiatory rite* of the church. Three immersions were by many considered necessary to the full performance of the rite. Compare the writer's note on Matt. 28 : 19.

EXAMPLE 236.

Zonaras ; Annotations on the Apostolic Canons (on Can. L.).*

"Three IMMERSIONS (BAPTISMS) the canon here calls the thrice sinking down in one initiation, that is, in one IMMERSION (BAPTISM).

He uses the word, in the first instance, to express simply an act of immersion, and in the second, this act as the christian rite.

* Of the twelfth century.

It thus appears, that the Christian Fathers understood this word in its ordinary, established signification in the Greek language, exhibited in Section I. from their own practice, as well as that of other Greek writers. Their figurative applications of the christian rite grew naturally out of its deep significance, in its various references to the doctrines and facts of the christian life. We are not to attach to the word itself ideas derived from the application of the rite.

GREEK TEXT.

μιᾶς μυήσεως ἐπιτελέσῃ, ἀλλὰ ἓν βάπτισμα εἰς τὸν θάνατον τοῦ κυρίου διδόμενον, καθαιρείσθω.

Zonaræ Annott. in Can. Apost. L. (*ibidem*).

Τρία βαπτίσματα ἐνταῦθα τὰς τρεῖς καταδύσεις φησὶν ὁ κανὼν ἐν μιᾷ μυήσει, ἤτοι ἐν ἑνὶ βαπτίσματι.

SECTION VI.
Requirements and Practice of the Church.

1.
The Eastern, or Greek Church.

Extract from Goar's "EUCHOLOGION, or Ritual of the Greeks."

"Office of the Holy IMMERSION (BAPTISM)."

(after the preliminary ceremonies)

"And when the whole body is anointed, the priest IMMERSES (BAPTIZES) him [the child], holding him erect and looking toward the east, saying:

The servant of God [*name*] is IMMERSED (BAPTIZED), in the name

---

GREEK TEXT.

ΕΥΧΟΛΟΓΙΟΝ, sive Rituale Graec. (*op. Goar, pp. 354, 355*).*

Officium Sancti Baptismatis.

* * *

Καὶ ὅτε χρισθῇ ὅλον τὸ σῶμα, βαπτίζει αὐτὸν ὁ ἱερεύς, ὄρθιον αὐτὸν κατέχων καὶ βλέποντα κατὰ ἀνατολάς, λέγων·

Βαπτίζεται ὁ δοῦλος τοῦ θεοῦ, Ὁ δεῖνα, εἰς τὸ ὄνομα

---

* *ΕΥΧΟΛΟΓΙΟΝ*, sive Rituale Græcorum, complectens ritus et ordines et. juxta usum Orientalis Ecclesiæ; Opera R. P. F. Jacobi Goar, ... nuper in Orientem missi Apostolici. Lutet. Paris. 1647.

THE EASTERN, OR GREEK CHURCH. 135

of the Father, and of the Son, and of the Holy Spirit; now and ever, and to ages of ages. Amen.

At each invocation, bringing him down, and bringing him up. And after the IMMERSING (BAPTIZING), the priest washes his hands, singing with the people: 'Happy they, whose sins are forgiven,'" etc.

The practice of this church has already been seen in the extracts given in Section V. The deviations from this practice (for convenience or other cause) were only occasional and exceptional, and without canonical authority.

GREEK TEXT.

τοῦ πατρὸς, καὶ τοῦ υἱοῦ, καὶ τοῦ ἁγίου πνεύματος. Νῦν καὶ αἰεὶ, καὶ εἰς τοὺς αἰῶνας τῶν αἰώνων. ἀμήν.

Ἑκάστῃ προσρήσει κατάγων αὐτὸν, καὶ ἀνάγων. Καὶ μετὰ τὴν βάπτισιν, νίπτεται ὁ ἱερεύς, ψάλλων σὺν τῷ λαῷ, Μακάριοι ὧν ἀφέθησαν αἱ ἀνομίαι κ. τ. λ.

2.

The Western, or Latin Church.

Extract from the Order of Sacraments, composed by Pope Gregory I.

"The font being blest, and he holding the infant by whom it is to be taken up, let the priest inquire thus:
What is thy name?
(*Answer*).
Dost thou believe in God, the Father Almighty, creator of heaven and earth?
Answ.—I believe.
And in Jesus Christ, his only Son our Lord, who was born and suffered?
Answ.—I believe.
Dost thou also believe in the Holy Spirit, the holy Catholic Church, the remission of sins, the resurrection of the body?

LATIN TEXT.

Sacramentarium Gregorianum, sive Sacramentorum ordo a sancto Gregorio I. Papa compositus. (*ed. Muratori, Vol. II. p. 73*).*

Benedicto fonte, et eo tenente infantem, a quo suscipiendum est, interroget sacerdos ita:
Quis vocaris?
Respondet.
(*Ille.*) Credis in Deum Patrem omnipotentem, Creatorem coeli et terrae?
Respondet: Credo.
Et in Jesum Christum, Filium ejus unicum, Dominum nostrum, natum, et passum?
Respondet: Credo.
Credis et in Spiritum Sanctum, sanctam Ecclesiam Catholicam, remissionem peccatorum, carnis resurrectionem?

---

* Liturgia Romana vetus, tria sacramenta complectens, Leonianum scilicet, Gelasianum, et antiquum Gregorianum; edente Ludovico Antonio Muratorio, Neapoli, 1776.

THE WESTERN, OR LATIN CHURCH.

Answ.—I believe.
Then let the priest baptize with a trine immersion, once only invoking the holy Trinity, saying:
And I baptize thee, in the name of the Father;
        (and let him immerse once)
And of the Son;
        (and let him immerse a second time)
And of the Holy Spirit;
        (and let him immerse a third time)."

For the early practice in this Church, see Examples 204–217, and the extract from the work of Brenner, at the end of this Section.

LATIN TEXT.

Respondet: Credo.
Deinde baptizet sacerdos sub trina mersione, tantum sanctam Trinitatem semel invocans, ita dicendo:
Et ego te baptizo in nomine Patris;
        Et mergat semel.
Et Filii;
        Et mergat iterum.
Et Spiritus sancti;
        Et mergat tertio.

3.

Anglican Church.

Extract from the first English "Book of Common Prayer, and Administration of the Sacraments," the first book of King Edward VI. 1549 (*Pickering's fac-simile, fol. CXVI.*).*

"Then the priest shall take the child in his hands, and ask the name. And naming the child, shall dip it in the water thrice. First dipping the right side: Second the left side: The third time dipping the face toward the font: So it be discreetly and warily done, saying.

N. I baptize thee, in the name of the Father, and of the Son, and of the Holy Ghost. Amen.

And if the child be weak, it shall suffice to pour water upon it, saying the foresaid words."

Extract from The Second Book of King Edward VI., 1552; as also in The First Book of Queen Elizabeth, 1559, and in that of King James, 1604, called "the Hampton Court Book" (*Pickering's fac-simile, vols II., III., and IV.*).

"Then the priest shall take the child in his hands, and ask the name, and naming the child shall dip it in the water, so it be discreetly and warily done, saying.

N. I baptize thee in the name of the Father, and of the Son, and of the Holy Ghost. Amen.

And if the child be weak, it shall suffice to pour water upon it, saying the foresaid words."

---

* "The book of the common prayer, and administration of the Sacraments, etc. after the use of the Church of England. Londini, in officina Edouardi Whitchurche Cum privilegio ad imprimendum solum. Anno Do. 1549." (*London, Wm. Pickering*, 1844.)

From the same, as revised and settled at the Savoy conference, under Charles II., 1662 (*Pickering's fac-simile, vol. V.*).

"Then the priest shall take the child into his hands, and shall say to the Godfathers and Godmothers,

Name this Child.

And then, naming it after them (if they shall certify him that the Child may well endure it) he shall dip it in the water discreetly and warily, saying,

N. I baptize thee in the Name of the Father, and of the Son, and of the Holy Ghost. Amen.

But if they certify that the child is weak, it shall suffice to pour water upon it, saying the foresaid words."

Practice of the Church in England, before the Reformation.

Canon of the Council of Calchuth, A.D. 816, ch. XI.

"Let the presbyters also know, when they administer the holy baptism, that they may not pour the holy water over the infants' heads, but let them always be immersed in the font; as the Son of God furnished by himself an example to every believer, when he was thrice immersed in the waves of the Jordan."

J. Lingard, History and Antiquities of the Anglo-Saxon Church, (Vol. I. p. 317).

"The regular manner of administering it was by immersion, the time the two eves of Easter and Pentecost, the place a baptistery, a small building contiguous to the church, in which had been constructed a convenient bath called a font. When an adult solicited baptism, he was called upon to profess his belief in the true God, by the repetition of the Lord's Prayer, and the

---

LATIN TEXT.

Concilia magnae Britanniae et Hiberniae (*ed. Wilkins, Vol. I. p. 171.*)

Sciant etiam presbyteri, quando sacrum baptismum ministrant, ut non effundant aquam sanctam super capita infantium, sed semper mergantur in lavacro; sicut exemplum praebuit per semetipsum Dei Filius omni credenti, quando esset ter mersus in undis Jordanis.

Apostles' creed; and to declare his intention of leading a life of piety, by making a threefold renunciation of the devil, his works and his pomps. He then descended into the font; the priest depressed his head three times below the surface, saying, I baptize thee in the name of the Father, and of the Son, and of the Holy Ghost."

"In the baptism of children the same rites were observed, with a few necessary variations.... The priest himself descended into the water, which reached to his knees. Each child was successively delivered undressed into his hands, and he plunged it thrice into the water, pronounced the mysterious words, and then restored it to its sponsors."... "Such were the canonical regulations with respect to the administration of baptism."

The following extract from Tyndale's "*Obedience of a Christian Man* (edition of 1571, p. 143), shows the practice of the English Church as late as the first half of the sixteenth century.

"The washing [of baptism] preacheth unto us that we are cleansed with Christ's bloodshedding, which was an offering and a satisfaction for the sin of all that repent and believe, consenting and submitting themselves unto the will of God. The plunging into the water signifieth that we die, and are buried with Christ, as concerning the old life of sin which is Adam. And the pulling out again, signifieth that we rise again with Christ in a new life full of the Holy Ghost, which shall teach us and guide us and work the will of God in us, as thou seest Rom. VI."

These three divisions of the Church are all that can be taken into account in this view. In respect to all three, the following statement by Brenner,[*] a Roman Catholic writer, deserves special regard. After a full investigation of the original authorities, he closes his work with a summary of the results, of which the first paragraph is as follows:

---

[*] Historical Exhibition of the Administration of Baptism, from Christ to our own times, p. 306.

"Thirteen hundred years was baptism generally and regularly an immersion of the person under the water, and only in extraordinary cases a sprinkling or pouring with water; the latter was, moreover, disputed as a mode of baptism, nay even forbidden."

GERMAN TEXT.

Brenner, Geschichtliche Darstellung der Verrichtung der Taufe, von Christus .bis auf unsere Zeiten; S. 306.

Dreizehn hundert Jahren war das Taufen allgemein und ordentlich ein Untertauchen des Menschen unter das Wasser, und nur in ausserordentlichen Fällen ein Besprengen oder Begiessen mit Wasser; letzteres ward ausserdem als Taufweise bezweifelt, ja sogar verboten.

SECTION VII.

Usage of the Versions.

---

1. In the oldest of the Latin versions known to us, we find this word literally translated into that language. Tertullian,* the earliest of the Latin Fathers, who cites from a vernacular version and not from the original Greek,† quotes the commission in Matt. 28 : 19, in the following manner (On baptism, ch. xiii): "*For a law of immersing was imposed, and the formula prescribed. 'Go* (says he) *teach the nations, immersing them in the name of the Father, and of the Son, and of the Holy Spirit.'*" John 4 : 2 is quoted as follows (On baptism, ch. xi.): "For we read, '*And yet he did not immerse, but his disciples.*'" In the same work, ch. xiv. he quotes the Apostle Paul, as having said: "*For Christ sent me not to immerse;*" and in ch. xx. he quotes the Evangelist as saying: "*Were immersed,*

---

* Born about the middle of the second century.
† Semler, Dissert. in Tertull. I. § IV. (*Op. Tertull. ed. Semler, vol. V. p.* 185.)

LATIN TEXT.

Tertull. de Baptismo c. XIII. (*ed. Semler, Vol. IV. p. 172*). Lex enim tinguendi imposita est, et forma praescripta. *Ite* (inquit) *docete nationes, tinguentes eas in nomen patris et filii, et spiritus sancti.*

Ejusdem c. XI. (*Vol. IV. p. 168*). Legimus enim: *Et tamen is non tinguebat, verum discipuli ejus.*

Ejusdem c. XIV. (*p. 172*). Sed de ipso Apostolo revolvunt, quod dixerit, *Non enim me ad tinguendum Christus misit*, quasi hoc argumento baptismus adimatur.

Ejusdem c. XX. (*p. 178*). *Tinguebantur*, inquit, *confitentes delicta sua.*

confessing their sins." In ch. xvi. of the same work, he quotes the Saviour's language in Luke 12 : 50, in the following manner: "There is indeed for us also a second bath, one and the same, namely of blood; of which the Lord says, '*I have to be immersed with a baptism,*' when he had already been immersed."

Cyprian, another of the Latin Fathers, born about half a century later, quotes Matt. 28 : 18-20, in the following manner (Epistle xxv.) : "The Lord, after his resurrection, when sending forth the Apostles, gives a command, and said: '*All power is given to me in heaven and in earth. Go ye, therefore, and teach all nations, immersing them in the name of the Father, and of the Son, and of the Holy Spirit; teaching them to observe all things, whatever I have commanded you.*'" In the same words he quotes this passage again, in Epist. LXIII. Gal. 3 : 27, he quotes in the following manner (Epist. LXXV): "For if the Apostle lies not, when he says, '*As many of you as were immersed in Christ, have put on Christ,*' then verily he, who was then baptized in Christ, has put Christ on."

It was, therefore, the earliest usage, in translations into the Latin language, to express the literal meaning of this

---

Latin Text.

Ejusdem c. XVI. (*pp. 173, 174*). Est quidem nobis etiam secundum lavacrum, unum et ipsum, sanguinis scilicet: de quo Dominus, *Habeo*, inquit, *baptismo tingui*, quum jam tinctus fuisset.

Cypriani Epist. XXV. (*ed. unus ex monach. congr. S. Mauri, p. 82*). Dominus post resurrectionem mittens apostolos mandat et dixit: *Data est mihi omnis potestas in coelo et in terra. Ite ergo et docete gentes omnes, tingentes eos in nomine patris et filii et spiritus sancti, docentes eos observare omnia quaecunque praecepi vobis.*

Ejusdem Epist. LXXV. (*p. 306*). Nam si non mentitur apostolus dicens, *Quotquot in Christo tincti estis, Christum induistis;* utique qui illic in Christo baptizatus est, induit Christum.

word. But the Greek name of the rite itself, and at a later period the Greek verb also, were retained in the current Latin versions; an example of the practice of the Romish Church, to express sacred things by what was superstitiously regarded as their sacred appellations, such as *azyma*, *pascha*, and the like. Of this weakness, injurious in every one of its tendencies, nearly all traces have, after long conflicts, been expunged from the English Bible.

2. This was also the usage of ancient Oriental versions; viz. the Syriac (last half of the second century), the Coptic (third century), and the Ethiopic (of the fourth century), according to the definitions, given in the best lexicons, of the words by which they severally translate the Greek terms.* Scholars differ in opinion only in regard to the Syriac word; and this difference respects only its *etymology* and *primary* meaning, for that it means to *immerse* in early Syriac literature is well known.†

3. The Teutonic versions.

At the head of these, as of Teutonic literature in general, stands the Gothic version of Ulfilas (bishop of the Moeso-Goths), made in the last half of the fourth century. In this version the Greek word is translated by *daupjan* (pronounced as *dowpyan*), which means *to dip*, like the Latin *mergere*, and the German *tau-*

---

* The rendering "*to stand*," which some scholars assert to be the meaning of the corresponding word in the Syriac version, is not claimed by them to be a translation of the Greek word, or to have been so regarded by the author of that version.

In the Sahidic (dialect of upper Egypt) the Greek word is transferred. Versions of a later date are not taken into account here; nor are those here referred to quoted as evidence of the proper meaning of the Greek word, which is established by the better testimony of native writers.

† Kirschii Chrestom. Syr. (ed. Bernstein, p. 378) : ܚܡܰܫ, fut. ܬܶܚܡܰܫ, 1) *mersus*, *immersus est; mersit, immersit se* c. ܒ *in* alqd. *Altitudini* (imo) *maris* ܚܡܰܫ *se immergit* p. 209 l. 5 [ܪܰܡܫܳܐ: ܚܕܡܨܡܨ], *aculeus sagittae immersit se in cerebrum eius, inhaesit in cerebro ejus*, Bar-Hebr. Chr. p. 558 l. 2 a f. (Cfr. Ar. غَمَسَ, quod trans. habet significationem *immersit, immisit* alqd, *recondidit* [stekken] *gladium in vaginam*). Transl. *mersit se dies*, i. e. inclinavit se, abiit, Ephr. opp. T. I. p. 81 l. 29. 2) *mergendo in aquam lavatus, ablutus est.* 3) *sacro lavario initiatus, baptizatus est.*

chen; in two instances (Luke 3 : 21, 7 : 29) by *ufdaupjan, to dip under,* like the Latin *submergere,* and the German *untertauchen.**

In its construction with other words also, this rendering corresponds with the Greek word. For example, Matt. 3 : 11, "*I indeed dip you in water.*" Mark 1 : 8, "*I dip you in water;*" v. 9, "*and was dipped by John in Jordan.*"†

By words of the same family, springing from the same etymological root, and having the same ground-meaning, the Greek word is translated in all the leading vernacular versions made for the Teutonic races. For example :

In the first lower-Saxon Bible (1470–80), it is translated by the word *doepen (to dip).*‡ John 1 : 33, "*But he who sent me to dip in water*" (not, '*with water*'); Matt. 3 : 11, "*And I indeed dip you in water*" (not, '*with water*').

In the *Augspurg German Bible* (1473–75), it is rendered by the word *tauffen (to dip).*§ John 1 : 33, "*He that sent me to dip in water*" (not, '*with water*'); Matt. 3 : 11, "*And I indeed dip you in water*" (not, '*with water*').∥

In Luther's German version (New Testament, 1522; entire Bible, 1534), the Greek word is rendered by *taufen, to dip.* So

---

* Gabelentz and Loebe, Glossarium der Gothischen Sprache : Daupjan, 1) tauchen, taufen, βαπτίζειν : Matt. 3 :11. ... 2. sich waschen, βαπτίζεσθαι : Mc. 7 : 4. Ufdaupjan, untertauchen, eintauchen, ἐμβάπτειν : Joh. 13 : 26 ; taufen, βαπτίζειν : Luc. 3 : 21, 7 : 29.

† Ulfilas, vet. et nov. Test. Versio Gothica ; Matt. 3 : 11, Ik allis izvis daupja ïn vatin (*Massmann's ed.*). Mark 1 : 7, Ik daupja izvis ïn vatin. (v. 9), Jah daupiths vas fram ïohanne ïn ïaurdane (*ed. Gabelentz et Loebe*).

‡ (John 1 : 33) Mer dye my sande to doepen in den waeter. (Matt. 3 : 11) Enn verwar ik dope uw in den water.

§ (John 1 : 33) Aber der mich sandt zu tauffen im wasser. (Matt. 3 : 11) Und furwar ich teuff euch im wasser.

∥ Copies of these ancient vernacular versions, now extremely rare, and of great interest in the history of Bible translation (being more than half a century older than Luther's version of the whole Bible), are in the library of the American Bible Union. The copy of the lower-Saxon Bible is of the edition that assimilates to the Dutch. Compare Panzer, Annalen der älteren deutschen Literatur, Nos. 12, 13.

Luther himself explains the word (Sermon on Baptism): "Then also without doubt, in German tongues, the word *Tauf* comes from the word *tief* (*deep*), because what one baptizes he sinks deep into the water."*

In the Dutch version (1526, revised 1562, and again by order of the States-General 1628-32), the Greek word is rendered by *doopen;* in the Swedish version (New Testament 1526, revised 1615, and more thoroughly 1711-28), by *dœpa;* in the Danish version (from Luther's, 1550, and 1589; from the original text, 1605), by *dœbe;* all of the same root as the word used by Ulfilas and Luther, and all meaning *to dip.*

The relationship of these words, with their ground-meaning, is shown on p. 400 of Meidinger's "Etymological and Comparative Dictionary of the Teuto-Gothic Languages (1833).† Under the root "Tief, *deep,*" he gives the family: "Dippen, *to immerse, to sink, to plunge.* Anglo-Saxon dippan, dyppan, *to plunge, to baptize;* dyfan, dufian, ge-dufian, *to plunge.* English to dip, to dive. Dutch doopen. Swedish doepa. Danish dyppe. Italian tuffare. Under the same root, he gives the family: "Taufen, *to baptize.* Anglo-Saxon dyppan, dippan, depan, dyfan. Swedish doepa. Danish doebe. Dutch doopen. Old-German doufan. Old-Gothic daupian, *to plunge, to bathe.*"

The same relationship (more fully carried out) is given by Diefenbach, Comparative Dictionary of the Gothic Language (*Vergleichendes Wörterbuch der Gothischen Sprache*) 1851, vol. II. p. 627, Nr. 24.

4. Versions for the use of the learned.

As in all versions of this class, so far as is known to the writer, the Greek word is uniformly rendered in this sense, when its literal meaning is professedly given, a few examples will suffice.

---

* Dann auch ohne Zweifel in deutschen Zungen das Wörtlein Tauf herkommt von dem Wort tief, dass man tief ins Wasser senkt was man tauft. Sermon vom Sacrament der Taufe; Werke, B. 21, S. 229 (*Irmischer's ed.*).

† "Tief, profond. Dippen, eintauchen, *enfoncer, plonger.* Ang. S. dippan, dyppan, *plonger, baptiser;* dyfan, dufian, ge-dufian, *plonger.* Eng. to dip, to dive, *plonger.* Holl. doopen. Swed. doepa. Dan. dyppe. *It.* tuffare." . . . . "Taufen, *baptiser.* Ang. S. dyppan, dippan, depan, dyfan. Swed. doepa. Dan. doebe. Holl. doopen. Alt-D. doufan. Alt-G. daupian, *plonger, se laver.*" (Meidinger, Dict. etymologique et comparatif des Langues Teuto-Gothiques. Franof s. M., 1833.)

Schott: the New Testament, with a critically edited Greek text, and a new Latin translation (1839).

Matt. 3 : 6, "were immersed by him in the Jordan."

V. 11 (and Luke 3 : 16), "I indeed immerse you in water; ... he will immerse you in the Holy Spirit and fire."

V. 13, "to be immersed by him."

V. 14, "I have need to be immersed by thee."

V. 16, "and Jesus, when he had been immersed."

Mark. 7 : 4, "except they immerse themselves in water."

Ib. "The immersing of water-pots, brazen vessels, and table-couches."

Ch. 10 : 38, "and undergo the immersion, that I must undergo."

John 1 : 25, "Why then dost thou immerse?"

V. 26, "I indeed immerse in water."

V. 28, "where John was immersing."

V. 31, "therefore I came immersing in water."

Ch. 3 : 22, "and there abode with them, and immersed."

V. 26, "behold, he immerses."

Latin Text.

Nov. Test. Graece, ... nova versione Lat. illustratum, auct. D. A. Schott. 1839.

Matt. 3 : 6, per eum Jordani immergebantur.

V. 11 (and Luke 3 : 16), Ego quidem aquae vos immergo; ... ille Spiritui sancto atque igui vos immerget.

V. 13, ut per eum immergeretur.

V. 14, mihi opus est, ut per te immergar.

V. 16, atque Jesus, quum immersus fuisset.

Mark. 7 : 4, nisi aquae se immerserint.

Ib. de immergendis poculis urceis, vasis aeneis, et lectis tricliniaribus.

Cap. 10, 38, et immersionem subire quae mihi subeunda.

John 1 : 25, cur tandem immergis?

V. 26, equidem aquae immergo.

V. 28, ubi Joannes immergebat.

V. 31, propterea veni aquae immergens.

Ch. 3 : 22, ibique cum iis commorabatur et immergebat.

V. 26, en, hic immergit.

Acts 1 : 5, "which ye heard from me, that John immersed in water," etc.

Ch. 11 : 16, "John indeed immersed in water, but ye shall be immersed in holy spirit."

Campbell (Pres. of Marischal College, Aberdeen), Trans. of the Gospels, Matt. 20 : 22, and Mark 10 : 38. "Can ye... undergo an immersion like that which I must undergo?"—Luke 12 : 50. "I have an immersion to undergo."

Fritzsche, on Rom. 6 : 3. "*I baptize one unto repentance* means: I immerse one, pointing out to him repentance (as needed), i. e. I bind one to the exercise of penitence."

Rom. 6 : 4, he paraphrases thus: "We are *therefore* (i. e. because, when we were baptized by immersion into water, Christ's death was presented before us *in an image of burial*) as was Christ, *deposited in a tomb by baptism, that we might be declared dead*" (p. 364). On p. 363, he quotes the following, as erroneous *constructions* given by others of these words: "*to be immersed in Christ and his death;*" "*to be immersed in Christ*

LATIN TEXT.

Acts 1 : 5, quod a me audivistis, Joannem quidem aquae immersisse.

Acts 11 : 16, Joannes quidem aquae immersit, vos autem Spiritui sancto immergemini.

Fritzschii in epist. ad Rom. vol. I. p. 362 : Matt. 3 : 11, βαπτίζω τινὰ εἰς μετάνοιαν valet immergo aliquem, *poenitentiam ei monstrans* (qua opus sit), i. e. poenitentiâ agendâ aliquem obstringo.

Fritzschii Com. in epist. ad Rom. vol. I. p. 364 : Sumus *igitur* (i. e. quia Christi mors quum baptizaremur mersu in aquam, *sepulturae simulacro*, nobis illata est ; v. ad v. 3), quemadmodum Christus, *in sepulchro repositi per baptisma, quo mortui declararemur.* Pg. 363 : Qui βαπτίζεσθαι εἰς Χριστόν et εἰς τὸν θάνατον αὐτοῦ Christo ejusque morti *immergi* enarrant, etc. ... Quodsi βαπτίζεσθαι εἰς Χριστόν Christo *immergi*

(i. e. into Christ's mystical body, the church;)" "*to be immersed in Christ*, (i. e. to be most closely conjoined with him by baptism, and as it were to coalesce in one);" "*to be immersed in Christ's death*, i. e. to come into this fellowship with Christ's death, that the death thou diest to sins may flow from that, as from a fountain."

Kuinoel (on Matt. 20 : 22) : "*To be submerged with the evils... with which I shall be submerged.* Afflictions and calamities, in the Holy Scriptures, are often compared to deep waters, in which they are submerged as it were, who are pressed by a weight of calamities. Hence, TO BE BAPTIZED is *to be oppressed with ills, with troubles*, or *to be immersed with ills.*"

LATIN TEXT.

valere dicas *in Christi corpus mysticum* (in ecclesiam Eph. 5 : 23, 30) *inseri*, etc. . . . Sin *Christo immergi* significare *arctissime cum Christo per baptismum conjungi et quasi in unum coalescere* cl. v. 5, et Gal. 3 : 27, contendas, . . . et *Christi morti immergi* interpreteris *in hanc cum Christi morte communionem venire, ut mors, quâ peccatis emoriaris, ex illa tanquam ex fonte profluat.*

Kuinoel Com. in Matt. 20 : 22. *Malis submergi . . . quibus ego submergar* . . . . Afflictiones et calamitates in literis sacris saepius comparantur gurgitibus aquarum, quibus veluti submerguntur, qui calamitatum onere premuntur. . . . Hinc βαπτισθῆναι, *malis, aerumnis opprimi s. malis mergi.*

SECTION VIII.

*Views of Scholars of different Communions.**

Alex. de Stourdza, Russian State-Councillor (of the Greek Church): Considerations on the doctrine and spirit of the orthodox Church.

"The distinctive characteristic of the institution of baptism is *immersion*, BAPTISMA, which can not be omitted without destroying the mysterious sense of the sacrament, and contradicting at the same time the etymological signification of the word, which serves to designate it."

"The church of the West has, then, departed from the example of Jesus Christ; she has obliterated the whole sublimity of the exterior sign; in short, she commits an abuse of words

FRENCH TEXT.

Alex. de Stourdza, Considerations sur la doctrine et l'esprit de l'Eglise orthodoxe. Stuttg. 1816. p. 87. (as quoted by Augusti, Denkw., Vol. VII., p. 227). " Le charactère distinctif de l'institution du baptême est *l'immersion*, βάπτισμα, qu'on ne saurait omettre, sans détruire le sens mysterieux du sacrement, et sans contredire en même temps la signification etymologique du mot, qui sert à le designer."

"L'église d'Occident s'est donc écarté de l'imitation de Jesus Christ, elle a fait disparaître toute la sublimité du signe extérieur, enfin elle commet un abus de mots et d'idées, en pra-

---

* The quotations in this Section are from the writings of distinguished scholars; men who wrote (with, perhaps, the exception of the first, who represents the views of a particular Church) in no partisan spirit, and to serve no party end. Their views will be accepted, by every competent judge, as fairly representing the testimony of unbiased christian scholarship, on the point in question.

and of ideas, in practicing *baptism* by *aspersion*, this very term being, in itself, a derisive contradiction. The verb BAPTIZO, *immergo*, has in fact but one sole acceptation. It signifies, literally and always, *to plunge*. Baptism and immersion are, therefore, identical, and to say: *baptism by aspersion* is as if one should say: *immersion by aspersion*, or any other absurdity of the same nature."

Maldonatus (Catholic), Commentary on the Gospels, Matt. 20 : 22. (*On the words, 'Can ye drink,' etc.*). "Mark says, that Christ added, *and be baptized with the baptism with which I am baptized;* which, by another metaphor, signifies the same thing, for baptism is also put for suffering and death, as Luke 12 : 50. Whence it is, that also martyrdom is called a baptism; a metaphor, as I think, taken from those who are submerged in the sea, to put them to death. For in Greek, to be baptized is the same as to be submerged."—Luke, 12 : 50. "To be baptized, therefore, which properly is to be submerged in water, is put for to suffer and to die, and baptism for affliction, for suffering, for death."

French and Latin Text.

tiquant *le baptême par aspersion*, dont le seul énoncé est déjà une contradiction derisoire. En effet le verbe βαπτίζω—*immergo*—n'a qu'une seule acceptation. Il signifie littéralement et perpetuellement *plonger*. Baptême et immersion sont donc identiques, et dire : *baptême par aspersion*, c'est comme si l'on disait : *immersion par aspersion*, ou tout autre contresens de la même nature."

Maldonati Comment. in quat. Evangel. (Matt. 20 : 22). Marcus ait, addidisse Christum : *et baptismo, quo ego baptizor, baptizari?* quod alia metaphora idem significat; nam et baptismus pro passione et morte poni solet, ut Luc. 12 : 50. Unde factum, ut et martyrium baptismus appelletur; metaphora, ut opinor, sumpta est ab iis, qui, ut moriantur, in mare submerguntur. Graece enim baptizari idem est, atque submergi.—(Luc. 12 : 50). Ideo ergo baptizari, quod proprie est aquis submergi, pro pati et mori : et baptismus pro afflictione, pro passione, pro morte ponitur.

Est (Catholic; Chancellor of the University of Douay), Com. on the Epistles (on Rom. 6 : 3). "For immersion represents to us Christ's burial; and so also his death. For the tomb is a symbol of death, since none but the dead are buried. Moreover, the emersion, which follows the immersion, has a resemblance to a resurrection. We are therefore, in baptism, conformed not only to the death of Christ, as he has just said, but also to his burial and resurrection."

The same work, on 1 Cor. 15 : 29. "Not much different is the exposition of those who explain the words '*for the dead*,' in this manner : and acting, or representing the dead; because the immersion and emersion, performed in baptism, are a kind of representation of death and resurrection."

The same work, on Col. 2 : 12. "For it is signified that believers, when they are baptized, by that very ceremony of baptism are buried with Christ; inasmuch as the immersion, which is performed in baptism, so represents Christ's burial, that it at the same time works in us what the burial of Christ signified, namely the death and burial of our old man. But because, not only does the immersion, which is performed in baptism, repre-

---

LATIN TEXT.

Estii Com. in Epist. N. T. Rom. 6 : 3. Nam immersio Christi sepulturam nobis repraesentat; adeoque et mortem. Sepulchrum namque mortis symbolum est, nec enim sepeliuntur nisi mortui. Quae autem immersionem sequitur emersio, similitudinem habet resurrectionis. Igitur in baptismo configuramur non tantum morti Christi, quod jam dixit, verum etiam sepulturae et resurrectioni.—1 Cor. 15 : 29. Non multum dissimilis est expositio eorum, qui illud *pro mortuis* ad hunc modum explicant: et agentes seu repraesentantes mortuos; eo quod immersio et emersio, quae fit in baptismo, sit mortis ac resurrectionis quaedam repraesentatio.—Col. 2 : 12. Et enim significatur fideles, dum baptizantur, ea ipsa baptismi ceremonia Christo consepeliri, quatenus immersio, quae fit in baptismo, ita sepulturam Christi repraesentet, ut simul efficiat in nobis id quod sepultura Christi significabat ; nimirum veteris hominis nostri mortem et sepulturam. Verum quia non solum immersio, quae fit in baptismo,

sent Christ's burial, but also the emersion presents an appearance of his resurrection, therefore he subjoins, "In whom also ye have risen again," etc.

Arnoldi (Catholic), Commentary on the Gospel of Matthew (on ch. 3 : 6). "Baptizein, *to immerse, to submerge*.... It was, as being an entire submersion under the water,—since washings were already a confession of impurity and a symbol of purification,—the confession of entire impurity and a symbol of entire purification."

Bishop Taylor (Church of England), Ductor dubitantium (The Rule of Conscience) Book III. Chap. IV. Rule XV., 13. (Bishop Heber's ed. vol. XIV. p. 62.)

"A custom in the administration of a sacrament, introduced against the analogy and mystery, the purpose and significance of it, ought not to be complied with. I instanced before in a custom of the Church of England, of sprinkling water upon infants in their baptism; and I promised to consider it again.... 'Straightway Jesus went up out of the water (saith the gospel); He came up, therefore he went down. Behold an immersion, not an aspersion.' And the ancient churches, following this of the gospel, did not, in their baptism, sprinkle water with their hands, but immerged the catechumen or the infant." After some references in proof of this assertion, he adds: "All which are a perfect conviction, that the custom of the ancient churches was not sprinkling, but immersion, in pursuance of the sense of the word in the commandment and the example of our

---

Latin and German Text.

repraesentationem habet sepulturae Christi; sed etiam emersio speciem praebet resurrectionis ejus, ideo subjungit, in quo et resurrexistis, etc.

Arnoldi, Commentar zum Evang. des h. Matthäus (Kap. 3 : 6). Βαπτίζειν, *eintauchen, untertauchen*..... Sie war als ein völliges Untertauchen unter das Wasser, da schon Waschungen Bekenntniss der Unreinigkeit und Symbol der Reinigung waren, das Bekenntniss gänzlicher Unreinigkeit und Symbol völliger Reinigung.

blessed Saviour." After showing that a partial application of water was allowed in cases of necessity, he says: "And this is the sense and law of the church of England; not that it be indifferent, but that all infants be dipped, except in case of sickness, and then sprinkling is permitted."

Towerson (Church of England), On the Sacraments; on the Sacram. of Bapt. Pt. III. 1 (p. 18). "As touching the outward and visible sign of baptism, there is no doubt it is the element of water, as is evident from the native significance of the word baptism, which signifies an immersion or dipping into some liquid thing."

Luther, On the Sacrament of Baptism (*at the beginning*). "First, the name *baptism* is Greek; in Latin it can be rendered immersion, when we immerse any thing into water, that it may be all covered with water. And although that custom has now grown out of use with most persons (nor do they wholly submerge children, but only pour on a little water), yet they ought to be entirely immersed, and immediately drawn out. For this the etymology of the name seems to demand."

Calvin, Institution of the Christian religion, Book IV. ch. 15; On Baptism, 19 (*at the end*). "Though the word baptize itself signifies immerse, and it is certain that the rite of immersing was observed by the ancient church."

LATIN TEXT.

Luther, de sacramento Baptismi, *init.* (Op. Lutheri, 1564, vol. I. fol. 319). Primo, nomen baptismus Graecum est; Latine potest verti mersio, cum immergimus aliquid in aquam, ut totum tegatur aqua. Et quamvis ille mos jam aboleverit apud plerosque (neque enim totos demergunt pueros, sed tantum paucula aqua perfundunt) debebant tamen prorsus immergi, et statim retrahi. Id enim etymologia nominis postulare videtur.

Calvini, Instit. Christ. Relig. Lib. IV. Cap. 15, de Bapt. 19. (Genevae 1612, p. 470). "Quamquam et ipsum baptizandi verbum mergere significat, et mergendi ritum veteri ecclesiae observatum fuisse constat.

Zwingli, Annotations on Romans 6 : 3. "*Into his death.* When ye were immersed into the water of baptism, ye were ingrafted into the death of Christ; that is, the immersion of your body into water was a sign, that ye ought to be ingrafted into Christ and his death, that as Christ died and was buried, ye also may be dead to the flesh and the old man, that is, to yourselves."

Philip Limborch (Prof. of Theol. among the Remonstrants), Christian Theology, Book V. ch. 67, On Baptism. "Baptism then consists in ablution, or rather in immersion of the whole body into water. For, formerly, those who were to be baptized were accustomed to be immersed, with the whole body, in water."

George Campbell (President of Marischal College, Aberdeen), Translation of the Gospels, Matt. 3 : 11. "The word BAPTIZEIN, both in sacred authors and in classical, signifies 'to dip,' 'to plunge,' 'to immerse,' and was rendered by Tertullian, the oldest of the Latin Fathers, 'tingere,' the term used for dyeing cloth, which was by immersion."

J. A. Turretin (Prof. of Theol. at Geneva), On Romans 6 : 3, 4. "And indeed baptism was performed, in that age and in those countries, by immersion of the whole body into water."

LATIN TEXT.

Zwinglii, Annott. in Epist. ad Rom. c. 6 : 3. (Op. Vol. IV. p. 420). *In mortem ejus.*) Quum intingeremini in aquam baptismalem, in mortem Christi inserti estis; id est, intinctio corporis vestri in aquam signum fuit, vos insertos esse debere Christo et ejus morti, ut quemadmodum Christus mortuus est et sepultus, et vos mortui sitis carni et veteri homini, id est, vobisipsis.

Limborchii, Theol. Christ. Lib. V. cap. 67, De Baptismo, XII. Consistit igitur baptismus in ablutione, vel potius immersione totius corporis in aquam. Olim enim baptizandi toto corpore aquae immergi solebant.

J. A. Turretini in Epist. ad Rom. Praelect. cap. 6 : 3, 4. Ac sane fiebat baptismus, illa aetate atque illis in oris, per immersionem totius corporis in aquam.

Meyer (Lutheran), Critical Commentary on the New Testament, (on Mark 7 : 4.) "Moreover, ἐὰν μὴ βαπτίσωνται is not to be understood of *washing the hands* (*Lightfoot, Wetstein*), but of *immersion*, which the word in classic Greek, and in the New Testament, everywhere means (compare *Beza*); i. e. here, according to the context, *to take a bath*. So also Luke 11 : 38. Comp. Sir. 31 : 25, Judith 12 : 7." On Matt. 3 : 11. "'Ἐν is, in accordance with the meaning of βαπτίζω (*immerse*), not to be understood *instrumentally*, but, on the contrary, as *in*, in the sense of the *element* wherein the immersion takes place."

Fritzsche (Lutheran), Commentary on the Gospel of Matthew, vol. I. p. 120. "Moreover Casaubon well suggested, that DUNEIN means to be submerged with the design that you may perish, EPIPOLAZEIN to float on the surface of the water; BAPTIZESTHAI [reflexive form of BAPTIZEIN] to immerse yourself wholly, for another end than that you may perish. But that, in accordance with the nature of the word BAPTIZESTHAI, baptism was then performed not by sprinkling upon but by submerging, is proved especially by Rom. 6 : 4."

German and Latin Text.

Meyer, krit. exeget. Kommentar über das N. T. Mark. 7 : 4. Dabei ist ἐὰν μὴ βαπτίσ. nicht vom *Händewaschen* (*Lightf., Wetst.*) zu verstehen, sondern vom *Eintauchen*, was das Wort im Classischen und im N. T. durchweg heisst (vrgl. schon *Beza*), d. i. hier nach dem Contexte: *ein Bad nehmen*. So auch Luk. 11 : 38. Vrgl. Sir. 31 : 25, Judith 12 : 7.—Matt. 3 : 11. Ἐν ist nach Maassgabe des Begriffs von βαπτίζω (*Eintauchen*) nicht *instrumental* zu fassen, sondern : *in*, im Sinne des *Elements*, worin das Eintauchen vor sich geht.

Fritzschii Com. in Evang. Matt. vol. I. pag. 120. Ceterum δύνειν esse eo consilio ut pereas submergi, ἐπιπολάζειν in aquarum superficie natare, βαπτίζεσθαι alio quam ut te perdas fine se totum immergere bene subindicavit *Casaubonus*. Sed praeter naturam verbi βαπτίζεσθαι baptismum non adspergendo sed submergendo illo tempore absolutum esse evincit maxime l. Rom. 6 : 4.

Conybeare and Howson (Church of England), The Life and Epistles of Paul, vol. I. p. 471. (Am. ed., p. 439). "It is needless to add, that baptism was (unless in exceptional cases) administered by immersion, the convert being plunged beneath the surface of the water to represent his death to the life of sin, and then raised from this momentary burial to represent his resurrection to the life of righteousness. It must be a subject of regret, that the general discontinuance of this original form of baptism (though perhaps necessary in our northern climates) has rendered obscure to popular apprehension some very important passages of scripture."

I remark, in conclusion:

1. That the rendering given to this word, in this revision, is its true and only meaning, as proved by the unanimous testimony of Greek writers, both pagan and christian.

2. That it accords with the religious instructions of the earliest christian writers, and with the requirements and practice of the whole christian church, till within a comparatively recent time.

3. That it is the rendering of ancient versions sanctioned by the use of the church, and still retained in the vernacular versions of northern Europe.

4. That it is the only rendering of the word in any version sanctioned by early use in the church, and is the only one used by scholars in their versions and expositions for the learned.

5. That recent and living scholars, without distinction of ecclesiastical relations, unite in asserting this to be the true meaning of the Greek word.

Such a rendering belongs to no one division of the church. It is catholic; sanctioned by all that can entitle any rendering to universal acceptation. Whatever else may be said of it, it can not, with any show of reason, be called sectarian.

SECTION IX.

Obligation to translate the word.

The obligation to translate this word rests on something more than grounds of philological correctness. There is, indeed, no reason of sufficient weight to justify, in any case, a departure from the simple rule of giving a faithful and intelligible rendering of the inspired word. No other rule can be recognized as right or safe. On the ground alone, were there no other, that the Greek word means '*to immerse*,' is the translator bound so to render it. The general rule no one disputes. It is an axiom, and needs no proof. It is simply the rule, when one professes to communicate the words of another, to tell the truth as to what he has said. Any author, purposely mistranslated or obscured, is falsified by his translator. Just so far as this is done, the translation is a literary forgery; for it conceals while it professes to exhibit what the author has said, or it represents him as saying that which he did not say. When applied to the Word of God, the rule is one of paramount force.

But in the form of the initiatory Christian rite, there are references vitally connected with the nature and development of the Christian life. To obscure the word which describes this form is, therefore, to obscure to the mind of the recipient, the nature of the rite, the specific ideas symbolized in it, and the obligations to which it binds him.

The word BAPTIZEIN, during the whole existence of the Greek as a spoken language, had a perfectly defined and unvarying import. In its literal use it meant, as has been shown, to put

entirely into or under a liquid, or other penetrable substance, generally water, so that the object was wholly covered by the inclosing element. By analogy, it expressed the *coming into a new state of life or experience*, in which one was as it were inclosed and swallowed up, so that, temporarily or permanently, he belonged wholly to it. The word was a favorite one in the Greek language. Whenever the idea of total submergence was to be expressed, whether literally or metaphorically, this was the word which first presented itself. The connection might be of the most elevated and serious, or of the most familiar and even ludicrous character. * It was a daily household word, employed in numberless cases where the use of the word '*baptize*' would be a profanation. Salt, wool, the hand, a pole, a cork, a nest, a fish-spear, a bladder, an ape, an insect, a salad, were with perfect propriety said to be BAPTIZED (IMMERSED). A man was BAPTIZED (IMMERSED) when he was ducked in sport or revenge (Exs. 26 and 60), or was accidentally submerged by a swollen stream (Ex. 13). A ship was BAPTIZED (SUBMERGED), when she was overloaded and sunk (Ex. 48). So, metaphorically, one was BAPTIZED (IMMERSED) in calamities, when he was swallowed up by them as by an ingulfing flood (Exs. 87, 88); in debts, when he owed vast sums and had no means of paying them (Ex. 133); in wine, when his faculties were totally overborne and prostrated by it (Ex. 142); with sophistries, when his mind was wholly confounded by them (Ex. 135). The relation in which it was used associated with it, for the time being, the ideas peculiar to that relation; but the word itself, protected by the daily and hourly repetition in common life of the act which it described, retained its primary meaning and force unchanged.*

It was this familiar term, understood by all because all used it in their every-day avocations, which our Saviour employed when prescribing the initiatory rite of his church. It conveyed to the minds of his disciples a meaning as clear and definite, as the words *to eat* and *to drink*, in his institution of the Supper.

---

* As shown, Section III. 1, 9, by its secular use in the Church Fathers, side by side with their use of it in reference to the Christian rite.

The claim, that he used it with any other meaning than that which has been exhibited in this treatise, originated in ignorance of the literature of the word. No one, it is presumed, with a full knowledge of the case, would assert that the Saviour employed it in a new sense, unknown to those whom he addressed; for that would be a charge that he used it with the intention, or at least with the certainty, of being misunderstood. To that mystical sense, supposed by many to have been shadowed forth in Christ's command, stands out, in the strongest possible contrast, the simple, distinct, corporeal sense, to which the word was appropriated by unvarying usage. The act which it describes was chosen for its adaptation to set forth, in lively symbolism, the ground-thought of Christianity. The change in the state and character of the believer was total; comparable to death, as separating entirely from the former spiritual life and condition. The sufferings and death of Christ, those overwhelming sorrows which he himself expressed by this word (Luke 12 : 50), were the ground and procuring cause of this change. These related ideas, comprehending in their references the whole work and fruit of redemption, were both figured by the immersion of the believer in water. In respect to both, it was called a burial. By it the believer was buried, as one dead with Christ to sin and to the world; and by it he pledged himself to newness of life, with him who died for him and rose again. Can it be supposed that to obscure these ideas, by virtually canceling the term on the clear expression of which the apprehension of them depends, is a trivial wrong against the body of Christ!

This view of the significance, and consequent importance, of the form of this Christian rite, is not peculiar to the body of professed followers of Christ to which the writer belongs. "And indeed," says Luther,* "if you consider what baptism signifies,

---

* Et sane, si spectes quid baptismus significet, idem [immersionem] requiri videbis. Hoc enim significat, ut vetus homo, et nativitas nostra plena peccatis, quæ ex carne et sanguine constat, tota per divinam gratiam demergatur, id quod copiosius indicabimus. Debebat igitur modus baptizandi respondere significationi baptismi, ut certum ac plenum ejus ederet signum. (*De Sacram. Bapt., Op. Tom. I. Fol.* 72.)

you will see that the same thing [immersion] is required. For this signifies, that the old man, and our sinful nature, which consists of flesh and blood, is all submerged by divine grace, as we shall more fully show. The mode of baptizing ought, therefore, to correspond to the signification of baptism, so as to set forth a sure and full sign of it." Matthies* (treatise on baptism) only repeats the expressed views of eminent Christian scholars of different communions, when he says: "In the apostolic church, in order that fellowship in Christ's death might be signified, the whole body of the one to be baptized was immersed in water or a river; and then, that participation in Christ's resurrection might be indicated, the body again emerged, or was taken out of the water. It is indeed to be lamented, that this rite, as being one which most aptly sets before the eyes the symbolic significance of baptism, has been changed."

The word '*baptize*' is an Anglicized form of the Greek BAPTIZEIN. On this account it has seemed to some that it must necessarily express the same meaning. It has been said, that no other word can so perfectly convey the thought of the Holy Spirit, as the one chosen by himself to express it in the original Scriptures; and that we are, therefore, at least right and safe in retaining it in the English version. A comparison of the meaning of BAPTIZEIN, as exhibited in Sects. I.–III. of this treatise, with the definitions of 'baptize,' as given in all dictionaries of the English language, and with its recognized use in English literature and in current colloquial phraseology, will show that this is far from being the case. The word 'baptize' is a strictly ecclesiastical term; broadly distinguished, by that characteristic, from the class of common secular words to which BAPTIZEIN belonged. It is a metaphysical term, indicating a mystical relation entered into with the church, by virtue of the sacramental application of water. In both these respects, it misrepresents the Saviour's manner and intent. Concealing the form of the Chris-

---

* In ecclesia apostolica, ut mortis Christi communio significaretur, totum baptizandi aquæ vel flumini immergebatur, et deinde, ut resurrectionis Christi societas innueretur, corpus iterum emergebat, seu extrahebatur ex aqua. Dolendum quidem est, hunc ritum, quippe qui aptissime symbolicam baptismi significationem ante oculos ponat, esse mutatum. (*Baptismatis Expos.* ₰ 16 *fin.*)

tian rite under a vague term, which means any thing the reader may please, it obscures the ideas thereby symbolized, and the pertinency of the inspired appeals and admonitions founded on them. The essence of the Christian rite is thus made to consist in this mystical church-relation, into which it brings the recipient. With this view associates itself, naturally and almost necessarily, the idea of a certain mysterious efficacy in the rite itself; and, accordingly, we find the belief prevailing in the majority of Christian communions that, through baptism, the recipient is, not externally alone, but mystically united to the body of Christ. Thus the rite ceases to be the symbol of certain great truths of Christianity, and becomes an efficacious sacrament. The tenacity with which this fatal error is adhered to, even in communions not connected with the state, is largely due to the substitution, in our English Bibles, of this vague foreign term of indefinite meaning, for the plain, intelligible English signification of the Greek word.*

Among the several words, all agreeing in the essential idea of *total submergence*, by which BAPTIZEIN may be expressed in English, the word IMMERSE has been selected for use in this Revision, as most nearly resembling the original word in the extent of its application. It is a common, secular word, used in the daily affairs of life, to express the most familiar acts and conditions. It is not an ecclesiastical term. It is not a metaphysical term. It describes, to every English mind, the same clearly marked, corporeal act as is expressed by the Greek word. It is used metaphorically with the same applications. We speak of a man as immersed in calamities, in debt, in ignorance, in poverty, in cares, etc., always with the idea of totality, of being wholly under the dominion of these states or influences. In all these applications, like the Greek word, through constant use in the literal sense, it suggests the clear image of the act on which they all are founded. It is, in short, the same potentiality in English as BAPTIZEIN in Greek,

---

* Other causes may produce, and have produced, the same perversion; but this is no reason why we should not remove the one within our reach.

having the same meaning and the same associations; being thereby fitted to make known to us the Saviour's will in prescribing the initiatory rite of his church, to exhibit the truths and relations symbolized by it, and the force of the inspired appeals founded on it, precisely as this was done to those who first heard and read the gospel in Greek.

AMERICAN BIBLE UNION,
350 BROOME ST., NEW YORK.

PUBLICATIONS.

Every friend of faithful versions should have the Primary Revisions of the Bible Union. The following is a list of our LARGE QUARTO EDITIONS, containing the Original Text, Common Version, and Revision, side by side, on each page, with Critical and Philological Notes. We will send any one of these large and beautifully bound volumes, FREE OF POSTAGE, to any part of the United States on receipt of the price.

PRICES BY MAIL, FREE OF POSTAGE.

MATTHEW AND APPENDIX, Complete,		$1 50
☞ The Appendix contains a literal translation of every known example of the use of BAPTIZEIN by the Greek authors.		
MARK, Complete,		80
LUKE, "		1 50
JOHN, "		90
ACTS, "		1 25
GALATIANS, " ☞ IN PRESS.		
EPHESIANS, "		50
THESSALONIANS, first and second Epistles, Complete,		60
TIMOTHY, first and second, and } " TITUS (bound together),		60
PHILEMON, "		25
HEBREWS, "		70
PETER, 2d Ep., ⎫ JOHN, 1st " ⎪ ☞ The Primary Revisions of these Books were the JOHN, 2d " ⎬ first issued by the Bible Union. They were bound together, and sold for $1 50. But, the pages not having JOHN, 3d " ⎪ been stereotyped, the edition is entirely exhausted, and JUDE, ⎭ we can not fill any orders for this volume. REVELATION,		
PROVERBS—Revision, Old Version, Hebrew Text and Notes,		85
JOB—I. Revision, Old Version, Hebrew Text and Notes,		1 00
JOB—II. Revision, with Notes for English Readers,		75
JOB—III. Containing JOB I. and II.		1 50
JOB—IV. 8vo, Revision in Paragraphs,		50
JOB—V. 12mo, Hebrew and English, on opposite pages,		75
JOB—VI. 32mo, Hebrew, Finest Edition Published,		50

NEW TESTAMENT REVISIONS, BOUND TOGETHER.

The Primary Revisions of the New Testament will be bound together complete, as soon as the remaining portions shall be issued. The first volume now ready, contains, with DR. CONANT'S APPENDIX, nearly 1000 quarto pages, equal to 2000 ordinary octavo pages. Strong and neat library binding, viz.,

MATTHEW, MARK, LUKE, JOHN, and APPENDIX, - $4 25
MATTHEW, MARK, LUKE, JOHN, and APPENDIX, Bound
 with ACTS, - - - - - - - - - 5 50

C. A. BUCKBEE,   WM. H. WYCKOFF,
Assistant Treasurer.   *Corresponding Secretary.*

Publications of the American Bible Union,
350 Broome Street, New York.

BOOK OF JOB, REVISED.

A quarto volume of 300 pages, equal to about 600 ordinary octavo pages. Containing the Revised Version, the Hebrew Text, and the Common Version, with Critical and Philological Notes, and Explanatory Notes for the English Reader. Price, sent by mail, $1.50.

Also, a quarto edition of the Revised Version (without the Hebrew Text and the Common Version) of Job, with an Introduction and Notes for English Readers. Price, sent by mail, 75 cts.

The Revised Version, by itself, octavo, price 50 cts. Hebrew Text, by itself, price 50 cts.

The work as a whole is a master-piece.—*The Israelite O.*
A noble specimen of sound scholarship.—*Religious Herald, Va.*
A valuable aid to Biblical scholarship.—*The Independent, N. Y.*
Not an idea could be omitted or changed.—*Am. Chr. Review, O.*
The Am. Bible Union is laboring faithfully.—*Masonic Review, O.*
We desire a similar service to all the Books of the O. T.—*Chr. Times, Ill.*
A rare pleasure to look over this new Version.—*Putnam's Monthly, N. Y.*
Eminent scholarship is at work upon it.—*Vermont Chronicle, Vt.*
It seems like an oasis in the desert.—*Christian Intelligencer, Va.*
A reliable improvement upon the Authorized Version.—*Guardian, Tenn.*
New light and beauty on many difficult passages.—*Tribune, N. Y.*
A valuable acquisition to every pastor's library.—*Gen. Evangelist, N. Y.*
A master-piece of profound scholarship.—*The Traveller, Mass.*
No lover of the beautiful can read it without pleasure.—*West. Recorder, Ky.*
Receives high encomiums from many secular journals.—*Zion's Adv., Me.*
The Hebrew Text is correct.—*The Israelite, O.*
The best Version of Job ever made.—*Chronicle, N. Y.*
The Introduction is admirable.—*The Baptist, Tenn.*
Its Notes are highly valuable.—*Gen. Evangelist, N. Y.*
Never read comments with which we were better pleased.—*Chr. Rev., N. Y.*
A version uniting elegance with correctness.—*Jewish Chronicle, London.*
The spirited rendering is sufficient to win all our sympathy.—*Lit. Ch. London.*
It can hardly be surpassed in English literature.—*Weekly Leader, Canada.*
We most heartily commend this version.—*Chr. Secretary, Conn.*
One of the ablest revisions that adorns the sacred literature.—*Courier, Ky.*
In the highest degree creditable to American scholarship.—*Journal, Ky.*
Dr. Conant has devoted thirty years' study of the original Hebrew.—*Express, N. Y*
The Notes are unusually full, and exhibit great erudition.—*Herald, N. Y.*
The wonder is that the work has not been done long ago.—*Fam. Gazette, N. Y.*
Many passages seem more clear in this new translation.—*Sentinel, N. J.*
The mechanism is simple and elegant.—*Advent Herald, N. Y.*
Philological and Biblical learning is accumulated in the notes.—*Jour. and Mess., O*
The scholar will see the absolute necessity for such a revision.—*Gazette, N. Y.*
A much clearer view of the meaning of the original.—*True Union, Md.*
It is beautifully printed.—*United States Democratic Review, N. Y.*
The introduction is a treat, indeed.—*Christian Age. O.*
Result of many years of careful study.—*Baptist Magazine, London.*
The living Spirit is more beautifully and accurately developed.—*Era, Mass.*
By all means procure a copy.—*Christian Union, Geo.*
The volume is a treasure.—*The La. Baptis', La.*
A great blessing to all our churches.—*Chr. Visitor, N. B.*

(1)

Publications of the American Bible Union,

350 Broome Street, New York.

BAPTIZEIN.

(*Originally issued as an Appendix to the Revision of Matthew.*)

A BOOK OF NEARLY 200 OCTAVO PAGES. PRICE, SENT BY MAIL, 50 CENTS.

No book of the size that has required such enlarged and accurate scholarship, and the toilsome research of so many years, has ever been published at less than double or fourfold this price. Many thousands of dollars have been used in the purchase of the books, and in other expenses, requisite in its preparation. Many journeys have been made, and the most celebrated libraries in Europe and America have been examined, to procure and prove the citations from ancient authors of which its arguments chiefly consist. Every precaution has been exercised to insure correctness, even in the most minute details. It may be safely averred, that no subject, requiring such extended research, has ever before been so completely exhausted and so transparently and impartially presented.

Writers on the use of the word BAPTIZO have generally been content to refer to a score or two of examples from ancient authors, and the majority of these they have not traced to their sources. But the investigations of Dr. Conant in the best libraries of Europe and this country, have enabled him to collect *two hundred and thirty-six examples*, and to authenticate each case beyond the possibility of doubt.

This book has been prepared both for the learned and the unlearned. Had the former not been satisfied, the verdict would not have been sustained by the literary world. Had it not been adapted to reach and inform the latter, the object of the publication would not have been attained. That object is, to afford to every man who can read the English language the opportunity of understanding the whole philological arguments regarding the meaning and the use of the word BAPTIZO, with all the learned proofs and authorities in the case, as completely and as accurately as the most eminent scholar. For this purpose, each example is translated in the most simple and literal manner, and the translation, with the citation of the author, book, and page, is placed conspicuously on the foreground, in the upper portion of each page. Below it the original is printed, for the inspection of the learned.

No one has yet been found to express a doubt of its thoroughness or of its impartiality. It is universally admitted to be the production of a master-mind in the maturity of its powers.

Publications of the American Bible Union,

350 Broome Street, New York.

BAPTIZEIN.

From the Southern Baptist Review, Tenn.

The Appendix evinces thorough scholarship and immense research. Its value can not be estimated. It contains every known example of *baptizo* to be found in the Greek classics, and examples of every use of it in the "Church Fathers." The baptismal controversy on the action of baptism is philologically settled.

From the Banner and Baptist, Atlanta, Ga.

This is the best production which we have received from the Bible Union Rooms, although we have received many valuable documents. The translation of *baptizein* "to immerse," will no doubt produce some excitement. The author has most ably fortified himself and his work in an Appendix. This Appendix we consider worth several times the price of Matthew revised. All our brethren should have this work.

From the Christian Union, Louisville, Ky.

The Appendix to Matthew is devoted to a thorough exploration of ancient Greek literature, for the use of *baptizein* and its derivatives. Nothing equal to it has ever appeared in the English language. It is alike unanswerable and invulnerable ; it is an inexhaustible magazine of armor for those engaged in the discussion.

From the Western Recorder, Louisville, Ky.

The Appendix brings the whole question within the comprehension of all, the plain English reader, as well as the most finished critical scholar. It has never been thus before. The common people have never before been permitted to enter the lists of the discussion. It is impossible to convey in writing the fullness and perfection of this argument. Nothing like it exists in any language on the subject. Every minister, every scholar, every intelligent reader of the Bible ought to study and master it. —*D. R. Campbell, D.D., LL.D., President of Georgetown College, Ky.*

From the Texas Baptist, Anderson, Texas.

The Appendix alone is worth to the Christian world, all that has ever been expended in the revision enterprise. It contains more *matter* than any other book ever published in the English language. It is in no sense a controversial book ; all, therefore, may read it. We would rejoice to see a copy of it in the hands of every minister, as well as every private Christian who speaks the English tongue.—*Rev. J. W. D. Creath.*

From the Freewill Quarterly

The philological argument respecting baptism is here exhausted. The material to be employed in the discussion of the subject by scholars was never before so accumulated within a small compass, or so admirably classified, or made so readily and easily available to minds of ordinary attainments and culture.

From the Chronicle, New York.

It is a monument to patient, persevering scholarship, of which any man might be proud. So far as the meaning of *baptizein* is concerned, it is final. The argument is conducted in no sectarian spirit. The original evidences are given without comment The controversy, so far as the *meaning* of the word is concerned, is settled forever.

From the Home Mission Record, New York.

The Appendix is a work of immense labor, and of great value. It settles definitely, conclusively, and forever, the true meaning of the word *baptizein*. Henceforth there is an end of controversy on that subject. The Bible Union have in this matter done a good work. We wish they would circulate one hundred thousand copies.

Publications of the American Bible Union,
350 Broome Street, New York.

BAPTIZEIN.

From the Christian Times, Chicago, Ill.

This collection of authorities from the ancient classical and ecclesiastical usage of *baptizo*, is by far the most complete ever before published. It in fact exhausts that department of inquiry—it settles the meaning of the usage of the Greek term. Every minister should have the work for the sake of these references, if for no other

From the Biblical Recorder, Raleigh, N. C.

The present work is destined to excite no little interest, and receive many a searching investigation, but we have no fears that it will not in the main come forth from the ordeal as "gold tried in the fire." We commend the whole volume to the careful study of all scholars of every denomination.

From the Journal and Messenger, Cincinnati, O.

The Appendix furnishes a most valuable treasury of argument on the baptismal question. It contains quotations from the Greek and Latin classics of *every instance* where the word *baptizo* or its equivalent occurs, with similar citations from the early Christian writers in each language. It contains also authority respecting the present practice in baptism of the Greek Church, also of the Latin Church, up to the Middle Ages, and of the English Church, till near the Reformation. These ample references will render the work very desirable to every minister.

From the Christian Freeman, Jacksonville, Ill.

The argument is purely philological and historical. We have long wished to see an argument of this character in support of the meaning of this word; an argument devoid of all denominational special pleading, and that can not offend any inquirer after truth. To any person having difficulties on the subject of immersion, we commend this Appendix, as the most satisfactory and least partisan source of information he can consult.

From the New Church Quarterly (Swedenborgian).

The Greek word *baptizo*, rendered "baptize" in the authorized version, is translated by Dr. Conant, "immerse;" and in the Appendix he cites a long array of authorities, Greek and Latin, sacred and profane, to show that this is the literal meaning. We cordially confess that his arguments seem to be conclusive, and that there is no escape from the admission that the original idea of the word is "immersion."

From the American Christian Review, Cincinnati, O.

The treatise on *baptizo* is the fairest, fullest, and, we think, the best, we have ever seen. It puts the humblest English reader upon the shoulders of all the learned, and enables him to see as far into the matter as the learned themselves can.

It ought to be put into a cheap book by itself, so that it can be circulated everywhere. It will certainly, with all candid people, be an end of the controversy on the meaning of that word: it will enable the preachers to end the controversy shortly. It is truly a master-piece.

From the Christian Era, Boston, Mass.

The Appendix, on the MEANING AND USE OF BAPTIZEIN, is the most exhaustive and condensed exhibition of the historical and critical argument for immersion on philological grounds, ever produced.

It is a critical Thesaurus, exhausting the resources of profane and ecclesiastical literature on this topic.

From the Witness, Indianapolis, Ind.

The Dissertation, showing that *baptizein* means *only* and *always to immerse*, is certainly one of great ability and research. The work rises above all sectarian prejudice. The issues are now put on a fair and firm basis. No doubt can be entertained by any one, any longer, that *baptizein* means, and *only* means, *to immerse*. We commend this work to the careful examination of all. Let those who sprinkle and pour for baptism, look well to this work. If you can take away the facts, do it.

Publications of the American Bible Union,
350 Broome Street, New York.

BAPTIZEIN.

From the Morning Star, Dover, N. H.

The Appendix furnishes a most valuable treasury of argument on the baptismal question. Such a review ought to settle this great question with all candid minds.

From the Christian Herald, Detroit, Mich.

This is a magnificent effort, on the part of Dr. Conant, worthy to be his monument, and must go far toward settling the controversy about the meaning of the word.

From the Mississippi Baptist, Jackson, Miss.

This Appendix gives the result of many years' research, and exhibits an amount of learning and scholarly ability in the collation of authorities that must command the admiration and respect of scholars throughout the world.

From the Christian Visitor, St. John, N. B.

Immerse, instead of *baptize,* is the change (in the proposed revision of Matthew) which, above all others, will call forth remark. But in an Appendix, luminous on every page with extended critical research, the Author (Dr. Conant) shows his authority for this change, and by evidence, the most conclusive, establishes the correctness of his position, and puts the question relating to the true signification of the original word *baptizein* to rest forever.

This Appendix alone is worth, to the Church of God, all that the Bible Union has cost in the shape of toil and money from the beginning to the present hour.

From the Christian Union, Louisville, Ky.

This is, by far, the ablest investigation of the Greek word, from which we get the English word *baptism,* that has ever been published.

From the Gospel Herald, London, England.

The Appendix proves by evidence more elaborate, in some respects, than has ever yet been given, that the meaning of the Greek word BAPTIZEIN is *immerse,* that this is its only import, and that fidelity requires it to be translated, and not transferred.

From the Mich. Christian Herald, Detroit, Mich.

The Appendix to Matthew's Gospel must stand an imperishable monument to the thorough research and accurate learning of the author.

From Zion's Advocate, Portland, Me.

There is one thing which must commend it—the reviser's bold treatment of the word baptize—sustained in an Appendix, in which every known instance of the use of the word baptize, by Greek authors, is considered.

Dr. Conant has thrown down the gauntlet. The question is before the world. If no reply is made, the question will be settled, settled once and forever.

From the Missouri Baptist, St. Louis, Mo.

Reader, do you wish to know, beyond doubt, what the apostles did when they baptized the people? Read this *Appendix.* Have you any curiosity to see the most chaste, comprehensive, and learned production of any age upon this subject? Read it. Would you like to examine over 220 Greek quotations, and a few from the Latin, with a reference or two to the Oriental and Teutonic? Here you have them, and all translated. Would you like to hear the voice of the classic, and the Greek of the common and of the religious life; the voice of early translations and of later ones; the voice of all Christendom for 1300 years; and the voice of scholars, of different ages and communions, upon the meaning and use of *baptizein?* Bend your ear to these clear-speaking, full-toned pages, and you can enjoy that pleasure.

Publications of the American Bible Union,
350 BROOME STREET, NEW YORK.

MATTHEW REVISED,
WITH BAPTIZEIN AS AN APPENDIX.

A quarto volume of about 300 pages, equal to nearly 600 ordinary octavo pages. Containing the Common Version, Greek Text, Revised Version, and Philological Notes. Price, sent by mail, $1.50.

From the Christian Review, N. Y.

This volume comes to us under the auspices of a Society of large membership and considerable power, and from the hand of a reviser of acknowledged scholarship. In no modern revision of the English Scriptures that has come to our knowledge, has there been so much of thoroughness. Evidences appear in every page of a scholarship comprehensive, patient, and enthusiastic. The reviser appears to have refrained, conscientiously and religiously, from introducing a single change that did not seem to himself to be demanded by fidelity to the original text, or by the requirements of English idiom. We have not detected a single expression in the revision of the twenty-eight chapters of this Gospel, that does not appear to have been most painfully selected as the one that, *in the judgment of the reviser,* was most precisely fitted to express the inspired thought of the adopted text.

From the Southern Baptist Review, Tenn.

This Revised Version is, in many respects, superior to the Common Version. The foot-notes are, in the main, judicious, and indicative of the author's qualifications for his work. Dr. Conant is the very man whose heart is inaccessible to the influence of sectarian considerations.

From the Christian Record, Ind.

The learning, research, and literary taste of Dr. Conant, are not to be questioned. If there were no other evidence, his recent labors for the American Bible Union would afford sufficient proof that he possesses all these qualifications for a reviser or translator in an eminent degree.

We do most heartily thank God for what has been accomplished, and we do most sincerely think that there is nothing to be desired more than a simple, faithful, pure translation of the word of God, into our own noble and almost universal language. We understand this to be the object of the American Bible Union. And we believe that every lover of the truth will hail with pleasure any and every effort that may be put forth in this direction ; and not only so, but earnestly pray to God for success.

From the Christian Times, Chicago, Ill.

We are free to say that we esteem it (the revision), in the main, a decided improvement on the old one. It brings out, in numerous instances, the sense of the original with a beauty and a force that almost take one by surprise. We are truly happy to place it on our shelves, as a tribute of American scholarship to sacred learning, and a most valuable help to the study of this portion of the New Testament.

From the Biblical Recorder, Raleigh, N. C.

The reviser is generally admitted to be among the first Hebrew and Greek scholars now living. His revision of Job has "won golden opinions" from the public press. The present work is destined to excite no little interest, and receive many a searching investigation. A full examination of the revision and notes was a work of weeks, instead of a few hours, even for a competent scholar.

We commend the whole volume to the careful study of all scholars.

From the Christian Union, Louisville, Ky.

This revision is one of the finest monuments of Biblical learning ever erected. The more we examine it, the higher it rises in our estimation. The industry of the reviser, his extraordinary collation of authorities, the remarkable learning and scholarly skill exhibited in every page, stamps this revision as one of the great works of this century.

Publications of the American Bible Union,
350 Broome Street, New York.

MATTHEW REVISED.

From the Morning Star, Dover, N. H.

Having used this volume in connection with the exercises of our class in the Greek Testament during the past term, we cheerfully give it a high commendation. We are especially pleased with the fidelity to the original, the accuracy and beauty of the Revised Version. The work must have cost immense labor, and exhibits throughout a marked success. If this may be regarded as a specimen of the Bible Union's great undertaking, the whole will be welcomed with great favor by the Christian public.

From the Christian Visitor, St. John, N. B.

All who examine the work will agree that it is, in all respects, a scholarly production of the very first grade.

From the Christian Freeman, Jacksonville, Ill.

Dr. Conant is an eminent member of the Final Committee, and this fruit of his labor possesses so many evidences of high scholarship and good taste, that we accept it as a flattering assurance of what the final work is to be.

From the Witness, Indianapolis, Ind.

This book was assigned to Dr. Conant, and has been executed by him. As to his ability and scholarship and honesty as a Christian man, we need not speak. He has done his work on this with great care and evident ability.

From the Banner and Baptist, Atlanta, Ga.

This is the *best* production which we have received from the Bible Union Rooms, although we have previously received many valuable documents.

From the American Christian Review, Cincinnati, O.

We are highly delighted with a large portion of his [Dr. Conant's] work. Indeed, the production is worth to the world all the funds we, as a brotherhood, have ever contributed to the Union.

From the Christian Herald, Detroit, Mich.

We have not a particle of doubt but that Dr. Conant has given us the most accurate version of Matthew in existence, and which will be hailed with great satisfaction, both by the learned scholars of the day, and by the common reader of the Scriptures.

From the American Baptist, New York.

The publication of this volume will do much to relieve the alarm of those who feared that their old-fashioned Bible was to be so changed that they could scarcely recognize it. The caution with which the reviser has introduced his emendations will secure favor for the volume.

From the Christian Era, Boston, Mass.

The revision of the Gospel of Matthew evinces great research, and marked candor. We have been struck with the generally terse and felicitous diction which it employs.

From the Home Mission Record, New York.

The Revised Version seems to have been executed with great care and fidelity. Comparatively few changes have been made, and those only where there seemed good and sufficient reason for making them.

From the New York Chronicle, New York.

The more it is examined, the more its profound scholarship and masterly research will appear.

From the Gospel Herald, London, England.

Among the valuable works which this Society (the American Bible Union) is publishing, none exceeds in interest "The Gospel of Matthew," by Dr. T. J. Conant. Such works, independently of being preparatory to so important a work as a revised translation for common use, are valuable additions to Biblical literature.

Publications of the American Bible Union,
350 Broome Street, New York.

MATTHEW REVISED.

From Zion's Advocate, Portland, Me.

Of the manner in which Prof. Conant has done his work, we need, perhaps, say but little. His reputation as a Biblical scholar is well established, and but few men would be willing to urge their own opinions, with much confidence, against his, on a question of philology.

From the True Union, Baltimore, Md.

It is the production of a profound scholar ; and, irrespective of its ultimate design, will be found a valuable work. The reviser keeps as closely as practicable to the Common Version, and retains, as much as possible, the fine old Saxon idiom.

From the Western Recorder, Louisville, Ky.

There is hardly a possibility of any further material improvement. Every page, every chapter, every verse, every word, every point, bears the impress of the most scrupulous care, and the most perfect human accuracy.

From the Journal and Messenger, Cincinnati, Ohio.

The plan which Dr. Conant proposes is the right one. We think that he has been generally successful in accomplishing his object, so far as we have been able to judge.

From the Plumas Standard, Quincy, California.

The reviser is Prof. T. J. Conant, whose reputation as a scholar is co-extensive with the world of education. This revision of Matthew, like all that comes from his pen, evinces a depth of erudition and careful research, such as few scholars in this age have attained. Where any departure is made from King James' Version, the reasons are given. The reviser has shown, not only a perfect command of our noble language, but a wonderful knowledge of the philology and customs of the ancients.

From J. H. Raymond, LL.D., President of the Polytechnic Collegiate Institute, N. Y.

This revision is made, throughout, in the Catholic spirit of a true scholar, who concerns himself not at all with questions of importance or unimportance, with moral or doctrinal, or ecclesiastical bearings, but simply and solely with the question of *accuracy*—who keeps steadily in view the two only questions pertinent to his work :
1. What is the true Greek to be Englished ?
2. What is the true English for that Greek ?

Dr. Conant follows the testimony of the *most ancient* witnesses, *i. e.*, of the oldest manuscripts and versions now extant, and the citations of Scripture found in the earliest Christian writings that have come down to us.

It is such a work as scholars love to look upon.

From Rev. George J. Johnson, Fort Madison, Iowa.

I have read the revised version of Matthew through twice, and am gratified with the book beyond measure. You know I have never been any kind of a friend to the Bible Union, and still have no faith in the general success of its undertaking. But I must acknowledge that if the Union shall never do any more, to have produced such a work as this now before me is not laboring for naught : it is so far a glorious success. I shall not attempt to review the revision critically, but will say this—So far as I can judge, it is faithful and elegant, and in many respects an improvement on the old version.

From Rev. Henry A. Hart, Maine.

I have been, heretofore, neither a friend nor a foe of the Bible Union. I have felt but little interest in the matter, and have not cared even to form an opinion. But since reading a copy of Conant's Revision of Matthew, I have changed my grounds. I am ready to take sides with the Union.

Publications of the American Bible Union,
350 BROOME STREET, NEW YORK.

MATTHEW REVISED.

From the Christian Union, Louisville, Ky.

We speak upon an extended experience, when we say, that never before has any English reader come as near the light that beamed from Matthew's Gospel upon the minds of those for whom it was originally written, as in this revision. The mere English reader may learn now from Matthew, what the scholar learns by much painstaking from Lachmann, Tregelles, Tischendorf, and Alford. This revision of Matthew is a monument of Biblical learning, of critical skill, of faithful and pious effort to give the English reader as perfect an idea of what the Holy Spirit said through this evangelist, as the original Greek readers had.

From the Freewill Quarterly.

The appearance of this Gospel by Matthew marks an era in the history and work of the Union. The revision generally shows great labor and care, and unquestionably brings us, in not a few instances, much nearer to the centre of the writer's thought and the great Spirit's lips. We can not help commending the manifest impartiality and conscientious scholarship of the translator. His motto seems to be—*Nothing to prejudice; every thing to truth.*

From the New Church Quarterly (Swedenborgian).

This new translation will be of extreme value, as embodying the results of the latest researches in Biblical learning, and, by the discussions it will provoke, can not fail to settle the truth, on points now involved in obscurity. We presume from Dr. Conant's acknowledged ability and painstaking scholarship the emendations it will require, will not be very important. We hope that all our readers who have any taste for the work will procure a copy of this book.

From the Advent Herald, Boston, Mass.

We hail every effort to perfect the rendering of the original Scriptures into our English tongue. The critical notes accompanying this work are invaluable.

From Zion's Advocate, Portland, Me.

Of the corrections of Bagster's edition of the Greek text, made by Dr. Conant, *Zion's Advocate* says,

Many, perhaps all, the omissions recommended, would be confirmed by the best authorities. In the New Version, the proper names are given as they are in the Old Testament. Words, whose meaning has changed, are replaced by others expressing the thought exactly and intelligibly. Ungrammatical expressions are corrected. Certainly, no one can object to eliminating from the Bible what we would not allow in a child's composition. Inexact translation, and faulty expressions are corrected. Surely, no one will object to having the exact sense of the original expressed in simple and intelligent language. Very many passages have been greatly improved, and these improvements were absolutely demanded.

From the Missouri Baptist, St. Louis, Mo.

The work will command respect.
Every page of it bears the impress of scholarship.
It will give satisfaction.
The mind of the Spirit is made clear and plain.
The notes are brief, clear, and to the point.

From the Mich. Christian Herald, Detroit, Mich.

It has been with mingled pleasure and profit that, for the last two months, we have, almost daily, examined a portion of Dr. Conant's Revision of Matthew; and, having finished it, we rise from our task with the conviction that it is, beyond all question, the best revision of Matthew's Gospel ever made in English.

Publications of the American Bible Union,
350 Broome Street, New York.

MARK REVISED.

This volume contains the Greek Text of Mark's Gospel, the Common Version, and the Revised Version, with Critical and Philological Notes. It makes a handsome quarto volume, equal to about 300 ordinary octavo pages. Price, sent by mail, 80 cts.

From the Christian Herald, Mich.

We have not failed to notice in the revision, in many places, a more felicitous, and in others, a far more accurate rendering of the original, the effect of which is to make the passages more intelligible to the general reader.

From the True Union, Md.

From a glance at its numerous criticisms and general appearance, we can but regard it as a valuable contribution to Biblical learning, and a sincere effort to obtain a pure version of the sacred Scriptures.

From the Christian Era, Mass.

There seems to have been great care used, and as far as we have been able to give any attention to it, we should judge the revision had been exceedingly thorough and judicious.

From the Louisiana Baptist, La.

The Version is a great improvement on that in common use.

From the Carolina Baptist, N. C.

The work is well executed, and the changes, for all of which authors are cited, are, in our estimation, decided improvements.

From the Daily Times, Ill.

The manner in which this revision is published, is certainly fair, to say the least. No scholar can fail to see that the translation is made with great carefulness. The typographical execution of the work is beautiful.

From the Christian Review, N. Y.

We regard it as an excellent peculiarity of this work, that it does not seem to seek unnecessary changes. We can not doubt that this and similar works will ultimately promote the cause of Biblical learning.

From Rev. Jesse Hartwell, D.D.

I am much pleased with the revision of Mark. None will hesitate to say it is a great improvement. Is the reviser not to be known? I should like to know his name and denomination. I am deeply interested in the work of revision. I hope the Lord will bless and direct those engaged in it.

From the Illinois Baptist, Ill.

The more we see of this important work, the greater are our anxieties to see the whole.

From Zion's Advocate, Me.

The whole Bible printed in this style, with marginal readings, embodying the results of great research, will be of great value to Biblical students.

From the Religious Herald, Va.

It bears traces of a hand free from the rashness which multiplies unnecessary changes, and the timidity which withholds changes for the better.

Publications of the American Bible Union,
350 Broome Street, New York.

LUKE REVISED.

A volume of nearly 300 quarto pages. It contains the Greek Text, Common Version, and the Revised Version, with numerous Critical and Philological Notes. Price, sent by mail, $1.50.

From the American Christian Review, O.

The revision with the notes shows a vast amount of labor. It is a valuable production, indeed.

From the American Baptist, N. Y.

The alterations are comparatively few, but are made with judgment and care.

From the American Sentinel, Me.

The *Bible Union Reporter*, containing portions of the new translation of Luke, we commend to the notice of our readers.

From the Lousiania Baptist, La.

Of the revision of Luke, xi., 33–36, the editor says : This is certainly a great improvement in translation, making the figure intelligible and very beautiful to every reader.

From the Boston Recorder, Mass.

This work of retranslating the Sacred Scriptures is steadily going forward.

From the Correspondent, Ala.

We have read some of these chapters with interest, and in the main with our hearty approval.

From the Bible Union Quarterly, N. Y.

The Committee appointed by the Bible Union to examine the Revision of Luke's Gospel report that : Its author has consulted a wide range of authorities, and has supported his departures from the Common Version, by much learning and a discriminating judgment. The style is easy, simple, and perspicuous. We admire the fidelity with which he adheres to the Common Version, where it can be done with justice to the original.

The Committee considers it superior to that version in the following particulars, not to mention others :

1. Accurate rendering of the inspired original. 2. Its style is more in harmony with modern usage. 3. The collocation is in many places much better. 4. It is more grammatically accurate. 5. It is in many places much more perspicuous.—P. CHURCH, D.D., *Chairman.*

From the Chicago Daily Times, Ill.

This paper says of the primary revision of Mark and Luke : We have here two quarto volumes, containing the two gospels indicated above, in the original Greek text, the Common English version, and the new and revised translation. We can not speak in too high terms of the faithful and conscientious manner in which the American Bible Union are fulfilling their mission, of giving to the world this new version of the Holy Scriptures. The work of translation is being performed by a number of the most eminent and profound Greek and Hebrew scholars, men whose scholastic attainments and deep erudition make them infinitely superior to the translators of the old "King James Version," so familiar to us from childhood. No student of the Bible, above all, no clergyman or minister, should be without these admirable translations of the gospels.

Publications of the American Bible Union,
350 Broome Street, New York.

ACTS OF THE APOSTLES.

This book is second in size of the books of the New Testament. The preliminary revision occupied a long time in its preparation, and was a work of great labor. Much light is thrown by it upon many dark and difficult passages. It will abundantly repay a careful perusal.

It contains the Greek Text, the Common Version, and the Revised Version, with Critical and Philological Notes. Price, sent by mail, $1.25.

From Challen's Monthly, Pa.

This large quarto so long and anxiously expected, has just issued from the press of the American Bible Union, and will be read with much interest.

More than ordinary care has been bestowed upon it.

The beautiful simplicity and historical truthfulness of Luke, in the original records of the planting and successful establishment of the Church of Christ, have been admirably translated into our language in this invaluable offering of the Board of the American Bible Union; and we accept it with peculiar satisfaction and pleasure. There is much in this translation which will solicit the earnest and, we trust, faithful criticism of the learned, and we doubt not but that it will pass through the fiery ordeal without much loss.

From the Christian Union, Ky.

Speaking of the revision of Acts and other portions issued in one volume, the editor says: "It contains some of the most valuable contributions ever made to Biblical science, and well deserves to be assiduously studied by all who wish to know what God has said to mankind."

From the Bible Union Quarterly, N. Y.

We take pleasure in adding that there is a great demand for this work, which increases as it is circulated.

From the Religious Herald, Va.

There are some notes of value; indicating correct opinions and large views, and a diligence of *collation* that is really wonderful and highly commendable.

From the New York Chronicle, N. Y.

This work is now before us. It is a beautifully bound quarto volume. The work has been prosecuted with an intense desire to make a faithful and perspicuous translation of the words of inspiration.

From the American Baptist, N. Y.

The most simple and appropriate terms to give expression to the meaning of the original, and every effort has been employed to make the ordinary reader acquainted with the mind of the Holy Spirit.

From the Chicago Daily Times, Ill.

It ought to receive the candid examination of all Biblical scholars. The typographical execution of the work is worthy of the highest praise.

From the Christian Index, Ga.

We accord to the reviser an extent of historical and philological knowledge which entitles his revision to a candid but fair criticism.

From the American Christian Review, O.

The Bible Union is furnishing work for critics. The simple aim of the Bible Union is to give to the world as pure a version as possible

(1)

Publications of the American Bible Union,
350 Broome Street, New York.

1 AND 2 TIMOTHY.

This volume contains the Greek Text, the Common Version, and the Revised Version of Paul's First and Second Letters to Timothy, with Critical and Philological Notes. Price, sent by mail, 60 cents.

From the Standard, Nashville, Tenn.

The revision is executed in a spirit of judicious and conservative scholarship. We can highly commend it.

One of the most noticeable features of this new version of Timothy, is the few changes that are made.

Quite a number of important changes in phraseology have, however, been introduced. The reader of the New Version will miss the words "church," "bishop," and other such ecclesiastical terms; and in their places he will find "congregation" and "overseer."

We have "love" in the place of "charity;" "demons" for "devils;" "appointed" for "ordained;" "silly fables" for "old wive's fables;" and many others which might be enumerated, and which commend themselves to the common reader no less than to the scholar and the critic.

1 AND 2 THESSALONIANS.

This volume contains the Greek Text, the Common Version, and the Revised Version of Paul's First and Second Letters to the Thessalonians, with Critical and Philological Notes. Price, sent by mail, 60 cts.

From the Christian Times, London.

This is a handsome thin quarto. The revised version is executed with great care, and if it were proposed to substitute it for the common English version, we should not entertain any insuperable repugnance.

From the Christian Repository, O.

One object of this publication is to invite the criticism of scholars, and to them it has a special value. But we can heartily recommend it to all; for, if the reader does not understand the original, the new version will often help him to gather the meaning of the old version.

EPHESIANS.

This book contains the Greek Text, the Common Version, and the Revised Version of Paul's Letter to the Ephesians, with Critical and Philological Notes. Price, sent by mail, 50 cts.

From the Christian Repository, O.

The Revised Version in many places is doubtless better than the Common Version. We hope to have the Bible in this form, and we will certainly prize it very highly. It is all that could be desired in typography. We never saw the Greek Text in such beautiful, large, clear type.

(1)

Publications of the American Bible Union,
350 Broome Street, New York.

PHILEMON.

A small volume, containing the Greek Text, the Common Version, and the Revised Version, with Critical and Philological Notes. This work is issued in quarto form, and also in a small pocket edition. Price, bound and sent by mail, 25 cts.

We think it a masterly and scholarly production.—*From the True Union, Md.*

It is a model for works of its kind.—*From the N. Y. Chronicle.*

From the Daily News, N. Y.

The proposed version, from the pen of Dr. Hackett, reflects great credit on his learning, critical acumen, and fine taste.

From the American Christian Review, O.

It is a very creditable production, and seems to be the fruit of much reading and a close study of the original. It bears the impress of an independent thinker.

From the Presbyter, Cincinnati, O.

We took our leisure to examine this little volume with some care, which has resulted in entire satisfaction with the author's labors.

From the Journal of Commerce, N. Y.

As a general remark, Prof Hackett adheres more rigidly to the literality of the original, than does the received version.

From the Independent, N. Y.

The work furnishes abundant proof of the author's accurate scholarship, exegetical insight, sober judgment, and carefulness to avoid rash and doubtful changes.

From the Boston Recorder, Mass.

We have examined with some care this production of one of our most careful and reliable Biblical scholars. We understand this important epistle better than before.

From the Methodist Protestant, Md.

This book is beautifully printed. The revision is from the pen of Dr. Hackett.

From the Christian Review, N. Y.

It bears on every page the impress of his (Dr. Hackett's) exact learning, cultivated taste, sound judgment, and nice philological tact.

From the Watchman and Reflector, Mass.

The superior merits of Dr. Hackett as an exegete are too well known to need any public commendation. He loves the Bible as the true word of God, and holds strongly to the broadest, deepest, and most spiritual views of divine truth. His judgment is cautious, sound, and clear; his philological acquirements are extensive and accurate; his taste is admirable. The work is a real gem of art.

From the Mississippi Baptist, Miss.

This is the completest work I have ever seen. It comes nearer giving the Greek idea in English than any of the revisions with which I have met.—*J. A. Oliver.*

From the Biblical Recorder, N C.

The work of Prof. Hackett is well done, and the volume is deeply interesting.

From the Western Watchman, Mo.

This volume, just issued by the American Bible Union, is from the hands of one of the most accomplished Biblical critics of the present day.

Publications of the American Bible Union,
330 Broome Street, New York.

HEBREWS REVISED.

A quarto volume, containing the Greek Text, the Common Version, and the Revised Version, with Critical and Philological Notes. Price, sent by mail, 70 cents.

From the Christian Review, New York.

We should be false to our convictions not to say that it is a great improvement on the Common Version. There has been no wanton or unnecessary tampering with the good old English of the Book so embalmed in the most sacred recesses of millions of Christian hearts.

From the Ladies' Christian Annual, Pa.

We accept, with special favor, this invaluable addition to the works already issued by the press in the employ of the American Bible Union.

From the American Sentinel, Me.

In some respects we think the translation superior to the Common Version. To all it will prove useful.

From the Southern Baptist, Tenn.

As it appeared in monthly parts, we noticed that it was highly commended for its fidelity to the original, and for its simple and pure English style. The Bible Union, in New York, is still continuing to progress in its work.

From the Christian Herald, Mich.

We have read the translation with much interest.

The English reader will discover a clearness, beauty, and logical force in the letter to the Hebrews, as it is here rendered, which he has not seen before.

From the Christian Secretary, Conn.

The Epistle to the Hebrews is received from the press of the Bible Union, in the style of their former issues. So far as we have examined this specimen, we like it

From the Israelite, O.

The Bible Society of New York has sent us a splendid copy of their edition of the Hebrew text of Job, and the new version of The Epistle to the Hebrews. The former is the most splendid edition of Hebrew Scripture we have seen in this country, and we accept it with many thanks.

From the Christian Ambassador, New York.

The typographical execution is excellent. The Text-Book in Greek and English is beautifully distinct, and the notes are in a plain type. Few editions of the Bible have been more handsomely printed, or on better paper.

From the New York Chronicle, N. Y.

It is believed to be among the choicest of the preliminary revisions yet put forth by the American Bible Union.

From the Knoxville Republican, Ill.

We thank the Union for the Biblical treat we have enjoyed. We invite all candid, Bible-loving men to read and carefully examine and compare this work with the common translation.

Between sixty and seventy versions and works of criticism, are quoted, as sustaining the changes made, and as helps to the critical reader, to enable him to determine for himself the propriety of these changes.

Publications of the American Bible Union,
350 Broome Street, New York.

HEBREWS REVISED.

From the Millennial Harbinger, Va.

We have hastily examined every page of it, and pronounce it to be a careful, learned, and greatly improved version of the second greatest epistle ever written by the greatest apostle, the most learned writer, as well as the largest author of the Christian Scriptures.

From the Illinois Baptist, Ill.

Its exact faithfulness to the original text, its pure vernacular English, as used by our best writers and speakers, and its tender regard for the commonly-received version, are strikingly manifest in each chapter and verse ; rendering it not only a living epistle, full of the pure words of inspiration, clothed in the familiar phraseology of the Family Bible, but also a work of the most superior literary merit.

No one can compare the Revised Version with the Greek, and with King James' Version, without being forcibly struck with its great superiority, both in faithfulness and diction.

The critical notes of the reviser are almost invaluable to the Biblical student.

From the American Baptist, New York.

Having compared it with the common translation, we now feel prepared to say that it is a very decided improvement on the version of King James.

From the Biblical Recorder, N. C.

The new translation is a decided improvement of the Common Version. It is better English. It is, in several instances at least, more faithful to the original, and it renders the meaning of some passages much more perspicuous.

From the N. W. Christian Review, O

We think that even the superficial reader can not fail to discover a manifest improvement on the authorized version of King James. To the scholar and theologian it must commend itself for the purity and clearness of its diction, and the faithfulness of its version, and, to the classical character, for its notes.

From the Commission, Va.

We have not had time to examine it, and can only, therefore, commend the mechanical execution. The publications of the Union are beautiful specimens of typography.

We feel an increasing conviction that the work they have undertaken will, ultimately, be well done. We are always glad to receive their publications.

From the Mountain Messenger, Va.

We do not feel qualified to *criticise* this work, but, no doubt, it will undergo the careful scrutiny of profound scholars, in this and other lands, before it is published as a finality.

From the True Union, Md.

There is no attempt to depart from the *style* of the old version apparently for the sake of differing ; no introduction of words of Latin origin, merely to supplant those of the Saxon stock.

From the Western Recorder, Ky.

Seldom have we read a work with so much real pleasure and profound gratitude.

From the Masonic Review, O.

No one can read it without being highly gratified with the beauty and force of the English used.

The religious public have nothing to fear from a *thorough* revision of the *translation* of the Sacred Scriptures by competent and God-fearing men. We wish the Union success ; for we believe their aims are pure, and the object commendable.

Publications of the American Bible Union,
350 Broome Street, New York.

DOCUMENTARY HISTORY OF THE AMERICAN BIBLE UNION,

Consisting of the reprint of its Constitution, Annual Reports, Quarterly Papers, Select Addresses, Tracts, etc., etc., in the form of the *Bible Union Quarterly*, the official organ of the American Bible Union, edited by WM. H. WYCKOFF, Corresponding Secretary, and C. A. BUCKBEE, Recording Secretary. The first three volumes complete, from the organization, in 1850, to 1860. Each volume contains over five hundred octavo pages. Volume one contains a beautiful steel engraved likeness of Rev. S. H. Cone, D.D., first President. Volume two contains one of Rev. Thomas Armitage, D.D., the present President, and volume three, one of the Corresponding Secretary, Wm. H. Wyckoff. Price, for each volume, sent by mail, $1.50.

From the Western Recorder, Ky.

The first two volumes contain a complete documentary history of the Union up to the close of 1856. The first volume contains an admirable likeness of Dr. Cone, the first President of the Society, and the second volume, one of Dr. Armitage, both from steel engravings in the best style of the art.

From the Christian Union, Ky.

Volume second is received. It is a beautiful book. We commend it to the perusal of all who love the cause of revision. They will acquire much useful knowledge, in relation to the Bible Union enterprise, by the diligent perusal of this volume.

From the True Union, Md.

Of the second volume, the editor says: This is an elegant volume, containing the documentary history of the Bible Union. It will be found deeply interesting to all those who desire to see a pure version of the Sacred Scriptures. An additional attraction to the volume is a beautiful engraving of the President, Rev. Thomas Armitage, D.D. We commend the volume to all our readers.

From the Bible Union Quarterly, N. Y.

The third volume of the Documentary History is now complete, bringing down the history, in the *Quarterly* form, to 1860. Whoever wishes to know all that the Bible Union has done, and the reasons for it, must study these volumes. They comprise facts and arguments, plans and proceedings, with which every friend of the cause ought to be familiar.

It will convince every one who reads these volumes, that the managers of the Bible Union have pursued a uniform, undeviating course, from the commencement of the enterprise, and have sought out and prosecuted the best possible measures to secure a most pure and faithful version of the word of God.

From the Christian Pleader, Sydney, Australia.

There is one piece of information which may be interesting to our readers. The most spiritual notion of their work is entertained by the conductors of the Union. The history of their enterprise and the manner in which they have conducted it will hereafter marvelously illustrate the power of prayer and faith. Nor can we doubt that this effort will mightily contribute to the glory of the latter days, and to the absolute overthrow of Satan and Antichrist.

(1)

www.ingramcontent.com/pod-product-compliance
Lightning Source LLC
Chambersburg PA
CBHW032138160426
43197CB00008B/690